GOING
TO
SALT LAKE CITY

TO DO

FAMILY
HISTORY
RESEARCH

GOING
TO
SALT LAKE CITY
TO DO
FAMILY
HISTORY
RESEARCH

J. Carlyle Parker

Third Edition, Revised and Expanded

Marietta Publishing Company
Turlock, California
1996

Marietta Publishing Company, Turlock, California
© 1989, 1993, 1996 by J. Carlyle Parker. All rights reserved

First Edition 1989. Second Edition 1993. Third Edition 1996

Printed in the United States of America

Library of Congress Cataloging-in-Publication Data

Parker, J. Carlyle.
   Going to Salt Lake City to do family history research / J. Carlyle
Parker. -- 3rd ed., rev. and expanded.
      p. cm.
   Includes bibliographical references.
   ISBN 0-934153-14-0 (acid free paper)
   1. Church of Jesus Christ of Latter-day Saints. Family History
Library--Handbooks, manuals, etc. 2. Genealogical libraries--Utah--
Salt Lake City--Handbooks, manuals, etc. 3. Genealogy--Library
resources--Salt Lake City--Handbooks, manuals, etc.
   I. Title.
Z733.C55P37 1996
026.9291'09792'258--dc20   95-25948
                                                                CIP
OCLC #33361524

Personal Ancestral File, *FamilySearch*, *Ancestral File*, *International
Genealogical Index*, *Family History Library Catalog*, *Family Registry*, and
TempleReady are trademarks of the Church of Jesus Christ of Latter-day Saints.

Some material in this publication is reprinted by permission of the Church of
Jesus Christ of Latter-day Saints. In granting permission for this use of
copyright materials, the Church does not imply or express either endorsement
or authorization of this publication.

$15.95, plus $2.50 for shipping if ordered direct from publisher.
Californians need to add $1.18, 7.375% sales tax.

Marietta Publishing Company, 2115 North Denair Avenue, Turlock,
                    CA 95382, (209) 634-9473, SAN 693-2002

Cover photo: The Family History Library, Salt Lake City, Utah

To

Janet

CONTENTS

ILLUSTRATIONS

FLOOR PLANS

MAPS

PREFACE

The Family History Library collection continues its rapid growth, with hundreds of cameras in many areas, including the former Soviet Block countries. The Library is still the world's largest genealogical library. The Library has also increased its number of Family History Centers throughout the world. The Library collection is estimated to be over seven million volumes.

The Library and its Centers are still open for the free use of the general public. The Centers have to charge a small fee in order for patrons to borrow microfilms from the Family History Library. Both the Library and Centers charge a modest fee for photoduplication, postage, computer printouts, and supplies.

For statistical reasons many of the Centers ask patrons to register as they enter the Center. These registration rolls are not used for solicitation in any form. There are no entrance fees, no free will offerings encouraged, and no call backs.

There is still much research that can be accomplished without even going to Salt Lake City. Many readers of the earlier editions of this work report how useful it has been in using their Family History Centers. Some of them had planned to go to the Family History Library, but their travel plans had to be altered and they have not yet had the opportunity. Nevertheless, they were happy with the research progress that they had made in their local Centers through the aid of this work.

As with the last edition, a random group (one hundred) of mail order purchasers was surveyed concerning improvements to this work, and many of their suggestions have been incorporated in this third edition.

Again, I am grateful to the staff of the Family History Library who have assisted me as I have used the Library, and to Teresa Upton for copyright clearances, and to Tom Daniels, who provided some of the Library's photographs. My very supportive wife, Janet, has helped with this work with good advice, suggestions, and proofreading assistance that is immeasurable. Janet's cousin, Edna Thea Roberts, provided some of her expert advice on Irish research.

Preface

It has been a pleasure to have helped researchers in the search for their roots. I hope that you, too, find the research techniques discussed in this work to be helpful, as others have reported them to be.

Constructive criticisms for improvement of this book are still welcome. Please write me at the publisher's address provided on the copyright page. Good luck and best wishes for successful research!

J. Carlyle Parker
Turlock, California
November 1995

PREFACE TO SECOND EDITION

The Family History Library continues to be the world's largest genealogical library. Since 1989, when *Going to Salt Lake City to Do Family History Research* was published, the Library's reported holdings have increased. The collection now consists of

> over 1.8 million reels of microfilm (the equivalent of about 6 million volumes),
> approximately 325,000 microfiches (the equivalent of about 81,000 volumes),
> over 235,000 volumes of books.

The total equivalent is about 6,316,000 volumes.

The Library will continue to grow at a rapid rate. It currently adds about 100,000 reels (the equivalent of about 350,000 volumes) of microfilm per year, about 62,000 microfiches (the equivalent of about 13,000 volumes) per year, and about 10,000 volumes of books per year, for a total equivalent of about 373,000 volumes per year. At this growth rate the Library will add the equivalent of over one million volumes every three years. The Library is open to the public free of charge, except for a few small service fees that will be mentioned within this book.

This work contains much material about Family History Centers. They serve as satellite research centers to the Family History Library. There are about 1,650 Family History Centers which offer services such as interlibrary loan of microforms, photocopy requests, and reference questionnaire requests. Because use of these centers is free except for small service charges for borrowing, photocopying, or computer printouts, there is much research that you can accomplish without even going to Salt Lake City. This book will help you know what that research is. Books and certain microforms in the Library in Salt Lake City cannot be borrowed. But even these are not entirely outside your reach. Through your local public library you may borrow these materials from other libraries, as they may exist elsewhere, or you may hire independent researchers to search these materials for you.

Preface to Second Edition

It is easier to research in Salt Lake City than in Denmark, England, the Netherlands, and Sweden because in those countries the research sources are not collected in one centralized national archive.

In the interest of obtaining suggestions for improvement of this book, inquiries were made of seventy-eight purchasers of the first edition in the United States and Canada. A special thanks to them for their suggestions, many of which have been incorporated in the second edition.

Since the first edition of this work I have had the privilege of opening another Family History Center, in Turlock, California. I now serve as its volunteer director and am no longer the librarian and director of the Modesto California Family History Center, where I served for twenty-one years.

I am grateful to librarians and researchers who responded to my inquiries concerning published and unpublished state-wide indexes of biographical sketches, included in chapter 8. For this I owe thanks to the librarians of the Tutwiler Collection of Southern History, Birmingham Public Library, Birmingham, Alabama; David A. Hales, University of Alaska Fairbanks; Maine Historical Society; Dr. Thomas Roderick of Bar Harbor, Maine; and Carla Rickerson, University of Washington, in addition to those named in the Preface on pages xviii-xix.

I am also grateful to the staff of the Family History Library who have assisted me as I have used the Library, and to A. Gregory Brown who provided most of the Library's photographs and floor plans. Sometime ago Kory L. Meyerink, Publications Coordinator of the Family History Library, invited me to permit him to review my works before publication. He has reviewed this work; and I am grateful to him for his suggestions, many of which have been implemented. Robert Davis and Ron Reed of the Museum of Church History and Art were very helpful in locating and permitting the use of the "Census Taker" photograph reprinted on page 80.

Preface to the Second Edition

I couldn't have completed this work without the advice, suggestions, and proofreading assistance provided by Janet, my very supportive wife, and my son, Bret, another professional librarian in the family. The third librarian in the family, my daughter, Denise, and her husband, Paul Paxton, helped me with some recent updates concerning Family History Library changes and Salt Lake City sights, restaurants, and hotels.

It is my continuing wish to help researchers in the search for their roots. I know that if the research techniques in this work are followed, positive results will occur if the materials needed are available in the Family History Library. I hope you find these techniques as helpful as others have.

Constructive criticisms for improvement of this book are still welcome. Please write me at the publisher's address provided on the copyright page. Good luck and best wishes for successful research!

J. Carlyle Parker
Turlock, California
December 1992

THE FAMILY HISTORY LIBRARY

PREFACE TO FIRST EDITION

The Family History Library in Salt Lake City is the world's largest family history and research library. It has nearly 1.5 million reels of microfilm and over two hundred thousand sheets of microfiche of courthouse, archival, and church records, as well as books and periodicals. The Library's book collection contains over 195,000 volumes and over eight million family group record forms. The scope of the Library's collection is worldwide, with its greatest strength relating to the United States, Canada, and Western Europe.

In some cases it is easier and more economical to do family history and genealogical research in the collection in Salt Lake City than to travel throughout the United States and in foreign countries trying to find the same resources in various county courthouses, churches, local libraries, or cemeteries. It is also easier to research in Salt Lake City than in Denmark, England, and Sweden because in those countries the research sources are not collected in one centralized national archive.

Proper preparation before a visit to the Family History Library in Salt Lake City can save precious time while researching there. It is a waste of time to do some routine tasks at the Family History Library that could have been done at home or at a nearby Family History Center or local public library. A Family History Center is a branch of the Family History Library. Nearly all Family History Centers have microfiche copies of the *International Genealogical Index*, the *Family History Library Catalog*, the *Family Registry*, and the *AIS* (Accelerated Indexing Systems) consolidated indexes to the 1790 through the 1850 United States federal census schedules.

Going to Salt Lake City to Do Family History Research was written as a guide for genealogists preparing to go and use the Family History Library in Salt Lake City, Utah. It addresses the preparation needs of all genealogists from beginners to advanced. It encourages the use of a Family History Center before traveling to Salt Lake City. Genealogists who do not have access to a Family History Center will still find this guide useful as it provides preparation instructions that can be done at home or at local public libraries.

Preface to First Edition

The instructions presented here have been tried and proven valuable to genealogists who enrolled in university courses taught by the author specifically for the purpose of preparing to go to the Family History Library. Those enrolled found that by doing their homework in this manner, in advance, once they arrived at the Library in Salt Lake City they could proceed directly to their most important research materials.

This guide reflects the research viewpoint of its author, who is a veteran of library service, a professional librarian, a genealogist, and the founder and volunteer director for over twenty years of the Modesto California Family History Center. This guide is not an official publication of the Family History Library nor of the Church of Jesus Christ of Latter-day Saints.

I am grateful to the many genealogists who have listened to most of these ideas presented here. I particularly appreciate those who enrolled in my California State University, Stanislaus courses that included a week's research at the Family History Library. They permitted me to experiment on them and confirm that these ideas are effective and productive.

Many individuals helped me in the preparation of *Going to Salt Lake City to Do Family History Research*. I am grateful to the staff of the Family History Library who have assisted me as I have periodically used the Library since 1955 and to A. Gregory Brown and Tom Daniels who provided the Library's photographs and floor plans. Thanks are also extended to Janet G. Parker, Denise Kay Paxton, and Bret H. Parker for their suggestions and proofreading. I also, like millions of genealogists throughout the world, express gratitude to the Church of Jesus Christ of Latter-day Saints for providing the Family History Library and its Family History Centers for people of all denominations to research their family histories.

I am also grateful to the following librarians who responded to my inquiries concerning published and unpublished state-wide indexes of biographical sketches included in chapter 8: Portia Allbert, Kansas State Historical Society, Topeka, Kans.; Lloyd DeWitt Bockstruck, Dallas Public Library; Dallas, Tex.; Donald Brown and John C. Fralish, Jr., State Library of Pennsylvania, Harrisburg, Pa.; John E. Bye, North

Dakota Institute for Regional Studies, North Dakota State University
Library, Fargo, N.Dak.; Andrea E. Cantrell, University of Arkansas
Libraries, Fayetteville, Ark.; Mary Ann Cleveland, State Library of
Florida, Tallahassee, Fla.; David C. Dearborn, New England Historic
Genealogical Society, Boston, Mass.; Carol Downey, Arizona
Department of Library, Archives and Public Records, Phoenix, Ariz.;
Laurel E. Drew, New Mexico State Library, Santa Fe, N.Mex.; Ann
Eichinger, South Dakota State Library, Pierre, S.Dak.; Alice Eichholz,
Montpelier, Vt.; W. Everard, New Orleans Public Library, New
Orleans, La.; P. William Filby, Savage, Md.; Eleanor M. Gehres,
Denver Public Library, Denver, Colo.; Peggy Medina Giltrow, New
Mexico State Library, Santa Fe, N.Mex.; James L. Hansen, The State
Historical Society of Wisconsin, Madison, Wis; Elizabeth P. Jacox,
Idaho State Historical Society Library and Archives, Boise, Idaho;
Thomas J. Kemp, Pequot Library, Southport, Conn,; Anne Lipscomb,
Mississippi State Department of Archives and History, Jackson, Miss.;
Kay Littlefield, Bangor Public Library, Bangor, Maine; Virginia H.
Ming, The Texas Collection, Baylor University, Waco, Tex.; Tom
Muth, Topeka Public Library, Topeka, Kans.; Reidun D. Nuquist,
Vermont Historical Society Library, Montpelier, Vt.; Gunther E. Pohl,
Great Neck, N.Y.; Wiley R. Pope, Minnesota Historical Society
Library, St. Paul, Minn.; Kathryn Ray, District of Columbia Public
Library, Washington, D.C.; M. Ann Reinert, Mid-Continent Public
Library, Independence, Mo.; Gwen Rice, Wyoming State Library,
Cheyenne, Wyo.; Dennis L. Richards, University of Montana Library,
Missoula, Mont.; Steve Rodhling, Charleston County Library,
Charleston, S.C.; Judy R. Roquet, Oregon State Library, Salem,
Oreg.; Stella J. Scheckter, New Hampshire State Library, Concord,
N.H.; Linda M. Sommer, South Dakota State Historical Society,
Pierre, S.D.; Sandra Stark, Illinois State Historical Library,
Springfield, Ill.; Madeleine B. Telfeyan, Rhode Island Historical
Society, Providence, R.I.; and Marvin E. Wiggins, Brigham Young
University Library, Provo, Utah.

It is my wish to help you in your research. I know that these research
techniques work, and I hope you find them as useful as others have.
Constructive criticisms for improvement of the guide are welcome.
Please write the author at the publisher's address provided on the
copyright page. Good luck and best wishes for successful research!

J. Carlyle Parker, Turlock, California, August 1989

INFORMATION BOOK AREA

INTRODUCTION

Before going to the Family History Library in Salt Lake City you should at least read "How to Use the Book," pages xxv-xxvi, and chapters 10, 11, and 12 of this book. You will be much better prepared if you also complete the steps outlined in chapters 1 and 2. If you have access to a Family History Center, before going to Salt Lake City you should complete as much as you can concerning the preparation suggestions made in chapters 3 through 7.

If a Family History Center is not available to you and you can locate copies of the Library of Congress catalogs mentioned in the "Local Public Library Users" section of chapter 5, it would help you to search them for family histories. The suggested "Additional Reading" at the end of each chapter is very important because the contents and use of some records are not fully explained in this book.

Please bear in mind that you do not have to go to Salt Lake City in order to use the Family History Library. Many researchers use the Family History Library in or near their own home towns through the services of Family History Centers, which serve as branch libraries of the Family History Library. Volunteers are available at Family History Centers to help you use their collections. The appendix of this work contains a city list of Family History Centers in the United States and Canada. For their locations please call your local Church of Jesus Christ of Latter-day Saints, or write the Family History Library, 35 North West Temple Street, Salt Lake City, Utah 81450 (801) 240-3702.

Microfilm and microfiche may be borrowed for a small service fee through the Family History Library's Family History Centers. Photocopied pages of books and indexes not available in microform may be obtained by mail either through direct correspondence with the Family History Library at the above address or through the use of the "Request for Photocopies" forms available at your local Family History Center.

Introduction

For the convenience of readers, some of the chapters of this book have been divided into three parts:

    I. Family History Center Users
   II. Local Public Library Users
  III. Home Library Users

These divisions have been made to assist researchers who do not have easy access to a Family History Center or public libraries with genealogical materials.

The book is written as if all readers were beginners. That, of course, will not be the case. Therefore, some readers will wish to skip parts of the book that are "old hat" to them. Nevertheless, many genealogical journal book reviewers of the second and first editions concur that there is something in each chapter for everyone, beginner or advanced.

Researchers should bear in mind that not all microforms that appear in the *Family History Library Catalog* are available in the Library. The Library does not have all cataloged microforms for records recently microfilmed. It also does not have microforms for records microfilmed in earlier years for Denmark, England, Finland, Germany, Iceland, Ireland, Netherlands, Norway, Poland, Scotland, Sweden, Switzerland, and Wales. Originals of microforms are stored in the Granite Mountain Records Vault, several miles from the Library. Since copies, not original microforms, are sent to the Library, these films cannot be retrieved at a moment's notice. As microforms are requested, copies are made and then become available for use at the Library.

If you plan to do research concerning foreign countries and recently microfilmed records for the United States and Canada, it may be important for you to write or call the Library, 35 North West Temple Street, Salt Lake City, Utah 81450 (801) 240-3702, a few weeks ahead of time to check whether they have your desired microfilm numbers in the Library. If they are not available, ask if they can be made available for your date of arrival. Also, provide them with your address and telephone number. Normally, the Library staff will do their best to meet your research needs.

Chapters two through seven include some instructions for assisting you in the use of the computer system, *FamilySearch*. Please do not let those instructions intimidate you from using this computer system. Most of the Family History Centers and the Family History Library have volunteers who will help you use the various reference tools on *FamilySearch*. If you find the computer instructions in this book too confusing or overwhelming, just forget about them and ask for help from one of the volunteers.

You may also wish to try to use *FamilySearch* by reading its menus, its search instructions that appear on the screens, or its help screens. There is also a short tutorial program, "A. Using the Computer," on the opening *FamilySearch* menu. Remember, you are never too old to learn.

It is imperative that you use *FamilySearch*, and, just like the "genealogy bug," the "computer bite" will not hurt. You'll find that the two "bugs" are a very good pair. In fact, chances are you'll become an avid computerist.

After you have read and worked through the entire book, please at least review the chapter summaries before each visit to the Family History Library.

FamilySearch COMPUTERS

HOW TO USE THIS BOOK

THE THREE HOUR APPROACH

If you only have three hours for reading this book, read the
introduction; chapter 10, "What to Take;" chapter 11, "At the Family
History Library;" chapter 12, "Library Miscellaneous Services and
Odds and Ends;" and the summaries at the end of each chapter.

THE TWO DAY APPROACH

If you only have two days for reading and preparation, besides the
above read chapters 1 and 2, which deal with the preparation of
pedigrees and family group sheets, and identifying counties or their
equivalents in other countries.

THE ONE WEEK APPROACH

If you only have one week for reading and preparation, besides the
above read chapter 3 and use the "*International Genealogical Index.*"

THE TWO WEEK APPROACH

If you only have two weeks for reading and preparation, besides the
above read chapter 4 and use the "*Ancestral File.*"

THE ONE MONTH APPROACH

If you only have one month for reading and preparation, besides the
above read chapter 6 and use the "*Family History Library Catalog:
Locality Catalog.*"

How to Use This Book

THE TWO MONTH APPROACH

If you have two months for reading and preparation, besides the above read chapter 5 concerning finding printed family histories and use the *"Family History Library Catalog: Surname Catalog."*

THE THREE MONTH APPROACH

If you have three months or more for reading and preparation, read the entire book, including all of the prefaces, and read the country outlines or state outlines of the *United States Research Outline* series in which you're interested. They are available in Family History Centers, or they may be ordered from the Family History Library, 35 North West Temple Street, Salt Lake City, Utah 81450, (801) 240-3702. Do other suggested projects, as needed, and read one of the following how-to-do-it books:

United States (titles for beginners first, advanced last)

Croom, Emily Anne. *Unpuzzling Your Past: A Basic Guide to Genealogy.* 2d ed. White Hall, Va.: Betterway Publications, Inc., 1989.
    FHL GENERAL BOOK AREA 929.1 C888u.

Allen, Desmond Walls, and Carolyn Earle Billingsley. *Beginner's Guide to Family History Research.* 2d ed. Conway Ark.: Research Associates (P.O. Box 303, 72033), 1991.
    FHL US/CAN REF AREA 929.1 A53b.

Stryker-Rodda, Harriet. *How to Climb Your Family Tree: Genealogy for Beginners.* Philadelphia: Lippincott, 1977. Reprint. Baltimore: Genealogical Pub. Co., 1983. Large print. Boston: G. K. Hall, 1990.
    FHL GENERAL BOOK AREA 929.1 St89h.

Crandall, Ralph. *Shaking Your Family Tree: A Basic Guide to Tracing Your Family's Genealogy.* Dublin, N.H.: Yankee Publishing, 1988.
    FHL US/CAN REF AREA 929.1 C85s.

Wright, Raymond S., III. *The Genealogist's Handbook: Modern Methods for Researching Family History*. Chicago: American Library Association, 1995.
FHL US/CAN REF AREA 973 D27gh.

Greenwood, Val D. *The Researcher's Guide to American Genealogy*. 2d ed. Baltimore: Genealogical Publishing Co., 1990.
FHL US/CAN REF AREA 973 D27g 1990.

A bibliography of state guides and additional foreign how-to-do-books may be found on pages 49-71 in J. Carlyle Parker's *Library Service for Genealogists*, Gale Genealogy and Local History Series, vol. 15 (Detroit: Gale Research Co., 1981, op. 2d edition in progress by Marietta Publishing Co.).
FHL US/CAN REF AREA 026.9291 P226L.

Foreign Countries and Ethnic Guides (a selected list)

Genealogical Society of the Church of Jesus Christ of Latter-day Saints. *Research Papers*. Salt Lake City, Utah: The Society, 1979-1988.
Many of these papers are available in Family History Centers; now available on microfiche and may be acquired by Family History Centers that do not have paper copies.

Redford, Dorothy Spruill. *Somerset Homecoming: Recovering a Lost Heritage*. New York: Doubleday, 1988. New York: Anchor Books, 1989.
FHL US/CAN BOOK AREA 929.273 L732r.
This work is not considered a how-to-do-it book, but the author writes in such detail concerning her African-American family history research that it can be used as such, as well as being interesting and inspirational reading.

Rose, James M., and Alice Eichholz, eds. *Black Genesis*. Gale Genealogy and Local History Series, Vol. 1. Detroit: Gale Research Co., 1978.
FHL US/CAN REF AREA 973 F27r.
A bibliographic guide.

How to Use This Book

Jonasson, Eric. *The Canadian Genealogical Handbook: A Comprehensive Guide to Finding Your Ancestors in Canada*. 2d ed. rev. and enl. Winnipeg: Wheatfield Press, 1978.
FHL US/CAN REF AREA 971 D27j 1978.

Gardner, David E., and Frank Smith. *Genealogical Research in England and Wales*. 3 Vols. Salt Lake City: Bookcraft, 1956-1966.
FHL BRITISH REF AREA 929.142 G172g.

Grenham, John. *Tracing Your Irish Ancestors: A Complete Guide*. Goldenbridge, Dublin, Ireland: Gill & McMillian Ltd., 1992 (available from Irish Books and Media, 1433 Franklin Cove East, Minneapolis MN 53404-2135, (800) 299-5305).
FHL BRITISH REF AREA 941.5 D27gj.

Falley, Margaret Dickson. *Irish and Scotch-Irish Ancestral Research: A Guide to the Genealogical Records, Methods and Sources in Ireland*. 2 Vols. Evanston, Ill.: The Author, 1961-62. Reprint. Baltimore: Genealogical Publishing Co., 1981.
FHL BRITISH REF AREA 941.5 D27f.

Hamilton-Edwards, Gerald Kenneth Savery. *In Search of Scottish Ancestry*. 2d ed. Baltimore: Genealogical Publishing Co., 1984.
FHL BRITISH REF AREA 941 D27ham 1984.

Miller, Olga, ed. *Genealogical Research for Czech and Slovak Americans*. Gale Genealogy and Local History Series, Vol. 2. Detroit: Gale Research Co., 1978.
FHL US/CAN REF AREA 943.7 D27m.

Jensen, Larry O. *Genealogical Handbook of German Research*. 2 vols. Pleasant Grove, Utah: The Author, 1978 and 1983. Distributed by Everton Publishers, Inc., P.O. Box, Logan UT 84323-0368.
FHL EUROPE REF AREA 943 D27j.
Available at Family History Centers: Microfiche 6000366-6000368 (v.1 only, 3 microfiches).

Suess, Jared H. *Handy Guide to Hungarian Genealogical Records*.
Logan, Utah: Everton Publishers, Inc., 1980.
FHL EUROPE BOOK AREA 943.9 D27s.

Colletta, John Philip. *Finding Italian Roots: The Complete Guide for Americans*. Baltimore: Genealogical Publishing Co., 1993.
FHL US/CAN BOOK AREA 973 F2cf.

Kurzweil, Arthur. *From Generation to Generation: How to Trace Your Jewish Genealogy and Family History*. Rev. ed. New York: HarperCollins Publishers, 1994.
FHL US/CAN REF AREA 929.1 K967f 1994.
The first edition (1980) is available from FHL through FHC: Microfilm 1059468 Item 4.

Platt, Lyman De, ed. *Genealogical-Historical Guide to Latin America*. Gale Genealogy and Local History Series, Vol. 4. Detroit: Gale Research Co., 1978.
FHL LATIN AMERICA REF AREA 980 D27p.

Ryskamp, George R. *Tracing Your Hispanic Heritage*. 1984.
Available from Hispanic Family History Research, 4522 Indian Hill, Riverside, CA 92501.
FHL US/CAN REF AREA 946 D27r.

Johansson, Carl-Erik. *Thus They Wrote; A Guide to The Gothic Script of Scandinavia: Denmark, Norway, Finland, Sweden*. Provo, Utah: Brigham Young University Press, 1970.
FHL SCANDINAVIA REF AREA 948 G37j.

Johansson, Carl-Erik. *Cradled in Sweden*. Rev. ed. Logan, Utah: Everton Publishers, Inc., 1995.
FHL SCANDINAVIA BOOK AREA 948.5 D27j 1995.
1977 edition available from FHL through FHC: Microfiche 6030093-6030095 (3 microfiches).

Suess, Jared H. *Handy Guide to Swiss Genealogical Records*. Logan, Utah: Everton Publishers, Inc., 1978.
FHL EUROPE REF AREA 949.4 D27s.

A MICROFILM READING AREA

LIST OF ABBREVIATIONS

AIS	Accelerated Indexing Systems
CAN	Canada
FGRC	Family Group Records Collection
FHCs	Family History Centers of the Family History Library of the Church of Jesus Christ of Latter-day Saints
FHL	Family History Library of the Church of Jesus Christ of Latter-day Saints, Salt Lake City, Utah
FHLC	*Family History Library Catalog*
FICHE	Microfiche
FILM	Microfilm
IGI	*International Genealogical Index*
II	Interval International Resort
JSMB	Joseph Smith Memorial Building
n.p.	No publisher
op	Out-of-print
PAF	*Personal Ancestral File*
Q	Oversize
RCI	Resort Condominiums International
REF	Reference
REG	Register
s.l.	Without place of publication
TIB	*Temple Records Index Bureau*

PART I

BEFORE YOU GO

Chapter 1

START WITH YOURSELF

Starting with yourself prepare a pedigree chart and a family group sheet. Write down the dates and places of births, marriages, and deaths, where appropriate. Please include the names of counties for the United States, Canada, and Great Britain, and the county equivalents for all other countries. Some pedigree charts and family group charts should be started before going to either the Family History Library or a Family History Center. Women's maiden names, instead of their married names, are used on pedigrees and family group sheets.

Work from what you know or have in your personal papers to the unknown. You should not start with a famous person with your surname and research his or her descendants. Such research can mislead you and waste a lot of time searching family lines that may not be your direct line.

Inquire at your local library, your local genealogical society, local LDS bookstore, or call a Church of Jesus Christ of Latter-day Saints to find out where you can obtain blank pedigree and family group forms. The following firms are a few among many that provide mail order service for genealogical supplies:

Alice's Ancestral Nostalgia, P.O. Box 510092, Salt Lake City, UT 84151, (801) 575-6510

American Genealogical Lending Library, 593 West 100 North; P.O. Box 329, Bountiful, UT 84011-0329, (801) 298-5446, FAX (801) 298-5468

Everton Publishers, Inc., P.O. Box 368, Logan, UT 84323-0368, (800) 443-6325, FAX (801) 752-0425.

Genealogy Unlimited, Inc., 1060 South 500 East, American Fork, UT 84003-9723; P.O. Box 537, Orem, UT 84059-0537, (800) 666-4363 or (801) 763-7132

Sample Pedigree Chart

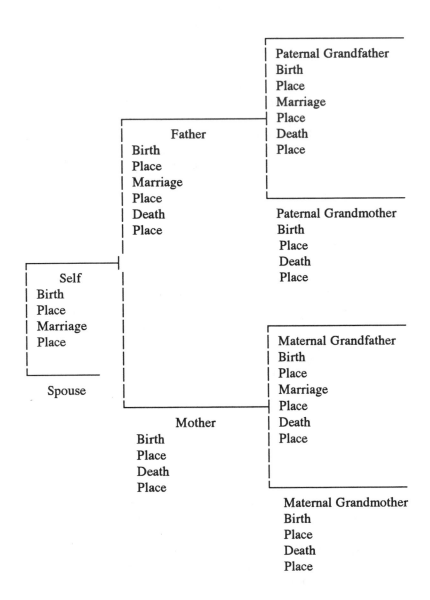

Hearthstone Bookshop, Potomac Square, 8405-H Richmond Highway, Alexandria, VA 22309, (703) 360-6900

S.E.L. Enterprises, 178 Grandview Avenue, Thornhill, Ontario, Canada L3T 1J1, (416) 889-0498

Personal papers that are the most useful in supplying data for the pedigree and family group charts are

baby books	journals
certificates	letters
citizenship papers	military records
deeds	newspaper clippings
diaries	probates
family Bibles	wills
funeral memorial cards	

PREPARE A LIST OF RESEARCH NEEDS

From the blank spaces on your pedigree and family group charts prepare a list of research needs of interest. Rank them in priority order to follow while at the library, including which family or families you wish to research first. Include the geographical places involved with these needs, objectives, and priorities. Faithful adherence to such lists may save you from the distractions that might otherwise sidetrack you from your primary goals. You should also regularly ask yourself, "Is this part of my research really necessary to achieve my goals?"

If you have a personal computer it may be more efficient to prepare a list of research needs on it, instead of the below typed or hand written cards. The inventory programs of the *Personal Ancestral File* (*PAF*) or other genealogical computer programs can assist in some aspects of the above lists. The *PAF* is written for MS-DOS and Macintosh computers and is an excellent computer program for family history research, and very reasonably priced. It is available from the Church of Jesus Christ of Latter-day Saints, Salt Lake Distribution Center, 1999 West 1700 South, Salt Lake City, Utah 84104-4233. Telephone number for VISA or Mastercard orders, (800) 537-5950; outside the United States and

3

Chapter 1

Canada call (801) 240-1174. For information on the availability of programs, telephone (800) 453-3860, ext. 2584.

Sample List of Research Needs in Priority Order

Names, places and dates of birth and death
of the two daughters of John Black Greer, perhaps
born in Glasgow, Scotland. Both died about 1850
under 8 years of age, perhaps St. Louis, Missouri.

Birth place of John Black Greer, perhaps
Ireland. Married Jean Leishman, 23 August 1856,
Binghamton, Broome, New York. Father of Jane
Greer Parkinson.

Birth date of John Parkinson, born Linn Co.,
Ohio, father of David, born 3 May 1871, Jefferson
Co., Iowa.

An excellent supplementary *PAF* user's manual is Joan Lowrey's *Personal Ancestral File 2.31 Users Guide* 5th ed. (La Jolla, Calif.: Joan Lowrey Enterprises (7371 Rue Michael, 92037, (619) 454-7046, FAX (619) 459-7514, joan__lowrey@f709.n202.z1.fidonet.org) 1995, FHL GENERAL BOOK AREA 005.3 L955). A helpful keyboard template for MS-DOS version of the *PAF* is available from Kathy Cook Consulting, P.O. Box 393, Escondido CA 92015.

Research objectives may also be prepared through the use of the notes mode of the *PAF*. Many other supportive utility programs for *PAF* are announced, questions answered, bulletin board systems and tips provided in the *International PAF Users' Group Quarterly*, 2463 Ledgewood Drive, West Jordan, UT 84084-5738 and *PAFinder Newsletter*, 4417 Pitch Pine Court, San Jose, CA 95136 (Silicon Valley PAF User's Group).

The *PAF* and other computer software for genealogical computing are nicely explained in Donna Przecha and Joan Lowrey's *A Guide to Selecting Genealogy Software*, 2d ed. (Baltimore: Genealogical Publishing Co., 1993, FHL in process).

PREPARE A LIST OF INDIVIDUALS

Prepare a list of individuals for whom you hope to find information. It is more practical to write each name on a 3"x5" card, separate slips of paper or computer lists. You may wish to limit individual cards to the last known ancestors on your pedigree. Put the surname in the upper left-hand corner of the card, followed by the first and middle names and some vital data below the name. Information should also include the name of the spouse and the child who is in the direct line being researched.

Sample Individual's Card

Greer, John Black

    b. perhaps in Glasgow, Scotland
    m. Jean Leishman, 23 August 1856, Binghamton, Broome, New York
    d. Cleveland, Cuyahoga, Ohio
    f. of Jane Greer, wife of Timothy Parkinson

PREPARE FAMILY SURNAME CARDS

Prepare a 3"x5" card or a computer entry for each family surname for which you would like to research and find a printed family history. Write the family's surname near the upper left-hand corner of the card.

Chapter 1

Under the surname write the names of prominent members of the family, the dates and places important in their lives, and their professions or other relevant information, such as outstanding accomplishments or service.

Sample Family Surname Card

>   Parkinson Family
>   Parkinson, John
>   born Linn Co., Ohio
>   father of David
>   born 3 May 1871
>   Jefferson Co. Iowa
>   Doctor

PREPARE A LIST OF GEOGRAPHICAL LOCATIONS

The final set of 3"x5" cards or computer lists that you should prepare is for each geographical location of research interest. Geographical cards or computer lists should contain in the upper left-hand corner the name of the state, the county, and the town or the name of the foreign country, the county, and the parish, village, or town, if known. Below the geographical location list the full names of some of the ancestors who lived there or the names of prominent members of the family, their occupations, if known, the years they lived there, and vital dates.

Sample Geographical Location Card

>   Ohio, Linn Co.
>   Parkinson, John
>   born Linn Co., Ohio
>   father of David
>   born 3 May 1871
>   Jefferson Co. Iowa
>   Doctor

At this point you should have prepared four different sets of cards or lists: research needs in priority order, individuals, family surnames, and geographical locations. These will be used in many different ways and will prove helpful in the research strategies explained later in this book.

After you have collected and organized the data found in your home, write or call relatives who may have done some genealogical research or have papers concerning your ancestors. Inquire whether they have pedigree charts or family group sheets that you can use to extend your ancestral lines. Also ask if they know of any printed biographical sketches, baby books, certificates, citizenship papers, deeds, diaries, family Bibles, family histories, funeral memorial cards, journals, letters, manuscript histories, military records, newspaper clippings, probates, wills, or magazine and periodical articles that include your ancestors.

You should keep copies of all of your correspondence. Some researchers find it useful to keep a "Correspondence Log" and a "Research Log" listing all of their correspondence and research, similar to the following:

Sample Correspondence Log

Date	Letter to	Subject	Date Rec'd Answer
1/3/92	Emily Smith	Place of marriage of Jane Greer	2/23/92

Chapter 1

Sample Research Log

Library	Source	Call #	Page in File	Date
FHL	1850 Census Elk Co. Penn.	444744	7	5/2/92

The research log can become the table of contents to your note file if you number your notes. Some researchers simply file their correspondence together with research notes in file folders under family surnames.

ADDITIONAL READING:

Wright, Raymond S., III. "Getting Started," chapter 2, pages 12-17 and "Computers and Genealogy," chapter 3, pages 25-33. In *The Genealogist's Handbook: Modern Methods for Researching Family History*. Chicago: American Library Association, 1995.
 FHL US/CAN REF AREA 973 D27gh.

SUMMARY:

Prepare pedigrees, family group sheets, and cards or lists of families, individuals, geographical locations, and ancestral research needs in priority order. Write or call relatives for additional family history information.

"Do you think that the Personal Ancestral File could handle my llamas' pedigrees?"
                    -- 1990 telephone question to author

Chapter 2

IDENTIFY COUNTIES

Because the majority of the records that relate to family history research are housed in county court houses (New England towns, some independent cities in various states, and some foreign countries are the exceptions), it is necessary to identify the county (or equivalent for foreign countries) for every place where the ancestors you wish to research were born, married, divorced, acquired or sold land, filed a will, died, were buried, and/or had a probate administered or by decree distributed. It is also helpful to know the counties where they lived in the United States during the census years of 1790, 1800, 1810, 1820, 1830, 1840, 1850, 1860, 1870, 1880, 1900, 1910, or 1920.

The geographical cards or lists outlined in chapter 1 can be used in the steps below to identify counties. County names (or equivalents), once identified, should be added to the geographical cards and to all geographical entries on pedigrees and family group sheets.

I. FAMILY HISTORY CENTER USERS:

One easy way to identify counties is by using the *Family History Library Catalog: Locality Catalog*. Consult the first few left-hand columns on the first microfiche of the state (or several microfiche for some countries) of the *Family History Library Catalog: Locality Catalog* and search for the name of the city or cities for which you need county names. County names (or equivalent) are given for all cities for which the Family History Library has materials; therefore it is not a complete list of cities or counties.

Sample
Family History Library Catalog: Locality Catalog
Geographical Entry on Microfiche

Warsaw, Missouri -----> Missouri, Benton, Warsaw

Chapter 2

This catalog is available also on the CD-ROM computer system, *FamilySearch,* (2.22) and is available in all Family History Centers, along with its microfiche edition. *FamilySearch* is available in the Family History Library, and in the Joseph Smith Memorial Building, South Temple and Main Streets, on a computer network mainframe (not online) that does not require the use of CD-ROM diskettes.

You may want to search *FamilySearch* at your local Family History Center for the names of your counties by looking at the "Locality Browse." To get to "Locality Browse" follow these instructions:

Select "**F. Family History Library Catalog**" from the FAMILYSEARCH MAIN MENU by pressing the letter "F" or by placing the computer highlight bar over the "Family History Library Catalog" line with the down arrow " ↓ " and by **pressing "Enter."**

The computer will request that you "INSERT COMPACT DISC." Locate the "Family History Library Catalog" CD-ROM diskette in a nearby rack and insert in the CD-ROM drive.

Select "**B. Locality Browse**" from the LIBRARY CATALOG MAIN MENU by pressing the letter "B" or by **pressing "Enter."**

"**A. Town and parish list**" from the LOCALITY BROWSE screen.

Press "Enter," type the name of the city of interest, press "Enter."

In a few seconds the name of the city, county, and state may be highlighted on the screen or you may need to read down the screen or press the page down key "PgDn" until you see your city and state, then make a note of the county's name. Press "F11" (=Menu) and continue your search for the second city by repeating the steps from selecting "Locality Browse" as explained above.

If a city is not listed in the *Family History Library Catalog: Locality Catalog*, the Family History Library does not have materials cataloged under the name of that city. However, the Library may have something cataloged for that city under the name of its county, and you may have to wait until you can consult the sources mentioned in Parts II and III of this chapter to determine the name of the county.

For those places not found in the *Family History Library Catalog: Locality Catalog*, you should check the following source, which the Family History Center may also have: *Bullinger's Postal & Shippers Guide for the United States & Canada: Containing Post Offices & Railroad Stations, With the Railroad or Steamer Line on Which Every Place or the Nearest Communicating Point is Located, and the List of Railroads & Water Lines With Their Terminal Points* (Westwood, N.J.: Bullinger's Guides, 1878, 1895, 1951, or 1961; FHL microfilm numbers: FHL US/CAN FILM AREA 1961 - 1320793 Item 7, 1951 - 483709, 1895 - 1033518, or 1878 - 1002373 Item 2). If you need to use it when you get to the Family History Library, it is in both the reference and the regular collections, with the call number: FHL US/CAN BOOK AREA 970 E8b.

For those really tough places to find, such as ghost towns or places that no longer exist and are not listed in available reference sources, a letter to the state library or the historical society library of the state involved may bring the needed answer. Most of those libraries maintain collections or card files for answering such difficult questions. Most public libraries can provide the state libraries' and state historical society libraries' addresses from the *American Library Directory* (New York: Bowker) FHL US/CAN REF AREA 973 J54a.

FOREIGN PLACE NAMES

Many of the Family History Centers have an excellent atlas with a detailed list of English parishes, *The Phillimore Atlas and Index of Parish Registers* (Chichester, England: Phillimore, 1984, FHL BRITISH REF AREA 942 E7pa). Most specific how-to-do-it books for foreign countries explain the use of that country's gazetteers and postal guides in genealogical research. The Family History Library also has atlases, gazetteers, and postal directories for many foreign countries to assist with place identification. Many of these are in microform and may be found in some Family History Centers or may be ordered. For those not available in microform you may have to wait until you go to Salt Lake City to gain access to them.

11

Chapter 2

The Subject headings under which they will be found in the *Family History Library Catalog: Locality Catalog* are as follows:

Gazetteers: FRANCE - GAZETTEERS

Geographical Names: FRANCE - NAMES, GEOGRAPHICAL

Ghost Towns: FRANCE - HISTORICAL GEOGRAPHY
                            FRANCE - HISTORY

Post Offices: FRANCE - POSTAL AND SHIPPING
                            GUIDES

Foreign country gazetteers and postal guides and directories may also be consulted by correspondence by completing a Reference Questionnaire available at a Family History Center. Obtain and complete the questionnaire and leave it at the Center for their mailing to the Family History Library. This service is free. The form, with an answer, will be returned to your mailing address; however, the Library's workload of correspondence is very heavy, so the answer may not be immediate.

COUNTY BOUNDARY CHANGES

As your research progresses you may find that you must learn something about county boundaries. You may be researching for ancestors in a particular county and find that the *Family History Library Catalog: Locality Catalog* only lists records for the county back to 1851, for example. At this point you need to know what county or counties are the parent counties. In order to determine this you need to use one or both of the following:

Everton, George B., ed. *The Handy Book for Genealogists.* 8th ed., rev. and enl. Logan, Utah: Everton Publishers, Inc., 1991.
   FHL US/CAN REF AREA 973 D27e 1991.

Ancestry's Red Book: American State, County, and Town Sources.
Edited by Alice Eichholz. Rev. ed. Salt Lake City: Ancestry
Publishing, 1992.
    FHL US/CAN REF AREA 973 D27rb.

The above works are usually the best two sources to answer the
problem of county boundaries. However, their information is limited to
the date of the county's creation and names of the county or counties
from which it was formed. You may need additional assistance
concerning difficult county boundary problems. A few states have
prepared detailed books on the subject. These books and references to
parts of other sources are listed in "A Selected Bibliography of
Statewide Place Name Literature, Old Gazetteers, Postal Service
Histories, Ghost Town Directories and Histories, and Boundary Change
Guides," in *Library Service for Genealogists*, ed. J. Carlyle Parker,
Gale Genealogy and Local History Series, vol. 15 (Detroit: Gale
Research Co., 1981, op, FHL US/CAN REF AREA 026.9291
P226L, 2d edition in progress by Marietta Publishing Co.), pages 29-
47.

Many county histories also include boundary change information, as
well as township boundary changes. For problems that can not be
resolved through the above sources, you should write the county clerk
of the county involved and ask for assistance.

Sample subject headings used in the *Family History Library Catalog:
Locality Catalog* relative to sources that identify county boundaries:

> CALIFORNIA - LAND AND PROPERTY - HISTORY
> KANSAS - HISTORICAL GEOGRAPHY

TOWNSHIPS

Some researchers may need to identify the county for a named
township, such as Washington Township, Ohio. John L. Andriot
compiled *Township Atlas of the United States, Named Townships*
(McLean, Va: Andriot Associates, 1977, FHL US/CAN REF AREA
973 E7an 1987, US/CAN FICHE AREA 6049121, (12 microfiches).

Chapter 2

It is the most useful reference source for assisting with named township problems. This atlas contains current outline maps for the twenty-two states with named townships, showing the names and locations of counties, and county maps showing the names and locations of their named townships and other minor civil divisions. The 223-page index contains entries for over 52,000 counties, districts, divisions, gores, grants, named precincts, plantations, towns, townships, and others.

There is a newer atlas by Andriot, *Township Atlas of the United States* (McLean, Va: Andriot Associates, 1979) for all townships for all states. However, it is not as detailed as the 1977 atlas for the twenty-two states with named townships.

If more information is needed concerning townships, you can turn to the county histories of the county concerned. Some county histories include a history of the townships and often explain their boundaries.

II. LOCAL PUBLIC LIBRARY USERS:

For county names in the United States check the indexes of the Rand, McNally and Co., *Commercial Atlas & Marketing Guide* (Chicago: 67th- 1936-). For counties or regional subdivisions in other countries check *Webster's Geographical Dictionary* or the *Columbia Lippincott Gazetteer*. For any cities not found in these sources you will have to check other atlases or maps that may be available at the public library. You may have to wait until you arrive at the Family History Library to check the place names not found.

III. HOME LIBRARY USERS:

Many counties can be determined through the use of maps or atlases that you have collected and have at home. The *National Five-Digit Zip Code & Post Office Directory*, which is available at your local post office, gives counties for all cities listed at the beginning of each state's listing.

14

If any of the above sources do not identify the county of a city which you need to research, you may also write the state library or the historical society library of the state for which you have a place name problem and enlist their assistance in determining the county.

ADDITIONAL READING:

Parker, J. Carlyle. "Identifying the Counties for Cities," chapter 5, pages 25-48. In *Library Service for Genealogists.* Gale Genealogy and Local History Series, vol. 15. Detroit: Gale Research Co., 1981, op. 2d edition in progress by Marietta Publishing Co.
    FHL US/CAN REF AREA 026.9291 P226L.

SUMMARY:

You must know the counties for all cities where ancestors were born, married, or died. Check maps and atlases at home, or the *Family History Library Catalog: Locality Catalog,* Rand McNally's *Commercial Atlas & Marketing Guide,* or the *National Five-Digit Zip Code & Post Office Directory* (2 vols., Washington, D.C.: U.S. Postal Service, 1992).

Q. "Where is Dover, California?"

A. "This little village was started in 1866 and at one time attracted considerable attention. It was situated on the San Joaquin River, above the mouth of the Merced River."
    -- *History of Merced County, California.* San Francisco: Elliott & Moore, 1881, page 118.

A Merced County, California, dock town for shipping winter wheat by steamer via the San Joaquin River to San Francisco (about 130 miles). Now, a cornfield.
    -- The author

FamilySearch, International Genealogical Index

TURLOCK CALIFORNIA FAMILY HISTORY CENTER

Chapter 3

INTERNATIONAL GENEALOGICAL INDEX

It is very important that a survey be made to determine what research
has already been completed. It is a waste of time to launch into in-
depth research without attempting to determine what has been done by
other researchers. One of the first sources that should be consulted is
the *International Genealogical Index (IGI)*.

The *International Genealogical Index* is available in all Family History
Centers, the Family History Library, the *FamilySearch* Center in the
Joseph Smith Memorial Building, and in the west wing of the fourth
floor of the Joseph Smith Memorial Building on the corner of South
Temple and Main Streets. A few public and several genealogical
libraries have also purchased the *International Genealogical Index* or
FamilySearch. However, if you have to wait until you arrive at the
Family History Library, microfiche copies and the *FamilySearch*
edition of the *IGI* are on all floors of the Library.

The latest edition of the *IGI*, 1993, contains 200 million name entries.
The first *Addendum* to the *IGI* was issued in 1994 and contains 40
million entries. The *IGI* is the largest and most useful genealogical
index available. Its entries cover deceased persons primarily born
between the early 1500s and the present.

The *IGI* is on microfiche and on *FamilySearch*. Until a microfiche
verse of the *Addendum* is provided, it is imperative that the
FamilySearch edition of the *IGI* be used for most searches.

The *IGI* consists of research submitted by LDS Church members or
entered from the Church's Name Extraction Program since October
1969, including many pre-1970 records that have been added by the
Church. It is international in scope and based on government, church,
and personal records. However, it contains more names for Denmark,
England, Finland, Germany, Iceland, Mexico, Netherlands, Norway,
Scotland, Sweden, Switzerland, United States, and Wales than for other
countries.

Chapter 3

Entries in the *IGI* and its *Addendum* do not totally represent all of the research submitted by members of the Church of Jesus Christ of Latter-day Saints. The 240 million deceased individuals' names, the combined total of the *IGI* and its *Addendum*, together represent about 95 % of the names submitted before 1970 and 98 % after 1970.

The following letters that begin batch numbers (found in the second from the right column on the microfiche copy of the *IGI* and on the source screen of the *IGI* and its *Addendum*) are for entries that are the most reliable, as they represent records abstracted through the world wide LDS Church extraction program based on primary genealogical sources: C, E, J, K, M (except M17 and M18), P, T5

The two versions of the *IGI* are usually not released simultaneously; therefore you should check the dates of each and use the latest release or edition. The date for the *IGI* microfiche is printed at the top of each microfiche. The date for the *FamilySearch IGI* appears on the program's first screen. As you make notes about ancestors found in the *IGI*, make sure that you also record the year that the *IGI* was published. The dates of the edition and/or addendum you have checked will be important to you when you need to recheck future addenda to the *IGI*.

Names in the *IGI* on microfiche are arranged alphabetically within each state where a vital event took place for the United States and Mexico; each province of Canada; the counties of Denmark, England, Finland, Ireland, Norway, Scotland, Sweden, and Wales; and by country for each of the other countries of the world. It is primarily useful for finding records of births or christenings and marriages. There are some death records included and some record entries based on the U.S. census schedules. The entries for Denmark, Finland, Iceland, Norway, Sweden, and Wales are listed separately by given names and by surnames (two alphabets for each country).

For checking the *IGI*, use the 3"x5" cards prepared in chapter 1 for individuals and select the ancestors for whom you wish to search. A search should include at least the last known ancestors on your pedigree. Each ancestor searched should be checked in the *IGI* under the state (province, county, or country) of birth and state (province, county, or country) of marriage. The surnames at the top of the microfiche, that can be read without a microfiche reader, are the first and last surnames that appear in the text of the microfiche.

Sample *International Genealogical Index* Entries

KENTUCKY

Vinson, Alexander Lucy Gibson H M 13 Sep 1817 Christian
Hopkinsville 7128123 96

Vinson, Benjamin Alexander Vinson/Lucy Gibson M B 29 Feb
1824 Muhlenberg   7802625 97

The first sample above is an entry for the marriage ("M") of Alexander Vinson (the husband, "H") to Lucy Gibson on September 13, 1817 in Hopkinsville, Christian County, Kentucky. The second sample is an entry for the birth ("B") of a male ("M"), Benjamin Vinson, to parents Alexander Vinson and Lucy Gibson in Muhlenberg County, Kentucky, February 29, 1824. Abbreviations like H, M, and B, as in the examples above, are explained at the top and bottom of the second and third columns respectively. If you are unable to understand *IGI* entries, ask a Family History Library or Family History Center volunteer to help you interpret them.

When using the *IGI*, record all of the information except for post-1970 dates in the columns labeled "b," "e," and "s." Those columns relate to the temple work done by members of the Church of Jesus Christ of Latter-day Saints and should be noted by LDS members. The reason that LDS members submit names of deceased relatives for temple work is because they believe that all persons should be provided the opportunity to accept Jesus Christ through baptism by immersion, to be married for eternity, and to receive additional religious ordinances that have to be done on earth. Latter-day Saints believe that these ordinances can be done by proxy in the Church's temples by living persons, for the deceased, who then have the choice and freedom to accept or reject these ordinances in the spirit life beyond the grave.

SOURCES SUBMITTERS USED

The numbers in the last two columns of the *IGI* are the "Batch Number" and the "Serial Sheet" number. Record these numbers in order to find the source of the *IGI* information: the patron's form on the batch microfilm or the microfilm or book number from which the genealogical information was extracted. The patron's form contains the name and address of the person or patron who submitted the data and a reference to the source of the data. It may be useful in some cases to consult the source used to submit the data.

The fastest way to find the source or sources used by submitters is through the use of the *FamilySearch IGI* and its *Addendum*. To find the sources after the ancestor's name is found **press "Enter" (=Details),** **then "Enter" again (=See Sources).** Please read all of the information on the "SOURCE INFORMATION" screen that will appear and, if you wish, print it by using "F2=Print/Holding File."

SUBMITTERS

In order to obtain the name and address of the person who submitted a name that has been indexed in the *IGI*, check the batch number in the next-to-last column of each entry. Patron-submitted names are identified by batch numbers wherein the first two digits represent the year of submission (<u>72</u>34444), with the following exceptions:

694, 725, 744, 745. 754, and 766

The names of persons who submitted names after May 1991 are not reported in any way. The person who submitted a common ancestor of yours may not be a direct relative, because in some circumstances Church members are permitted to submit names for all persons with the same surname as an ancestor of theirs within a ten-mile radius of that ancestor's residence or within the same county in the United States where that ancestor resided.

The patron's forms were microfilmed and the paper copy destroyed. The microfilm number of the microfilmed patron's form is listed as the "Input Source" on the microfiche copy of the *IGI Batch Number Index*, opposite the batch number. The *IGI Batch Number Index* is a small, separate microfiche publication, usually filed with or near the *IGI*.

Sample *IGI Batch Number Index* Entry on Microfiche

BATCH NUMBER	INPUT SOURCE
7200322	820079
7200323	820068

The serial sheet number is used like a page number to locate the exact patron's record within the batch number on the microfilm.

There are three ways to access a patron-submitted record, but in any case you must determine the microfilm number for the submitted record. The "Input Source" may be checked while researching at the Family History Library, or beforehand, by requesting a photocopy via the Library's "Request for Photocopies" form, or by ordering the microfilm through the Family History Center's interlibrary loan program.

A large part of the entries in the *IGI* are not patron-submitted but were extracted from vital and parish records by LDS Church volunteers. The sources used for entries that are not patron-submitted may also be found on the *IGI Batch Number Index*. It lists some printouts of records. The printouts contain the same information found in the *IGI*. However, if you would like to use an alphabetical list of a single record or part of a record, it may be useful to use a printout microfilm.

Chapter 3

PARISH AND VITAL RECORDS LIST

Another useful supplement to the *IGI* for determining what records have been extracted is the *Parish and Vital Records List*. It is also a small microfiche publication and is arranged in alphabetical order by country and sub-arranged by state or province and county. It provides the years extracted from each type of record; the Family History Library call number for the microfilm or book used; and, for a few records, a microfilm number for a computer print-out of a listing, in alphabetical order, of the names extracted. It is available at Family History Centers, the Family History Library, and in the Joseph Smith Memorial Building, and in some genealogical libraries and genealogical departments of public libraries.

Sample *Parish and Vital Records List* Entry on Microfiche

UNITED STATES
MAINE

CO.   TOWN/   PERIOD RECD PRINTOUT PROJECT SOURCE
        PARISH FROM-TO TYPE CALL NO.

ANDRSC TURNER 1776-1875 BIR 0883819   C50327-1 012262

The *IGI* batch numbers that start with the letter "A" with sealing ("s") dates between 1942 and 1970 may be traced through the Archive (main) Section of the Family Group Records Collection (FGRC listed in the source column of the *IGI* as "AR REC"). The person who submitted the data may no longer be available; however, the form will contain other useful information. The Family Group Records Collection is explained in chapter 11, pages 134-35.

The *IGI* batch numbers T000001 through T000010, and T000150- may also be traced to the Family Group Records Collection.

Occasionally the word "FILM" is given in the serial sheet column, in which case a microform number will be provided in the batch number column. Some *IGI* entries include the symbols " ∆ ," "#," "∂," and " > ." The " ∆ " stands for "Entry altered from source" (after evaluation for clearer meaning); and the "#," "∂," and " > " represent "Relative named in source." The symbols also indicate:

> "#"   that the names of parents or grandparents are included
>
> "∂"   that some dates may have been estimated
>
> " > "   that additional information is only available to direct descendants of the person listed in the *IGI* from Special Services, Temple Department, 50 East North Temple Street, Salt Lake City, Utah 84150.

These symbols will not appear with most entries added to the *IGI* before its 1984 edition and many entries added to the *IGI* between the 1984 and the 1988 editions. These symbols are also provided and explained in the detail windows of the *IGI* on *FamilySearch*.

IGI ON *FAMILYSEARCH*

The *IGI* and its *Addendum* are available on the CD-ROM computer system, *FamilySearch*, and, along with the *IGI* on microfiche, are available in all Family History Centers and the Family History Library. The *FamilySearch* is provided in the Joseph Smith Memorial Building. The *FamilySearch* computer terminals available in the Family History Library, and in the Joseph Smith Memorial Building, South Temple and Main Streets, are on a computer network mainframe (not online) that does not require the use of CD-ROM diskettes.

The Centers, the Library, and the Joseph Smith Memorial Building have volunteers who will help you with the *FamilySearch*. Also a few genealogical libraries and genealogical departments of public libraries have the *IGI* or the *FamilySearch* and the *Addendum*.

At your Family History Center you should search for the names of your ancestors on the *IGI* of the *FamilySearch* (2.22) and its *Addendum* by making the following choices (selections):

Chapter 3

"International Genealogical Index" from the FAMILYSEARCH
MAIN MENU by pressing the letter "C" or by placing the computer
highlight bar over the "International Genealogical Index" line with the
down arrow " ↓ " and by **pressing "Enter."**

"Press F4 to begin a search" at the *International Genealogical Index*
screen.

At the SELECT REGION OR COUNTRY OF THE WORLD TO
SEARCH screen **PRESS "Enter" for North America or move the bar
down, with the arrow key, to the desired country and press
"Enter."**

At the SURNAME SEARCH MENU select one of the following:
   A. Individual Search (Birth/christening information, etc.)
   B. Marriage Search
   C. Parent Search (Individual search sorted by parents' names)
      (You may find children grouped together by parents in
      this search.)

Of course, the selection is made by moving the down arrow to A, B, or
C. The next screen after selecting any of the above will ask for "Given
Name;" **type in given name(s) and press "Enter."** The typing area
bar will advance to the "Surname," at which you must **type in the
surname and press "Enter."** The type area bar will advance to the
"Year of Event (birth, christening, marriage, etc.)." **If you know the
date, type it in.** If you do not know the date, you should estimate it
and **press "Enter."** It is best not to use the "F10=Filter" option, as it
slows a search for a specific individual.

Press either "F12=Start Search" or "Enter."

You will be asked to insert one of the CD-ROM diskettes. When using
computers that use the CD-ROM diskettes make sure that you closely
follow the screen directions for inserting and ejecting the "disc." Some
Centers and libraries will have their *IGI* on CD-ROM diskettes in
caddies (cases) for placing in the disc drive and others will not. Please
leave the diskettes in their caddies or handle with care those that are not
in caddies.

When searching the "C. Parent Search" make sure you type in the maiden name of the mother. It apparently does not matter on which line you type either parent. However, if no parents are found one way it may be wise to type the other.

Please pay attention to the screen helps, particularly "F6=Individual Search," "F7=Marriage Search," or "F8=Parent Search." Using these function keys enables you to repeat the search two additional ways without retyping names from "F4=Search."

After you have searched the *IGI* for one name you should immediately search the *Addendum* for the same name by pressing **"F9."** After the computer has completed its search of the *Addendum*, search your second name in the *Addendum* by pressing **"F4."** Press the type of search and pay attention to the OPTIONS, "Begin a new search" or "Modify previous search." If the next person you are searching has the same given name or surname, it is faster to move the bar down to "Modify previous search" and press "Enter." Type in the new given name(s) or surname, hit the space bar to erase any unwanted letters that may follow the name(s) typed and press either "F12" or "Enter." After searching the *Addendum* for the second name, press "F9" again to search the second name in the *IGI*. Follow this back and forth process with all your *IGI/Addendum* searching.

To print a name press "F2=Print/Holding File." If you select "A. Print Individual Record (highlighted person)" or "A. Print Marriage Record (highlighted person)" the PRINT OPTIONS warn you that printing the source(s) takes extra time. You need the source(s), so follow the screen instructions for printing them, keeping in mind the time elements of the warning. If you wish to consult the source to see if the person who submitted the data may be able to assist you in your research, order the input source microfilm or submit a "Request for Photocopies--International Genealogical Index and Sources" order form for a copy of the patron-submitted form. If the data is not patron-submitted, you may wish to order the input source in order to read possible additional data from the input source that was not extracted, such as notes about your ancestor or burial data.

Chapter 3

Researchers with computers with genealogical software that can receive GEDCOM data may download to their formatted disks, in all sizes, any printable data from the *IGI* by following the prompts for preparing a "HOLDING FILE."

For additional information concerning finding an IGI source, please consult: *Finding an IGI Source*. Research Outline. 2d ed. Series IGI, No. 2. Salt Lake City: The Church of Jesus Christ of Latter-day Saints, 1992. 4 pages.

I. FAMILY HISTORY CENTER USERS:

The *International Genealogical Index* is on microfiche and *FamilySearch*, available at the Family History Centers, the Family History Library. The *FamilySearch* Center in the Joseph Smith Memorial Building, and in the west wing of the fourth floor of the Joseph Smith Memorial Building, South Temple and Main Streets, does not have the microfiche edition.

II. LOCAL PUBLIC LIBRARY USERS:

A few public and genealogical libraries have purchased the *IGI* on microfiche or *FamilySearch*. Make sure as you use it that you check and record in your notes the copyright date of each edition or *Addendum* used.

III. HOME LIBRARY USERS:

If you are impatient you can hire the *IGI* consulted by mail through the services of many of the genealogists who advertise in the *Genealogical Helper* or other genealogical magazines. However, that should not be necessary since my hope is that you'll be in Salt Lake City soon. The microfiche edition of the *IGI* and the *FamilySearch* edition of the *IGI* are available on all floors of the Family History Library. *FamilySearch* computer terminals are also available in the Joseph Smith Memorial Building, South Temple and Main Streets, using a computer network mainframe (not online) that does not require the use of CD-ROM diskettes.

Individuals may also purchase parts of the *IGI* on microfiche for non-commercial use. Write the Family History Library, 35 North West Temple Street, Salt Lake City, UT 84150. Some individuals have *FamilySearch* in their homes for testing for the Family History Library. This home testing program includes a substantial fee; and, if the home use program is extended to more home users, it will probably require a substantial annual fee.

ADDITIONAL READING:

Additional information concerning the *IGI*'s use is found in the following Research Outlines and pamphlets which are available at the Family History Library and Family History Centers:

International Genealogical Index (on microfiche). Research Outline. 2d ed. Series IGI, No. 1. Salt Lake City: The Church of Jesus Christ of Latter-day Saints, 1992. 4 pages.

International Genealogical Index (on compact disc). 4th ed. Salt Lake City: The Church of Jesus Christ of Latter-day Saints, 1993. 5 pages.

Parish and Vital Records Computer Printout. Research Outline. Series IGI, No. 4. Salt Lake City: Corporation of the President of The Church of Jesus Christ of Latter-day Saints, 1988.

FamilySearch: International Genealogical Index (on compact disc) Getting Started. 2d ed. Salt Lake City: Corporation of the President of The Church of Jesus Christ of Latter-day Saints, 1990. 20 pages. In *"FamilySearch"* [manuals in binder].

Using the IGI: Instructions for the 1992 Edition. Salt Lake City: The Church of Jesus Christ of Latter-day Saints, 1992. 4, 4, 45, 9 pages.
    The collection of publications is also available with the microfiche edition of the *IGI* as Z0001, *Instructions for 1992 Edition*.

Chapter 3

For researchers who do not have access to a Family History Center, an excellent article about the *IGI* is Elizabeth L. Nichols' "The *International Genealogical Index*," *The New England Historical and Genealogical Register* 137 (July 1983): 193-209, FHL GENERAL BOOK AREA 929.3 N515i. There is updated information in her more recent article, "*International Genealogical Index (IGI)* 1988 Edition is Distributed to Family History Centers," *Genealogical Helper* 42 (September/October 1988): 5-9.

SUMMARY:

Check the *International Genealogical Index* and its *Addendum* for all of the ancestors for whom you wish to do research, under the geographical location of their birth and marriage. Not everyone will find their ancestors indexed. However, such a large percentage of researchers do find completed research in the *IGI* and *Addendum* that it is imperative that the search be made. Many skeptical researchers have been amazed to find, through the use of the *IGI* and *Addendum*, that someone else has worked on their ancestral lines.

"This stuff [the *IGI*] can give you a real high!"

-- Hippie researcher, Modesto California
Family History Center, early 1970s

Chapter 4

ANCESTRAL FILE

Another step to take in the survey of completed research is to consult *FamilySearch*'s *Ancestral File*. Your individual and family surname 3"x5" cards or your lists may be used in your search of the *Ancestral File*. Next to the *IGI*, the *Ancestral File* is the second largest index that should be used for surveying completed research.

The *Ancestral File* is only available on *FamilySearch* (2.22) at the Family History Library, Family History Centers, and a few public and genealogical libraries. It is also available in the *FamilySearch* Center in the Joseph Smith Memorial Building, and in the west wing of the fourth floor of the Joseph Smith Memorial Building on the corner of South Temple and Main Streets. At the Library and in the Joseph Smith Memorial Building, *FamilySearch* is on a computer network mainframe (not online) that does not require the use of CD-ROM diskettes.

You should search it for the names of your ancestors, as it is another way of determining what research has already been done concerning your families and of finding the names and addresses of possible relations who have done and submitted the research data, starting in 1979. It contains approximately fifteen million names. Other than for corrections and minor additions, the file has no documentation, although submitters' names and addresses are given. The *Ancestral File* has submission, as well as computer input, errors.

The *Ancestral File* is a computer data base which started with contributions of four generations of ancestors by members of the Church of Jesus Christ of Latter-day Saints. Data is still being added to this data base. The *Ancestral File* has expanded far beyond four generations, and the Family History Library encourages all researchers to contribute their pedigrees and family group sheets for inclusion in it.

To use the *Ancestral File* make the following choices (selections) in order, or ask a volunteer for help:

Chapter 4

"**Ancestral File**" from the FAMILYSEARCH MAIN MENU by pressing the letter "B" or by placing the computer highlight bar over the "Ancestral File" line with the down arrow " ↓ " and by **pressing "Enter."**

Please record the date of the edition that appears on the *Ancestral File* screen.

Next press "**F4=Search**" at the ANCESTRAL FILE window screen, which will begin your search.

Press "**Enter**" for "**By SIMILAR last name spelling**" at the SEARCH window, as it will inform you of variant spellings, which you should learn from it and record in your notes.

Type the first and middle names (example: Mary Ann) in the colored bar labeled, "Given Name(s)" on the "Ancestor's name:" line of the SEARCH BY SURNAME AND GIVEN NAME screen. **Press "Enter."**

The colored bar will move to the "Surname (Last Name)." **Type in the name** and **press "Enter."**

The bar is now in the "Birth Year:" and if you know the year or can estimate a year of birth of your ancestor, type it in, as it speeds up the search. Press "**Enter**" or "**F12=Begin Search.**" If you do not know or can not estimate the date press "Enter" or "F12=Begin Search." Follow the directions on the screen for which CD-ROM diskette to place in the CD-ROM drive.

If the person you are searching is in the *Ancestral File*, the name will appear on the screen highlighted with the bar; if not, the highlight bar will appear over a similar name. At this point you have the following numbered options:

1. **Press "Enter=Details."** This selection will produce a window with the name of the person and various data concerning him or her; date of birth and often place of birth or "LIVING," if not deceased at the time of the record submission; marriage date; sex; AFN (*Ancestral File*

30

number); names of father, mother, and spouse (often just "LIVING," if that is the case at the time of record submission). Information concerning living persons is very limited and restricted by the program in order to protect their privacy rights.

Another press of the **"Enter"** will bring up more details about the individual, including places for "Chr:," [christened] "Died:," and "Bur:" [buried]. Yet another **"Enter"** often provides additional information which should include your paging down, "PgDn," to the end of the file. The result may be nothing or as much as the name of spouse, and date and place of marriage.

However, you may be directed to CHANGE COMPACT DISCS. Follow those instructions to the letter. After the computer ejects the disc currently in the CD-ROM, replace it with the one requested. The computer takes some time to read the new disc, followed by a **"PLEASE WAIT"** window, as if it knows you may be too excited to wait for the results. WAIT! Pressing other keys to push it along faster will just get you into a time-consuming mess. The detailed window adds information for christening, death, burial, and the names of all spouses. At this window pressing "F9 = Sources" will bring up source information, which usually provides the name and address of the person or persons submitting the data, including the microfilm number of data microfilmed; research interest; the names of related family organizations; and notes and history of changes in the records, if any have been made. Only those items in bolder print contain some information and can be activated.

The **pressing of the "ESC"** (escape) key will return you to previous screens.

2. **"F6 = Family."** Pressing "F6" brings up the FAMILY GROUP RECORDS window and the choice of the person with a spouse or as a child with parents. Move the bar with the down arrow and make your choice with "Enter." After the family group records information appears, the windows for brief and detailed individual information are available for anyone on the record by moving the bar over their name and pressing "Enter." Also the **"F7 = Pedigree"** function can be selected for anyone on the family group record.

31

To exit the "Family" part of the program press "F5 = Index" which will return you to your list of names.

3. **"F7 = Pedigree."** This function of the *Ancestral File* is one that is exciting and perhaps the most useful. The person you select becomes the first person on the pedigree and you WAIT with interest as the computer builds a five generation pedigree right before your eyes. Following the names of the five generations are arrows that indicate that additional generations follow that name. To extend a line move the bar over the arrow following their name with the up, down, left and right arrow keys and press "Enter." The windows for brief and detailed individual information, plus a window for children ("F11"), are also available for anyone on the pedigree record by moving the bar over their name and pressing "Enter."

4. **"F8 = Descendancy."** Also this function may be selected for anyone on the pedigree, with the arrow keys, and by pressing "Enter." The preparation, printing, or downloading of a descendancy chart by the computer is very time consuming. Please remember, computer time is usually just a one hour slot and you will not be permitted to infringe on the next researcher's time. The "F8 = Descendancy" function may also be chosen from the beginning list of names in the **"F10 = Go-back"** function, which permits you to return to names and the functions that have been used for those persons during your search and to reactivate those functions.

The pedigree on the screen provides only names; however, a printout through the use of **"F2 = Print/copy"** includes their dates and places of birth, marriage, and death. From the PRINT/COPY window choose **"Print Pedigree Chart" and press "Enter."** The PRINT PEDIGREE CHART gives you several choices. One important one is to select a **6 generation CHART TYPE** if your pedigree indicates with an arrow at the end of a fifth generation person that additional generations are available. To choose a 6 generation printout, move the bar with the down arrow over **"6 Generations per page"** and press "Enter" and "F12" to print. Another window will appear with more selections and the ability to print family group records for each couple. If you have a full pedigree chart, please choose **"Do NOT print family group records" and press "Enter"**, as it takes a great deal of time and costs a lot for all of the family group records, as you are charged for all printouts.

The next window, PEDIGREE CHART NUMBER, permits you to number them as you wish. If in doubt or you don't care how they are numbered, type 1 in the "Chart Number:" bar and press "F12." While the printer is printing or the computer is compiling a file for downloading to a disk, you may proceed with your searching. If you want to print all of the family group records and have enough time and money to do so, then move the bar over either "Print family groups with LDS dates" or "Print family groups without LDS dates" and press "Enter." A screen with a list of the selected options will appear. Press either "Enter" if it is okay or "Esc" to cancel it if it is not okay. If you press "Esc" it will return you to the print selection menu again.

Researchers with computers and genealogical software that can receive GEDCOM data (Genealogical Data Communications, a computer standard for transferring genealogical information) may download to their formatted disks, in all sizes, any printable data from the *Ancestral File* by following the prompts of "Create GEDCOM file of ancestors."

Ancestral File may also be used to edit, revise, change, and make additions to itself. Inquire at a Family History Center or write the Family History Library, 35 North West Temple Street, Salt Lake City, UT 84150 (801) 240-3702 for the instructions, *FamilySearch: Contributing Information to Ancestral File*" (3d ed., Salt Lake City: The Church of Jesus Christ of Latter-day Saints, 1992) and *FamilySearch: Correcting Information in Ancestral File*" (Salt Lake City: Corporation of the President of The Church of Jesus Christ of Latter-day Saints, 1991).

FAMILY REGISTRY

The *Family Registry* is another source to check in your surveying completed research. It was introduced in 1983 by the Family History Department of the Church of Jesus Christ of Latter-day Saints for researchers and representatives of family organizations as an aid to the coordination of research. Thousands of people have registered their research needs. The twenty-sixth edition, published in March 1992, contained 336,341 registrations. Registration was not restricted to members of the LDS Church; seventy-six percent of the registrants were not members. The *Family Registry* is available on microfiche in the Family History Library and its Centers in the United States and Canada and in some genealogical libraries and genealogical departments of public libraries.

When the *Family Registry* was introduced it was organized in two parts: the "Registration Forms" and an "Index." Upon receipt, the "Registration Forms" were given a number and then microfiched in numerical order. The "Index" is arranged in alphabetical order, by surnames (for the registration of family organizations) and by ancestors (for individuals). Each index entry for individuals includes vital dates (the year only); the country (including foreign countries) and state; sex; researcher who submitted the information, and a registration number.

Sample *Family Registry* Index Entry

NAMES SEX DATES/PLACES RELATIVES REG.NO. CONTACT
PERSON

WEEKS F B.1769?-USA/NC F.JABEZ WEEKS FR 13288
TAMAR   D.1852 -USA/LA M.MARY RHODES   LURLINE
          M.1796   SP.DANIEL SANDERS   STANLEY
                                                ROUTE 2 BOX 75
                                                DIANA
                                                TX   75640
                                                USA
                                                PH:214 968-6438

Besides the above information, the "Registration Forms" usually
contain the complete dates for vital events, the city and county where
those events took place, the date the form was submitted, an alternate
name and address in case the person who submitted the form was no
longer available for contact, and additional notes that might be helpful
in research. Registration forms received after March 20, 1985 and
numbered after 96641 were indexed but were not added to the
"Registration Forms" part of the *Family Registry*. That part ends with
microfiche sheet number 248 of microfiche collection number 6050001.
The microfiche number for the index is 6050000. A list of the
abbreviations used in the index appears in frames D 01 and E 01 of
each microfiche.

I. FAMILY HISTORY CENTER USERS:

The *FamilySearch*'s *Ancestral File* is available in Family History
Library and its Family History Centers in the United States and
Canada. It is highly recommended that you search it before traveling to
the Family History Library. It is also available in the *FamilySearch*
Center in the Joseph Smith Memorial Building, and in the west wing of
the fourth floor of the Joseph Smith Memorial Building, South Temple
and Main Streets.

Other resources that help researchers get together are the *Family
Registry*, *Computerized "Roots" Cellar*, and the *Genealogical Helper*,
which contains the "Bureau of Missing Ancestors" column. The
Computerized "Roots" Cellar is also published in each issue of the
Genealogical Helper, online search (801-752-6095, n,8,1,ansi), CD-
ROM, and microfiche. Both the *Computerized "Roots" Cellar* and the
Genealogical Helper are publications of the Everton Publishers, Inc.,
P.O. Box 368, Logan, UT 84323-0368 (800) 443-6325, FAX (801)
752-0425.

Chapter 4

II. LOCAL PUBLIC LIBRARY USERS:

Some public and genealogical libraries have acquired the *Family Registry* and *Computerized "Roots" Cellar.* Many of them also subscribe to the *Genealogical Helper,* of which the "Bureau of Missing Ancestors" column should be checked through the index to each copy of the magazine. You will probably have to wait until you are able to do research at the Family History Library in order to use the *Ancestral File* on *FamilySearch.*

Some of these libraries have also been able to expand their online computer services to the public, some free and others for a fee, where genealogists can use the genealogy files of *America Online, Genie, Prodigy,* or *CompuServe.* A few libraries have also been able to extend to the public the services of Internet and the World-Wide Web, with connections to many genealogical accounts.

III. HOME LIBRARY USERS:

A subscription to the *Genealogical Helper* may be useful. It is published by the Everton Publishers, Inc., P.O. Box 368, Logan, Utah 84323-0368, (800) 443-6325, FAX (801) 752-0425. If you wish to check the *Family Registry* while at the Family History Library, copies are available on the main floor near the Information (Reference) Desk. Make sure that you have a pedigree and the cards explained in chapter 1 in order to effectively use the *Ancestral File* on *FamilySearch.* It would also be helpful to read the *Genealogical Helper*'s regular feature, "Family History Library News."

Computers have opened many doors for genealogists, even in their homes. Some of the library computer services mentioned above are available for home use. Many genealogists through their employment have access to the Internet. No matter to which they have access, in some cases they have the possibility of contacting others who are researching the same family lines.

ADDITIONAL READING:

All of the following are available at the Family History Library and its Centers:

FamilySearch: Using Ancestral File." 3d ed. Salt Lake City: The Church of Jesus Christ of Latter-day Saints, 1994. 4 pages.

"Ancestral File: Getting Started." 3d ed. Salt Lake City: The Church of Jesus Christ of Latter-day Saints, 1992. 41 pages. In *"FamilySearch"* [manuals in binder].

FamilySearch: Correcting Information in Ancestral File." Series AF, No. 4. Salt Lake City: Corporation of the President of The Church of Jesus Christ of Latter-day Saints, 1991. 4 pages.

FamilySearch: Contributing Information to Ancestral File." Salt Lake City: The Church of Jesus Christ of Latter-day Saints, 1992. 4 pages.

SUMMARY:

The *Ancestral File* on *FamilySearch* is a very popular file and will probably grow at a rapid rate, as everyone is invited to submit their research to it. However, it does have some errors. The "Research interest" and "Family organizations" functions of the *Ancestral File* that appear on the "Sources" window are not yet operational. When they have been fully developed they may replace the *Family Registry*. Write the contributors to the *Ancestral File* and the registrants of the *Family Registry* who are researching the same ancestors. The *Ancestral File* is the largest single source for locating common ancestors. Through its use, many researchers have found other researchers and genealogists who are researching common lines. All researchers should consult it.

Please remember to structure your computer time in order not to infringe on the time of others. Usually the maximum use of *FamilySearch* in the Family History Library is limited to one hour. While at the Family History Library, if you need to use *FamilySearch* for an extended amount of time, it would be advantageous to walk over

Chapter 4

to the Joseph Smith Memorial Building and use *FamilySearch* in the west wing of the fourth floor where your use of it is not limited.

FamilySearch CENTER

JOSEPH SMITH MEMORIAL BUILDING

Chapter 5

DOES YOUR FAMILY HAVE
A PRINTED HISTORY?

Another aspect of surveying completed research is determining if a family's research has already been published or is available as a manuscript family history. Many hours of research can be saved if a family history is found. Some family histories contain errors; nevertheless, they can still help answer puzzles about who and from where, even if researchers need to verify some of the data.

Family histories usually contain some information concerning the countries of origin. Most genealogical libraries in the United States also include some family histories for families in foreign countries.

I. FAMILY HISTORY CENTER USERS:

Arrange your family surname cards, or computer lists prepared from instructions in chapter 1, in alphabetical order and consult the *Surname Catalog* of the *Family History Library Catalog* for each family. The *Surname Catalog* contains seven times as many references to allied or collateral lines as do the Library of Congress catalogs mentioned later in this chapter. The Family History Library has an estimated 43,000 family histories in book form alone. The Library also has additional family histories that are only available in the collection in microform. A study some time ago indicated that twenty-three percent of the Library's family history collection is not found in other major genealogical collections.

This catalog is available on the CD-ROM computer system, *FamilySearch* (2.22), and in a microfiche edition available in all Family History Centers. *FamilySearch* is available in Family History Centers, the Family History Library, in the *FamilySearch* Center in the Joseph Smith Memorial Building, and in the west wing of the fourth floor of the Joseph Smith Memorial Building, South Temple and Main Streets, and in some genealogical libraries and genealogical departments of public libraries. Both versions of the catalog are prepared and released at different dates. You should check the dates of each and use the latest release or edition. The date for the microfiche is printed at the top of each microfiche. The date for the catalog on *FamilySearch* appears on the LIBRARY CATALOG MAIN MENU. The catalog is also available on all floors of the Library on microfiche.

Sample
Microfiche
Family History Library Catalog: Surname Catalog Entry

COLE

```
                                        +----------------+
                                        :US/CAN
King, Larry, 1909-                      :BOOK AREA
    Keith kinfolks : descendants of James   :929.273
    Keith, Sr., from 1720 to 1979 / by      :K269a
    Larry King. -- Hendersonville,      +----------------+
    Tenn. : King, c1979. -- [16],
    363 p. : ports.
```

James Keith (b. ca. 1720) immigrated from England to
    Virginia "...(brought) as an infant by relatives of
    a guardian." Many descendants moved westward.
Includes index.
Includes Alderman, Buckner, Cole, Hylton, King,
    Sutphin and related families.

Also on microfilm. Salt Lake City :   US/CAN
    Filmed by the Genealogical Society of   FILM AREA
    Utah, 1986.   1321234
    on 1 microfilm reel ; 35 mm.   item 6.

Bibliographic 3"x5" cards should be prepared for the family histories that you would like to consult at the Family History Library. Bibliographic cards should contain the call number (also microform

number), author's full name, book title, place of publication,
publisher, date of publication, number of pages, and a note about
whether or not the book or microform has an index.

Sample Family History Bibliographic Card

Alison Family	U.S. & Can Q area 929.273

Morrison, Leonard Allison.
    The history of the Alison or Allison
family in Europe and America. A.D. 1135-1893;
giving an account of the family in Scotland,
England, Ireland, Australia, Canada, and the
United States. Boston, Mass., 1893.
    312 p. index. illus., ports.
	AL48n
	
	U.S. & Can
	film area
	1036444
	item 12

FHLC Microfiche 9/94

SURNAME CATALOG ON *FAMILYSEARCH*

If your Family History Center has *FamilySearch*, you may want to
search for family histories in it through the following computer choices
(selections), or ask a volunteer for help:

"Family History Library Catalog" from the FAMILYSEARCH
MAIN MENU.

When the INSERT COMPACT DISC screen prompt "Insert the
following disc into drive G: Library Catalog," appears, do it. Then
with the down arrow ↓ move the highlight bar down to select
"Surname Search" from the LIBRARY CATALOG MAIN MENU.

Press "Enter," type the surname of the family of interest, and press
"Enter."

Chapter 5

In a few seconds the surnames and a few names of individuals with the designated surname and variant spellings may appear on the screen. You should read down the screen or press the page down key "PgDn," checking the individuals' names for anyone of interest. If you find an individual of interest, move the computer highlighted bar with the up "↑" or down arrow "↓" keys over that name, and if only one record relates to that person press "F8=Full Display" for a full display of the book about whom or in which the individual appears. You will usually have to page down in order to read the entire record. If the record is of interest, please make the necessary bibliographic notes in order to obtain the work for use, or print the record by pressing "F2=Print/Copy." Select "Print the full list or record" from the PRINT MENU by pressing "Enter." While the printer is printing you may proceed with your searching and queue up additional print commands. Researchers with computers may download to their formatted disks, in all sizes, any entries from the *Family History Library Catalog* by following the prompts of "Copy data to disk." Entries may then be transferred to most word-processing programs, but not to the *Personal Ancestral File.*

If two or more records are available for one person, press "F7=Title/Notes" and the system will display brief author and title with summaries ("CONTENTS") of all of the records. Arrow down until you have read all the records or select the one(s) you wish to display, then display it (them) using "F8."

After searching the individuals return to the top of the list of surnames by pressing "F5=Begin" and then the "Home" key, which is usually on the right of the keyboard. The "Exact Match" entry usually cites a large number of records. The most efficient way to search a large collection of records is to limit the number of records displayed by pressing the "F6" key which permits you to "Add Key-word," really two words or phrases. By typing in one or two of your related or collateral lines, the maternal lines, or a name of a prominent family member or first immigrant on a pedigree (examples Keith, King, and James Keith), you can reduce that large file to a very small number, often one, maybe none. This type of collateral line search will often bring up a book that is about your family.

UPDATE INFORMATION

May 12, 1998; February 3, 1997; October 22, April 12, 1996

All family histories and single biographies in bound format (domestic and foreign, 70,000 volumes) are now shelved in the *FamilySearch* Center on the fourth floor (west wing) of the Joseph Smith Memorial Building.   pages 43-45

In a February 1996 software release, The Family History Library changed "F5 = Begin" to "F4 = Begin" for searching the *Family History Library Catalog* on *FamilySearch*.   page 42

NEW *FamilySearch* FILE, *SCOTTISH CHURCH RECORDS*
At the same time The Family History Library added to *FamilySearch* a ten million name index, *Scottish Church Records*, which permits you to do individual, marriage, and parent searches of Church of Scotland records from the late 1500s through 1854. It is estimated that sixty percent of the population for the period is included in the index. If it applies to your research, please consult it as needed or read the Library's four page pamphlet, *Scottish Church Records*, for details concerning its use.   page 26

A new sign at the end of the second floor microfilm cabinets in the Family History Library reads: "For US/CAN film number higher than 1942968 please go to Floor B1, Row 26." Row 26 is straight ahead and to the left from the elevator alcove.   page 125

US/CAN books with "A1" on the second line of the call number have been moved to the beginning of the collection, rows 2 and 3, to the right of the Automated Resource Center, 124, main floor.   page 127

The Best Western Salt Lake Plaza Hotel is the new name of the Howard Johnson Hotel. All but one of the telephone numbers are the same as published. The (800) 654-2000 number has been changed to (800) 528-1234. The Doubletree Hotel has purchased the Red Lion Hotel. Its 800 number is now (800) 222-8733 and FAX (801) 532-1953. The Doubletree Hotel at 215 West South Temple Street is now the Wynham Hotel, (801) 531-7500, (800) 996-3426, FAX (801) 528-1289.   pages 179-81

Does Your Family Have a Printed History?

A useful addition to your **"Add Key-word"** search is the name of a city, county, state, region, country of origin, or long-time residence to limit the number of records displayed. If you really want to search through several hundred records, it is faster to do it with the microfiche edition. You should read some of the family history entries on microfiche sometime.

FOREIGN COUNTRIES FAMILY HISTORIES

The Family History Library call numbers listed below, for family histories of the various countries represented in its collections, are included for your browsing convenience of the shelves of the Library. The list is arranged in alphabetical order by country, with identification of the area where the family histories in book form are shelved in the Family History Library.

Please remember that there are many more additional family histories in microform. Also many of the family histories in book form have been microfilmed for circulation to the Family History Centers and for preservation. Also remember that is it impossible to browse the microform collections; you must use the *Family History Library Catalog: Surname Catalog* in order to find the microform family histories.

Book Area FHL Call Number

Africa	AFR./MID EAST 929.268
Albania	EUROPE 929.14965
Argentina	LATIN AMERICA 929.282
Australia	BRITISH 929.294
Austria	EUROPE 943.2436
Bahamas	LATIN AMERICA 929.27296
Barbados	LATIN AMERICA 929.272981
Belgium	EUROPE 929.2493
Bermuda	LATIN AMERICA 929.27299
Bolivia	LATIN AMERICA 929.284
Brazil	LATIN AMERICA 929.281

Canada	US/CAN 929.71
Chile	LATIN AMERICA 929.283
China	ASIA 929.251
Columbia	LATIN AMERICA 929.2861
Costa Rica	LATIN AMERICA 929.27286
Cuba	LATIN AMERICA 929.27291
Czechoslovakia	EUROPE 929.2437
Denmark	SCANDINAVIA 929.2489
Ecuador	LATIN AMERICA 929.2866
England	BRITISH 929.242
Finland	SCANDINAVIA 929.24897
France	EUROPE 929.244
Germany	EUROPE 929.243
Greece	EUROPE 929.2495
Guatemala	LATIN AMERICA 929.7281
Honduras	LATIN AMERICA 929.7283
Hungary	EUROPE 929.2439
Iceland	SCANDINAVIA 929.24912
India	ASIA 929.254
Ireland	BRITISH 929.2415
Italy	EUROPE 929.245
Jamaica	LATIN AMERICA 929.27292
Japan	ASIA 929.252
Korea	ASIA 929.2519
Mexico	LATIN AMERICA 929.272
Netherlands	EUROPE 929.2492
New Zealand	BRITISH 929.2931
Nicaragua	LATIN AMERICA 929.27285
Norway	SCANDINAVIA 929.2481
Peru	LATIN AMERICA 929.285
Poland	EUROPE 929.2438
Portugal	EUROPE 929.2469
Puerto Rico	LATIN AMERICA 929.27295
Russia	EUROPE 929.247
Scotland	BRITISH 929.241
Spain	EUROPE 929.246
Sweden	SCANDINAVIA 929.2485
Switzerland	EUROPE 929.2494
United States	US/CAN 929.73

Uruguay	LATIN AMERICA 929.2895
Venezuela	LATIN AMERICA 929.287
Wales	BRITISH 929.2429

II. Local Public Library Users:

Find out if your public library or Family History Center has a copy of any of the following:

U.S. Library of Congress. *Genealogies in the Library of Congress: A Bibliography.* Edited by Marion J. Kaminkow. 2 vols. Baltimore: Magna Carta Book Co., 1972.
FHL US/CAN REF AREA 016.9291 K128g.

U.S. Library of Congress. *Genealogies in the Library of Congress: A Bibliography. Supplement, 1972-1976.* Baltimore: Magna Carta Book Co., 1977. FHL US/CAN REF AREA 016.9291 K128g supp.

U.S. Library of Congress. *Genealogies in the Library of Congress: A Bibliography. Second Supplement, 1976-1986.* Baltimore: Magna Carta Book Co., 1987.
FHL US/CAN REF AREA 016.9291 K128g supp. 1987.

U.S. Library of Congress. *Genealogies Cataloged by the Library of Congress Since 1986: With a List of Established Forms of Family Names and a List of Genealogies Converted to Microfilm Since 1983.* Washington, D.C.: Library of Congress, 1992.

Complement to Genealogies in the Library of Congress Baltimore: Magna Carta Book Co., 1981.
FHL US/CAN REF AREA 016.9291 K128c.

These titles should be checked against your family surname cards or lists.

Chapter 5

15378   SHARP. Know your relatives: the Sharps, Gibbs,
Graves, Efland, Albright, Loy, Miller, Snodderly, Tillman,
and other related families. By Genevieve Elizabeth
(Cummings) Peters. (Arlington? Va.) 1953. 169 p. 28 cm.
58-49595.

CS71.S53 1953

Sample *Complement to Genealogies* Entry

SHARP. Christian Sharp family genealogy. By Eli Sharp.
Kansas City, Mo., 1952. 5 leaves.   FW

(FW = This book is available at the Allen County
Public Library, Fort Wayne, Indiana.)

These bibliographies are arranged by family surname. To use them
simply look up surnames of interest. Check all of the names, dates,
and places that are mentioned in each entry for each surname to see if
an ancestor can be recognized, or a place where ancestors lived. The
first two volumes of the *Genealogies in the Library of Congress* and the
Complement to Genealogies in the Library of Congress have addenda
that must also be checked. When reading the entries in these
bibliographies, all the notes should be read as well; they may contain
clues about who the principal ancestor was and in which part of the
country an ancestor may have resided. If you know that the ancestor
for whom you are looking was from New York and that the family
moved west through Ohio, Nebraska, and Colorado to California, a
family history about a family from Georgia is probably not yours.

Does Your Family Have a Printed History?

For any book that appears to be of interest, write down the author's full name, the title of the book, publisher, place and date of publication, number of pages, the Library of Congress call number (example: CS71 B213 1976).

Sample Family History Bibliographic Card

Sharp Family   CS71.S53 1953
  Know your relatives: the Sharps, Gibbs, Graves,
Efland, Albright, Loy, Miller, Snodderly, Tillman, and
other related families. By Genevieve Elizabeth
(Cummings) Peters. Arlington, Va., 1953. 169 p.

Your public library may purchase the microfilm edition of the *Family History Library Catalog: Surname Catalog*.

While at the Family History Library take the family surname cards or lists and the bibliographic cards prepared from the above catalogs and check them against the *Family History Library Catalog: Surname Catalog*. Prepare additional bibliographic cards for family histories of interest and add FHL book or microfilm numbers to any books listed on bibliographic cards that were prepared from the Library of Congress Catalogs.

III. HOME LIBRARY USERS:

You may write to the Family History Library, 35 North West Temple Street, Salt Lake City, Utah 84150, and ask them to photocopy portions of the *Family History Library Catalog: Surname Catalog*. There is a small fee for this service. You may also purchase the microfiche edition of it for use at your nearest library that has a microfiche reader or on your own reader.

Chapter 5

ADDITIONAL READING:

Parker, J. Carlyle. "Finding Family Histories," chapter 8, pages 105-117. In *Library Service for Genealogists*. Gale Genealogy and Local History Series, vol. 15. Detroit: Gale Research Co., 1981, op. 2d edition in progress by Marietta Publishing Co.
FHL US/CAN REF AREA 026.9291 P226L.

SUMMARY:

Checking the *Surname Catalog* of the *Family History Library Catalog* for a family history before you go to Salt Lake City for research is very important. The *Surname Catalog* will help you locate the most important books and microfilm to read in the Library and save you from a long catalog search while you're there.

If the *Family History Library Catalog* is not readily available to you, check the *Genealogies in the Library of Congress: A Bibliography*, its supplements, *Genealogies Cataloged by the Library of Congress Since 1986: With a List of Established Forms of Family Names and a List of Genealogies Converted to Microfilm Since 1983*, and the *Complement to Genealogies in the Library of Congress*. After you have used either the *Family History Library Catalog: Surname Catalog* or the Library of Congress bibliographies, you should check the other.

"Whew! I don't know which is harder, this [research] or housework."

-- Female researcher overheard in the Family History
Library bookstacks, 1992

Chapter 6

FAMILY HISTORY LIBRARY CATALOG

Use of the *Family History Library Catalog* is imperative because of the Library's vast collections of books and records on microfilm and microfiche. If you try browsing your way through the book collection you will waste hours of research time. Browsing through microforms is impossible because there are very few library-generated titles on the microfilm boxes, and all microforms are arranged in numerical order and not arranged in subject or geographical order.

The *Family History Library Catalog* is available in all Family History Centers. A few public and genealogical libraries have also purchased the *Family History Library Catalog*. However, you may have to wait until you arrive at the Family History Library to use it.

The *Family History Library Catalog* is on microfiche and on *FamilySearch* and is divided into four sections: *Locality Catalog*, *Surname Catalog* (already explained in chapter 5), *Subject Catalog*, and *Author/Title Catalog*. The later two catalogs are currently (1995) not on *FamilySearch*. Checking the *Family History Library Catalog: Locality Catalog* can be done simply by utilizing the 3"x5" geographical cards or computer lists that were discussed in chapter 1.

Locality Catalog on microfiche

Look in the *Family History Library Catalog: Locality Catalog* for vital records of the geographical areas and periods of time that relate to your ancestors of interest. Vital records are the most important resource for genealogical research. They include the registration of births, marriages, deaths, and divorces, as well as U.S. mortality census schedules (June 1, 1849-May 31, 1850; June 1, 1859-May 31, 1860; June 1, 1869-May 31, 1870; June 1, 1879-May 31, 1880) and mortuary records. Microfilmed vital records are the cheapest, often the fastest, and in many cases the easiest way to obtain this information about ancestors. The Library has large collections of civil and church vital records from the sixteenth through nineteenth centuries. Records in the library's largest collections are from the United States, Canada, Mexico, Philippines and most countries of western Europe (including the Azores of Portugal), and Poland.

However, the records at the Family History Library that are available for public use usually protect the current rights of privacy. Therefore, available microfilm often does not include twentieth century records that might contain information about living persons.

The subject headings for vital records used in the *Locality Catalog* of the *Family History Library Catalog* are like these examples:

OHIO, ROSS - VITAL RECORDS
OHIO, ROSS, CHILLICOTHE - VITAL RECORDS.

Sample
Family History Library Catalog: Locality Catalog
Entry on Microfiche

OHIO, ROSS - VITAL RECORDS

```
                                        +--------------+
                                        :US/CAN
Ohio.  Probate Court (Ross County).     :FILM AREA
   Birth records, 1867-1908; index to   +--------------+
   birth records, 1867-1908. -- Salt Lake
   City : Filmed by the Genealogical Society
   of Utah, 1962. -- 3 microfilm reels ; 35 mm.
```

Microfilm of original records in the Ross
   County courthouse, Chillicothe, Ohio.
Records are not in order by date.
Includes indexes at the beginning of each
   volume.

```
Index, v. 1-2    1867-1908 ------------- 0281655
Births, v. 1-3   1867-1889 ------------- 0281656
Births, v. 4-5   1889-1908 ------------- 0281657
```

As you identify materials of interest you should make bibliographic cards for them. Also make note of the date of the *Family History Library Catalog* that you have used, since the catalog is updated periodically. This date is in the caption at the top of each microfiche and can be read without a microfiche reading machine. This may help resolve problems that you might encounter while using the Family History Library due to a change in the catalog, such as a changed call number. The microfiche and *FamilySearch* versions of the catalog are prepared and released at different dates. You should check the dates of each and use the latest release or edition. The date for the catalog on *FamilySearch* appears on the LIBRARY CATALOG MAIN MENU. Make sure that the county, or its equivalent for other countries, appears somewhere on your bibliographic cards.

Sample Bibliographic Card

Ohio, Ross Co.   U S & Can
  Births   film area

    Index, v. 1-2   1867-1908   0281655
    Births, v. 1-3   1867-1889   0281656
    Births, v. 4-5   1889-1908   0281657

FHLC Microfiche 9/94

An avid genealogist who started using this system because of the author's class assignments in a 1982 course recently reported that she still uses it but uses yellow 3"x 5" cards for books and white for microforms. A reader who has utilized the card system avoids one of its pitfalls, spilling them all over the floor of the Family History Center or Family History Library, by punching a hole in them and attaching them onto a key ring.

Chapter 6

Long catalog entries with many volumes, books, years, etc., should be photoduplicated for your convenience while doing research at the Library for referring from the index of a group of microform records to the microforms that it indexes. Often it is easier to copy these long catalog entries from the microfiche edition of the *Locality Catalog*, as you can get more lines per page than from the CD-ROM edition.

Both the county and city subdivisions of a state should be searched for vital records. In addition, for some states and countries it may be necessary to look under the state or country name because the records may have been collected at the state or country level.

If government vital records are not listed in the *Family History Library Catalog: Locality Catalog* or when they fail to provide needed information, researchers should try to determine the religion of their ancestors and turn to church records for vital data and other information collected, recorded, and preserved by churches. Because church records in the United States have not been as widely microfilmed as civil records, it is not as easy to locate them as it is civil or government records, but it is not an impossible task.

The subject headings for searching church records in the *Family History Library Catalog: Locality Catalog* are like these examples:

> OHIO, ROSS - CHURCH RECORDS
> OHIO, ROSS, CHILLICOTHE - CHURCH RECORDS

Besides the church records that substitute for vital records (baptisms, christenings, marriages and their banns, and church burials) the locality subject heading subdivision "CHURCH RECORDS" includes other miscellaneous records, such as church membership lists and church censuses that may also be helpful in genealogical research.

Other supplementary vital records are cemetery and sextons' records. Researchers can turn to these records when government and church records are not available at the Family History Library, or, if available, do not include your people. Many cemetery records have been collected and published by various genealogical and hereditary societies and by individuals. Often these cemetery records are based on headstone inscriptions. Occasionally, they are based on the records of the cemetery's sexton.

The sextons' records may be the better of the two, as there are many cemetery burial plots not marked with headstones. However, headstone inscriptions may contain additional information, including relationships, that may not be provided in the sextons' records. The following are the subject headings under which cemetery records may be found in the *Family History Library Catalog: Locality Catalog*:

> OHIO, ROSS - CEMETERIES
> OHIO, ROSS, CHILLICOTHE - CEMETERIES

Other useful supplementary records are wills and probates. You should bear in mind that wills and probates may not include the exact date of death and usually do not contain the names of deceased, disowned, or lost children. Wills and probate records are cataloged in the *Family History Library Catalog: Locality Catalog* under the following subject headings,

> OHIO, ROSS - PROBATE RECORDS
> OHIO, ROSS - PROBATE RECORDS - INDEXES

Land records often include the sale of property from parent to child and may provide information concerning relationships, but rarely death dates. Land records subject headings in the *Family History Library Catalog: Locality Catalog* are:

> OHIO, ROSS - LAND AND PROPERTY
> OHIO, ROSS - LAND AND PROPERTY - INDEXES

Photoduplicate the entries to all indexes to probates, guardianships, and land records from the microfiche edition of the *Family History Library Catalog: Locality Catalog*. It is better to copy the microfiche edition of the *Locality Catalog* than the CD-ROM edition because you get more information on a page.

Chapter 6

When using the *Family History Library Catalog: Locality Catalog* on
CD-ROM and searching long catalog entries, such as a collection of
128 microfilm reels of marriage records with lots of lines for a large
collection of records, you may be able to speed up your search through
the use of the **F3=Word** function of the computer. **Press "F3"** then
type a date, name, first few letters of name, or a phrase of words, **press
"Enter"** to begin your search to quickly determine if a long entry has
something of interest to you, rather than paging down many times
through the entry. If the first search using the F3=Word concept does
not locate the information you wish to find, you can repeat the search
with a different word, etc., by pressing the **"Home"** key, which moves
back to the beginning of the catalog entry. Then press "F3" again, type
another date, etc. If your search stops part way though the file with
either close to what you wish or what you wish, continue the search to
the end of the file, if necessary, by **pressing "F3"** again. The word or
date you just searched will reappear, simply press "Enter," retype the
word, and the search will continue. A repeat of this process many be
made for one word, etc, until the end of the entry.

The Library also has the following additional sources that supplement
vital records: adoption records, Bible records, census schedules,
guardianships, retroactive military pension applications, naturalization
records, obituaries and necrologies, orphan records, and passenger
lists. The following list provides the *Family History Library Catalog:
Locality Catalog* subject headings for these records:

Subject or Record Type	Locality Subject Heading Subdivision
Adoptions	COURT RECORDS
	GUARDIANSHIP
Baptism records	CHURCH RECORDS
Cemetery records	CEMETERIES
Census schedules	CENSUS
Death notices	OBITUARIES
Family Bibles	BIBLE RECORDS
Guardianships	GUARDIANSHIP
Military retroactive pension applications	MILITARY RECORDS - PENSIONS

Naturalization records	NATURALIZATION AND CITIZENSHIP
Necrologies	OBITUARIES
Obituaries	OBITUARIES
Orphan records	ORPHANS AND ORPHANAGES
Parish registers	CHURCH RECORDS
Passenger lists	EMIGRATION AND IMMIGRATION
Sextons' records	CEMETERIES

It is efficient use of the *Locality Catalog* to read it backwards, starting with the "Vital Records" of city, county, or state and moving towards the front of the locality catalog through "Probate Records," "Land Records," "Church Records," "Census Records," and "Biography." Following this backwards reading method, the records, except for "Church Records" are arranged generally in order of importance.

FAMILYSEARCH

If your Family History Center has *FamilySearch* (2.22), you may want to search the *Family History Library Catalog* for vital records, probate records, or land records by the names of your counties, looking at the "Locality Search." Please ask a volunteer for help if you have any problems using any of the computer programs on *FamilySearch*. To get to "Locality Search" choose (select) in the following order:

"**Family History Library Catalog**" from the FAMILYSEARCH MAIN MENU by placing the computer highlight bar over the "Family History Library Catalog" line with the down arrow " ↓ " and by **pressing "Enter."**

A computer window will appear: "INSERT COMPACT DISC." The computer's compact drive wants the *Family History Library Catalog* put in its mouth. Please feed it the diskette.

Then choose **"Locality Search"** from the LIBRARY CATALOG MAIN MENU by **pressing "Enter."**

If you wish to limit your search to a town or parish, then choose "**Town and parish records**" from the LOCALITY REQUEST screen by **pressing "Enter."**

Chapter 6

However, for research in the United States, except for the New England states and a very few independent cities, such as Richmond, Virginia, you should skip town records, as such a search is too limiting. Search first for research materials at the county subject subdivision of the catalog, then the town or city, and finally at the state subject subdivision.

Therefore, arrow down so that the bar is over **"County or non-Canadian province records" and press "Enter,"** and type in the name of the county of interest, and **press "Enter."**

FamilySearch provides another helpful asset to its program, the truncation of localities. The typing of the long place names, such as Connecticut, may be reduced to four letters plus an asterisk, such as, "Conn*" (without the quotation marks or a period). The following are several examples of how the asterisk may be used:

Turl*	Stanislaus	California
Turlock	Stan*	California
Turlock	Stanislaus	Cali*
Durham	Strafford	New Hamp*

For any set of localities only one truncation may be used. This truncation program can help save time and assist with the problem of not knowing how to spell the names of some localities, especially foreign place names.

If you wish to limit your search to vital records, type that into the barred area to the right of **"Topic:" and press "Enter."**

However, **you should leave the "Topic:" area blank and simply press "Enter."** A search of just one topic may be too limiting, perhaps misleading, and not as thorough as a search of **"ALL"** topics.

At the **"Country/State:"** bar, type in the state of the United States, province of Canada, or name of foreign country.

In all of the above processes type out full place names, not abbreviations. Press "Enter" and usually a screen of historical information will appear; press **"F6=Topic(s),"** then "Enter."

The screen will normally display a long list of topics; page and arrow down to the last and usually most useful topic, "Vital records." From "Vital records" use the following process to read back to the top of the list the records that may be of interest to you:

With the bar over **"Vital records"** press **"F7 = Author/Title"** for topics with two or more records or **"F8 = Full Display"** for topics with only one record.

When searching two or more records on the "F7 = Author/Title" screen, arrow down as you read each record and with the bar over the entry you wish to choose to read press "F8 = Full Display." Make the necessary notes or print the record by pressing **"F2 = Print/Copy."** Select "Print the full list or record" from the PRINT MENU by pressing "Enter." While the printer is printing you may proceed with your searching and queue up additional print commands. Researchers with computers may download to their formatted disks, in all sizes, any entries from the *Family History Library Catalog* by following the prompts of **"Copy data to disk."** Entries may then be transferred to most word-processing programs, but not to the *Personal Ancestral File*.

To return to the list of topics, press "F6 = Topic(s)," move the bar with the up arrow "↑" and press "Enter" at your next record(s) of choice. It is faster to search through multiple records on the microfiche edition of the *Family History Library Catalog*.

After viewing the full text of a catalog entry in the "Full Display" section of the program you may return any time to the author/title section of the catalog by pressing **"F7 = Author/Title"**.

SURNAME CATALOG

There may be other works that have been or will be brought to your attention in your research that may not be easily found through the use of the *Locality Catalog* of the *Family History Library Catalog*. The *Author/Title Catalog* of the *Family History Library Catalog* may be used if an author or title is known, or the *Surname Catalog* of the *Family History Library Catalog* if only a family name is known. The *Author/Title Catalog* is not available on *FamilySearch*.

Chapter 6

The *Subject Catalog* of the *Family History Library Catalog* contains, in part, the following selected list of subjects that may be of interest to some researchers:

> COLLEGE, used as the second word following the
>> name of the college; example: ST. MARY'S COLLEGE
>> (ST. MARYS, KANSAS). A useful subdivision of this
>> type of entry is BIOGRAPHY, where you would find
>> biographical sketches of graduates and those who
>> served in various wars.
>
> CONFEDERATE STATES OF AMERICA - HISTORY,
>> MILITARY
>> NAVY - HISTORY
>> REGISTERS. Subject headings used for some
>>> Confederate Civil War records.
>
> CONVICTS - AUSTRALIA.
>
> DICTIONARIES - ENGLISH, used as the subject heading
>> subdivision for English language dictionaries of
>> another language; example: FINNISH LANGUAGE -
>> DICTIONARIES - ENGLISH.
>
> GENEALOGY, used for some general genealogical
>> how-to-do-it books.
>
> INDIANS, used as the second word following a tribal
>> name; example: CAYUGA INDIANS.
>
> INDIANS OF NORTH AMERICA - NEBRASKA and
>> nearly all of the other states of the union.
>
> INDIANS OF NORTH AMERICA - UNITED STATES
>> United States. Bureau of Indian Affairs.
>> Indian census rolls, 1885-1940. 692 reels.
>
> Minorities; examples: ACADIANS - QUEBEC -
>> GENEALOGY.
>> AFRO-AMERICANS - VIRGINIA.
>> AMERICAN LOYALISTS - CANADA.
>> AMERICAN LOYALISTS - NEW JERSEY.
>
> Religions' general records, histories, etc. (nationwide);
> examples:
>> MORMONS - GENEALOGY - SOURCES.
>> QUAKERS - UNITED STATES.
>> WALDENSES - ITALY.

UNIVERSITY - STUDENTS, used as the second word
following the name of the university and
subdivided by STUDENTS; example: ACADIA
UNIVERSITY - STUDENTS. This heading usually
covers works containing biographical sketches
of graduates.

The *Subject Catalog* is not presently available on *FamilySearch*.

MILITARY INDEX

Two vital record files are also available on *FamilySearch*. The *Military Index* contains the death records of United States military service persons who died or were declared dead in the Korean (1950 to 1957) and Vietnam (1957-1975) conflicts. It contains birth and death dates, race, residence at the time of enlistment, rank, branch of service and number, and place of death. For casualties of the Vietnam conflict, their religious affiliation and marital status were added. A one-page publication available at Family History Centers and the Family History Library that explains the index is *FamilySearch: Military Index* (Series FS, No.2, Salt Lake City: Corporation of the President of The Church of Jesus Christ of Latter-day Saints, 1991).

SOCIAL SECURITY DEATH INDEX

The second file is the *Social Security Death Index*, which contains brief information on 49.3 million deceased persons, 1937-1994, best coverage of which is from 1962-1994. Nearly a million names are added each year. It provides for, but does not always give, birth and death dates, the state in which application was made, the last place of residence, and/or where a death benefit was sent.

Women's married names, instead of their maiden names, are used for searching the *Social Security Death Index*. The application card of those listed may be obtained by sending the ancestor's Social Security number with a check or money order payable to the Social Security

Chapter 6

Administration for $7.00 to the Freedom of Information Officer, 4-H-8 Annex Building, 6401 Security Blvd., Baltimore, MD 21235.
The data on these files can be limited geographically by state by pressing the "F10=Filter" key after having typed in the "Surname" or "Birth year." Both files may be either printed or downloaded to computer disks. These indexes are a United States government document and may be available in some public and university libraries. The Family History Centers and the Family History Library also have a four page pamphlet, *Social Security Death Index* (Series FS, No. 3, Salt Lake City: Corporation of the President of The Church of Jesus Christ of Latter-day Saints, 1990).

I. FAMILY HISTORY CENTER USERS:

You can save a great deal of time at the Family History Library if, before you go to Salt Lake City, you consult the *Family History Library Catalog* and prepare bibliographic cards or computer lists for the materials you wish to use at the Family History Library. The *Family History Library Catalog* is available in all Family History Centers.

II. LOCAL PUBLIC LIBRARY USERS:

A few public and genealogical libraries have purchased the *Family History Library Catalog*. However, you may have to wait until you arrive at the Family History Library before you will have access to it, or follow the directions below in section III.

III. HOME LIBRARY USERS:

You may write to the Family History Library, 35 North West Temple, Salt Lake City, Utah 84150, and ask them to photocopy portions of the *Family History Library Catalog*. The microfiche edition of the catalog may also be purchased from the Library in total or in part by individuals for non-commercial use. The Family History Library offers classes on how to use the *Family History Library Catalog*.

ADDITIONAL VIEWING AND READING:

Using the Family History Library Catalog. Salt Lake City: The Church of Jesus Christ of Latter-day Saints, 1994. 44 pages.

Family History Library Catalog (on Microfiche). Resource Guide. Salt Lake City: The Church of Jesus Christ of Latter-day Saints, 1993. 4 pages.

How to Use the Family History Library Catalog. Salt Lake City: The Church of Jesus Christ of Latter-day Saints, 1987.
   A 24-minute videocassette, available at the Family History Library and most Family History Centers.

FamilySearch: Family History Library Catalog (on compact disc). 4th ed. Series FHLCAT, No. 2. Salt Lake City: The Church of Jesus Christ of Latter-day Saints, 1995. 4 pages.

Nichols, Elizabeth L. "The Family History Library Catalog." *Everton's Genealogical Helper* 48 (September/October 1994): 6-14.

"FamilySearch: *Family History Library Catalog* (on compact disc) Getting Started." 3d ed. Salt Lake City: Corporation of the President of The Church of Jesus Christ of Latter-day Saints, 1992. 24 pages. In *"FamilySearch"* [manuals in binder].

"FamilySearch: *Social Security Death Index.*" 2d ed. Series FS, No. 3. Salt Lake City: The Church of Jesus Christ of Latter-day Saints, 1994. 4 pages.

"FamilySearch: *Social Security Death Index* (on compact disc) Getting Started." 2d ed. Salt Lake City: Corporation of the President of The Church of Jesus Christ of Latter-day Saints, 1990. 13 pages. In *"FamilySearch"* [manuals in binder].

Additional information about vital records may be found in chapter 10, pages 151-79 of Val D. Greenwood's *The Researcher's Guide to American Genealogy* (2d ed., Baltimore: Genealogical Publishing Co., 1990. FHL US/CAN REF AREA 973 D27g 1990). Greenwood

Chapter 6

covers church records in chapter 20, pages 423-63; cemetery records in chapter 24, pages 545-55; probate records in chapters 13-15 and 18, pages 255-320 and 379-96; and land records in chapters 16-18, pages 321-96.

Newman, John J. *American Naturalization Processes and Procedures, 1790-1985.* Indianapolis, Ind.: Family History Section, Indiana Historical Society, 1985. FHL US/CAN REF AREA 973 P4n.

U.S. National Archives and Records Service. "Passenger Arrival Lists," chapter 2, pages 39-57. In *Guide to Genealogical Research in the National Archives.* Washington, D.C.: National Archives Trust Fund Board, 1983. FHL US/CAN REF AREA 973 A3usn. FHL US/CAN FICHE AREA & FHCs 6051414 (4 microfiches).

Also in the above guide, chapters 4-9, pages 71-146 is a discussion of military records available at the National Archives and its regional centers, many of which are available from or at the Family History Library.

Tracing Immigrant Origins. Research Outline. Series FHR 8. Salt Lake City: The Church of Jesus Christ of Latter-day Saints, 1992. 31 pages.

Colletta, John Philip. *They Came in Ships: A Guide to Finding Your Immigrant Ancestor's Arrival Record.* Salt Lake City: Ancestry, 1993. FHL US/CAN BOOK AREA 973 W27c.

SUMMARY:

Consulting the *Family History Library Catalog, Locality Catalog* before you go to Salt Lake City for research is perhaps the most important thing that you can do to save time while in Salt Lake City. It should be checked particularly for vital records for all places where ancestors lived, as well as supplemental vital records, such as church records, cemetery and sextons' records, wills and probates, land records, adoption records, Bible records, census schedules, guardianships, retroactive military pension applications, naturalization records, obituaries and necrologies, orphan records, and passenger lists.

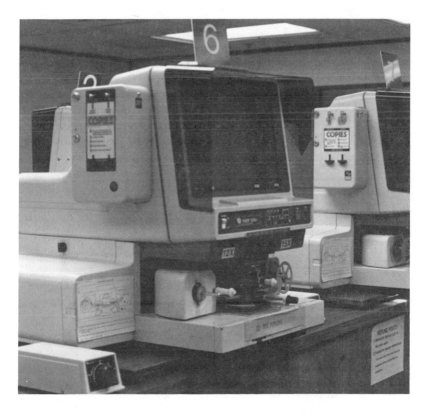

MICROFILM PHOTOCOPY MACHINES

CENSUS TAKER

Martha Porter and children with U.S. census taker, Orderville, Utah 1910.
Photograph by F. Alvin Porter, 1878-1976.

Reprinted by permission. Museum of Church History and Art, The Church of Jesus
Christ of Latter-day Saints.

Chapter 7

ARE YOUR ANCESTORS IN THE
U.S. FEDERAL CENSUS SCHEDULES?

If any one of your ancestors lived in the United States during the years
1790, 1800, 1810, 1820, 1830, 1840, 1850, 1860, 1870, 1880, 1900,
1910, or 1920, he or she probably can be found in the federal census
schedules. The census schedules from 1850 to 1920 are the most
useful, as they include the names of all members of households at the
time of the census and increase in the amount of genealogical
information with each succeeding census. The earlier census schedules
give only the names of the heads of households and the age and sex of
the members of the households. All of the microfilm copies of the U.S.
federal census schedules are available at the Family History Library;
the National Archives, Washington, D.C.; and its twelve regional
archives. Some large public libraries also have microfilm copies of the
U.S. federal census schedules. The schedules may also be borrowed,
for a small fee, from the Family History Library for use in the Family
History Centers.

The Family History Library also has some state census schedules that
were taken in the mid-census years; for example, Kansas 1855, 1865,
1875, and 1885. There are also census schedules available at the
Family History Library for Canada (1841-1901), England, Scotland,
and Wales (1841-1891); and Denmark (1787-1911), Iceland (1762-
1901), Ireland (1901) and Norway (1664-1900). A substitute for census
records for Sweden are clerical surveys, which were prepared by the
churches.

There are many published state-wide indexes for the United States
federal census schedules for the years 1790 through 1850. Some for
more recent years have also been published, and many are currently in
preparation for 1860 and 1870 and a few for Canada and England. A
bibliography of hundreds of U.S. federal census schedule state-wide
indexes is included in chapter 12, pages 139-89, "Census Schedules," in
Library Service for Genealogists by J. Carlyle Parker (Gale Genealogy

and Local History Series, vol. 15, Detroit: Gale Research Co, 1981, op, FHL US/CAN REF AREA 026.9291 P226L; 2d edition in progress by Marietta Publishing Co.).

At some point you will need to use the 1880, 1900, 1910, or 1920 Soundex and Miracode card indexes to the U.S. federal census schedules. The 1880 index includes only families with children age 10 and under. All families are indexed in the 1900 and 1920 census schedules. Index cards of the Soundex and Miracode were created only for the names of the heads of households and for persons residing in the same household with surnames different than the head of the household.

The 1880, 1900, and 1920 Soundex cards are formatted and contain nearly the same information and are self-explanatory. Notes made from the Soundex should always include the county, city, the enumeration district number, and the sheet number and line number. These numbers are necessary to locate your ancestor on the census schedule for the county of residence. The line number is not provided on the 1910 Soundex cards.

However, the Soundex and/or Miracodes for the 1910 schedules are only available for the following twenty-one states:

Alabama	Kentucky	Oklahoma
Arkansas	Louisiana	Pennsylvania
California	Michigan	South Carolina
Florida	Mississippi	Tennessee
Georgia	Missouri	Texas
Illinois	North Carolina	Virginia
Kansas	Ohio	West Virginia

Staff members of the Family History Library have prepared the following very essential reference tool to assist in the use of the 1910 schedules for states for which there are no Soundex and/or Miracodes: G. Eileen Buckway, compiler, *U.S. 1910 Federal Census: Unindexed States: A Guide to Finding Census Enumeration Districts for Unindexed Cities, Towns, and Villages,* compiled by C. Eileen Buckway; assisted by Marva Blalock, Elizabeth Caruso, Ray Matthews, and Kenneth

Nelson (Salt Lake City: Family History Library, 1992, FHL US/CAN REF AREA 973 X2bu 1910 and microfiche 6101540, 8 microfiches).

After the Soundex or Miracode has been used, it is important that the census schedules be checked to determine if any errors were made in the Soundex or Miracode transcription and for additional information contained in the schedules.

Before you use a Soundex or Miracode you need to determine the soundex codes for all of your surnames of research interest and add the number to your 3"x5" cards or computer lists.

SOUNDEX CODES

The easiest single source to use for determining soundex codes is Bradley W. Steuart's *The Soundex Reference Guide: Soundex Codes to Over 125,000 Surnames* (Bountiful, Utah: Precision Indexing, 1990, FHL US/CAN REF AREA 973 D27so). It may be available in your Family History Center or public library.

A part of the computer program, *Personal Ancestral File (PAF)*, completes a soundex code with record speed. The *PAF* is also available at Family History Centers with *FamilySearch*. The soundex codes may be found through the following choices (selections) by pressing:

"1" for Family Records from the ACCESS MENU. After this choice the program will ask you to "Put Your Family Record data disk in drive A." You may insert a blank formatted disk.

"9" for Facts and Fun from the MAIN MENU.

"2" for SOUNDEX from the FACTS AND FUN MENU.

Type in surname of interest and press return and soundex code will appear on the screen, example: S563.

An "Error" message may also appear, press "Enter" and the program will then report "No Match Found." Again press "Enter" which will return you to the FACTS AND FUN MENU.

67

Chapter 7

Press "2" again for SOUNDEX (type in another surname).

To end the search choose the following:

"0" for Return to Main Menu from the FACTS AND FUN MENU.

"0" for Return to System from the MAIN MENU.

"Enter" at Backup Reminder!

"O" for Return to System from the ACCESS MENU

Don't forget to remove your disk.

The accuracy of both of the above are superior to the use of the standard instructions which follow, taken from the copyright-free U.S. federal census catalogs listed in part II, "Local Public Library Users," of this chapter:

Guide to the Soundex System

The Soundex filing system, alphabetic for the first letter of surname and numeric thereunder as indicated by divider cards, keeps together names of the same and similar sounds but of variant spellings.

The Bureau of the Census created and filmed Soundex index cards for the entire 1920 census. The Soundex is a coded surname (last name) index based on the way a surname sounds rather than how it is spelled. Surnames that sound the same but are spelled differently, like SMITH and SMYTH, have the same code and are filed together. The Soundex coding system was developed to find a surname even though it may have been recorded under various spellings. The National Archives has assigned a separate microfilm publication for each state and territory.

The Bureau of the Census used two separate Soundex cards, the "family card" and the "individual card." Both types of cards are arranged numerically by the Soundex code and then alphabetically by the first name of the head of the household on the family cards and the first name of the individual on the individual cards.

Every Soundex code consists of a letter and three numbers, such as S-650. The letter is always the first letter of the surname, whether it is a vowel or a consonant. Disregard the remaining vowels and W, Y, and H and assign numbers to the next three consonants of the surname according to the Soundex coding guide. If there are not three consonants following the initial letter, use zeros to fill out the three-digit code.

Most surnames can be coded using the Soundex coding guide. Names with prefixes, double letters, or letters side by side that have the same number of the Soundex coding system are described below.

To search for a particular name, you must first work out the code number for the surname of the individual. No number is assigned to the first letter of the surname. If the name is Kuhne, for example, the index card will be in the "K" segment of the index. The code number for Kuhne, worked out according to the system below, is 500.

Soundex Coding Guide

The number   Represents the letters

1	b, p, f, v
2	c, s, k, g, j, q, x, z
3	d, t
4	l
5	m, n
6	r

Chapter 7

The letters a, e, i, o, u, y, w, and h are not
coded.

The first letter of a surname is not coded.

Every Soundex number must be a 3-digit number.
A name yielding no code numbers, as Lee, would thus
be L000; one yielding only one code number would
have two zeros added, as Kuhne, coded as K500; and
one yielding two code numbers would have one zero
added, as Ebell, coded as E140. Not more than
three digits are used, so Ebelson would be coded as
E142, not E1425.

Names with Double Letters

When two key letters or equivalents appear together,
or one key letter immediately follows or precedes
an equivalent, the two are coded as one letter, by
a single number, as follows: Kelly, coded as K400;
Buerck, coded as B620; Lloyd, coded as L300; and
Schaefer, coded as S160.

If several surnames have the same code, the cards for them
are arranged alphabetically by given name. There are
divider cards showing most code numbers, but not all. For
instance, one divider may be numbered 350 and the next
one 400. Between the two divider cards there may be
names coded 353, 350, 360, 364, 365, and 355, but instead
of being in numerical order they are inter-filed
alphabetically by given name.

Names with Prefixes

If the surname has a prefix, such as "van," "Von," "de,"
"le," "Di," "D'," "dela," or "du" code it both with and
without the prefix because it might be listed under either
code. The surname vanDevanter, for example, could be V-
531 or D-153. Mc and Mac are not considered prefixes.

Names With Letters Side by Side That Have
The Same Number on the Soundex Coding Guide

A surname may have different letters that are side by side
and have the same number on the Soundex coding guide;
for example, PF in Pfister (1 is the number for both P and
F); CKS in Jackson (2 is the number for C. K. and S).
These letters should be treated as one letter. Thus in the
name Pfister, F should be crossed out; in the name
Jackson, K and S should be crossed out.

The following names are examples of Soundex coding and
are given only as illustrations.

Name	Letters Coded	Code No.
Allricht	l, r, c	A 462
Eberhard	b, r, r	E 166
Engebrethson	n, g, b	E 521
Heimbach	m, b, o	H 512
Hanselmann	n, s, l	H 524
Henzelmann	n, z, l	H 524
Hildebrand	l, d, b	H 431
Kavanagh	v, n, g	K 152
Lind, Van	n, d	L 530
Lukaschowsky	k, s, s	L 222
McDonnell	c, d, n	M 235
McGee	c	M 200
O'Brien	b, r, n	O 165
Opnian	p, n, n	O 155
Oppenheimer	p, n, m	O 155
Riedemanas	d, m, n	R 355
Zita	t	Z 300
Zitzmeinn	t, z, m	Z 325

Native Americans, Orientals, and Religious Nuns

Researchers using the Soundex system to locate religious
nuns or persons with American Indian or oriental names

should be aware of the way such names were coded. Variations in coding differed from the normal coding system.

Phonetically spelled oriental and Indian names were sometimes coded as if one continuous name, or, if a distinguishable surname was given, the names were coded in the normal manner. For example, the American Indian name Shinka-Wa-Sa may have been coded as "Shinka" (S-520) or "Sa" (S-000). Researchers should investigate the various possibilities of coding such names.

Religious nun names were coded as if "Sister" were the surname, and they appear in the State's Soundex/Miracode under the code "S-236." Within the State's Soundex/Miracode code S-236, the names are not necessarily in alphabetical order.

Sample 1910 MIRACODE for Oklahoma Entry

OKLAHOMA		OKLAHOMA CITY		049	0218	0317
J162 JEFFERSON	ALLEN	H	M 32	TEXAS	OKLA
	MARY		W	30	TEXAS
GRAHAM	HENRIETTA	SD	15	TEXAS
DAVIS	SAMMIE	SS	11	TEXAS

J162 is the Miracode code for the surname Jefferson; 049 is the volume number, not necessary to note; 0218 is the enumeration district; 0317 is the number of the family in order of visitation. Both of the latter numbers should be noted in order to find the family in the census schedule. Oklahoma is the county. The state is not recorded on each card.

DATES OF CENSUS COLLECTION OF DATA

Occasionally it helps to know the date for which data was to be recorded by the census taker in order to make a value judgment of whether to search it or not. For example, if you were searching for an ancestor who was born in December of the census year, he/she would not normally be included. When using the census schedules please record the exact date when it was taken, from the leaf or page on which an ancestor is found.

The following is a selection from the "Instructions to Marshals-Census of 1820" concerning the date for which data was to be recorded:

> Your assistants will thereby understand that they are to insert in their returns all the persons, belonging to the family on the first Monday in August, even those who may be deceased at the time when they take the account; and, on the other hand, that they will not include in it, infants born after that day.
> -- *Twenty Censuses: Population and Housing Questions, 1790-1980* (Washington, D.C.: Bureau of the Census, 1979), p. 11.

The above census publication does not include such a statement of instruction concerning the 1790, 1800, and 1810 census. However, it may have been the same. Similar instructions in *Twenty Censuses* concerning the recording of information for 1820 census were given to the marshals of the 1830 (p. 12), 1850 (p. 14), 1870 (p. 18), 1880 (p. 22), 1890 (p. 27), 1900 (p. 32), and 1910 (p. 42) federal censuses. However, the date on which census data was to be based was changed to June 1 for the 1850-1900 censuses; April 15, 1910, January 1, 1920, and April 1, 1930 and 1940.

Beginning in 1850 the printed heading for each leaf of the census schedule contained the following statement: "The name of every person whose usual place of abode on the first day of June 1850, was in this family." This same statement also appears on the 1860 census schedule leaves. For the 1870, 1880, 1900, 1910, and 1920 censuses the word "usual" was omitted. In 1900 and continuing in 1910, 1920, and 1930, the following phase was added to "The name ... family." in the leaf headings of the schedules: "Include every person living on June 1, 1900. Omit children born since June 1, 1900." Of course, the date was changed to April 15, 1910 and January 1, 1920 for those schedules.

In the 1940 census "The name ... family." statement contained two changes, "abode" to "residence" and "family" to "household."

The following list is provided to simplify all of the above dates for which data was to be recorded in each decennial United States census, in addition to very brief indexing information:

Data Collection Date		Indexing
1790	August 2	Accelerated Indexing Systems
1800	August 4	AIS
1810	August 6	AIS
1820	August 7	AIS
1830	June 1	AIS
1840	June 1	AIS
1850	June 1	AIS
1860	June 1	Not complete
1870	June 1	Some done
1880	June 1	Majority soundexed
1890	June 1	Indexed, but very few schedules survived a fire
1900	June 1	Soundexed
1910	April 15	Part soundexed and miracoded
1920	January 1	Soundexed
1930	April 1	No indexing done and not yet available on microfilm
1940	April 1	No indexing done and not yet available on microfilm

The changes of census collection dates for 1900-1930 and the date the census was taken may effect the ages listed in the schedules. They may not be 10 years apart for each census year for all persons. Also the census taker may not have followed the above instructions, recording ages as of the day he or she visited the family instead of basing the ages on the data collection date. Some persons may have not remembered their ages and those of other members of the household; others may have "fudged" on their age.

I. Family History Center Users:

If census schedules are ordered for use in a Family History Center, their microfilm numbers will have to be ascertained.

The fastest way to determine the Family History Library's microfilm numbers for the federal census schedules is to consult the binders at a Family History Center labeled: U.S. CENSUS, 1790-1880; U.S. CENSUS, 1900; U.S. CENSUS, 1910; and U.S. CENSUS, 1920. These microfilm numbers are also included in the *Family History Library Catalog: Locality Catalog* on microfiche and *FamilySearch* under the subject heading "United States - Census - (year)." State census schedule microfilm numbers are listed in the *Family History Library Catalog: Locality Catalog* under the name of the state, subdivided by "Census - (year)."

Most of the older Family History Centers have the *AIS* (Accelerated Indexing Systems) consolidated indexes on microfiche for the 1790 through 1850 federal census schedules, including some earlier and later census schedules. It may be useful to check these indexes before going to the Family History Library to find the exact county and leaf number (which consists of the front and back of one leaf, or the equivalent of two pages) where your ancestors are listed. Please remember that indexes are not always perfect.

The *Family History Library Catalog: Locality Catalog* on microfiche and *FamilySearch* also have the microfilm numbers for the census schedules of some foreign countries under the subject heading "(name of country) - Census - (year)."

Family History Centers also have a separate set of microfiches for the determining the microfilm numbers for the census schedules of part of Great Britain:

Index of Place-names Showing the Library Microform Numbers for the 1841-1891 Census Records of England, Wales, Channel Islands and the Isle of Man: Arranged by Names of Places and Showing the Parish in Which Situated. 5 vols. Salt Lake City: Family History Library, 1992. Computer print-out. FHL BRITISH REG TABLE 942 X2pi.

Microfiche. Salt Lake City: Genealogical Society of Utah, 1993. FHL
BRITISH FICHE AREA 6024509 (5 microfiches). Contents: v. 1. A-C
-- v. 2. D-H -- v. 3. I-M -- v. 4. N-S -- v. 5. T-Z.

As your research with the census progresses you may find that you
must learn something about original counties and their boundaries.
Suppose you are researching for ancestors in a particular county and
find that that county is not listed in the federal census schedule catalog
for 1870, or that the community in which they lived is not in its present
county or the county in which they were reported to have lived. Then
you need to know what county in 1870 included the place where your
ancestor was living. The following work may be able to help you solve
your problem:

Thorndale, William, and William Dollarhide. *Map Guide to the U.S.
Federal Censuses, 1790-1920*. Baltimore: Genealogical Publishing
Co., 1987. FHL US/CAN REF AREA 973 X2th.
    Shows 400 U.S. county boundary maps for the census decades from
    1790 to 1920 superimposed on modern county boundaries.

II. LOCAL PUBLIC LIBRARY USERS:

Some local public libraries will have copies of the National Archives,
Catalog of Federal Census Schedules. There is no way to match the
reel numbers in these catalogs with the microfilm numbers in the
Family History Library. However, you can get an idea of what is
available. Some of the larger public libraries, the National Archives,
and its regional archives have collections of printed state-wide indexes
to the federal census schedules which should be checked for ancestors
in appropriate volumes.

The catalogs for the federal census schedules are as follows:

U.S. National Archives. *Federal Population Censuses 1790-1890: A
Catalog of Microfilm Copies of the Schedules*. Publication 71-3.
Washington, D.C.: Gov't. Print. Off., 1971-   GS4.2:P31/2/790-890.

U.S. National Archives. *1900 Federal Population Census: A Catalog of Microfilm Copies of the Schedules*. Washington, D.C.: Gov't. Print. Off., 1979.

U.S. National Archives and Records Service. *The 1910 Federal Population Census: A Catalog of Microfilm Copies of the Schedules*. Washington, D.C.: National Archives Trust Fund Board, 1982.

U.S. National Archives and Records Service. *The 1920 Federal Population Census: A Catalog of Microfilm Copies of the Schedules*. 2d ed. Washington, D.C.: National Archives Trust Fund Board, 1992 (title page reads "1991," copyright page reads "Second edition, 1992).

Many libraries are able to obtain microfilm copies of the U.S. federal census schedules through interlibrary loan from their state libraries or through the rental services of the National Archives Microfilm Rental Program, P.O. Box 30, Annapolis Junction, MD 20701-0030, (301) 604-3699 or the American Genealogical Lending Library, Box 329, Bountiful, Utah 84011-0329, (801) 298-5446, FAX (801) 298-5468.

III. HOME LIBRARY USERS:

You could purchase the above National Archives catalogs. However, the author would not recommend it. Just wait until you can go to either the Family History Center or a public library and use the above catalogs, or go to the National Archives in Washington, D.C. or to one of its twelve regional archives in Anchorage, East Point (near Atlanta), Waltham (near Boston), Chicago, Denver, Fort Worth, Kansas City, Laguna Niguel (near Los Angeles), New York City, Philadelphia, Pittsfield (Massachusetts), San Bruno (near San Francisco), or Seattle.

If you can't wait to read a federal census schedule and do not have access to a Family History Center, and if you cannot obtain them through the services of your public library, you can join either the National Archives Microfilm Rental Program, P.O. Box 30, Annapolis Junction, MD 20701-0030, (301) 604-3699 or the American Genealogical Lending Library, P.O. Box 329, Bountiful, Utah 84011-

Chapter 7

0329, (801) 298-5446, FAX (801) 298-5468. The American
Genealogical Lending Library also has some state census schedules.

ADDITIONAL VIEWING AND READING:

How to Use the U.S. Census. Salt Lake City: The Church of Jesus
Christ of Latter-day Saints, 1985.
  A 12-minute videocassette, available at the Family History Library
  and most Family History Centers.

U.S. National Archives and Records Service. "Census Records,"
chapter 1, pages 9-38. In *Guide to Genealogical Research in the
National Archives*. Washington, D.C.: National Archives Trust Fund
Board, 1983. FHL US/CAN REF AREA 973 A3usn. FHL
US/CAN FICHE AREA & FHCs 6051414 (4 microfiches).

Parker, J. Carlyle. *City, County, Town, and Township Index to the
1850 Federal Census Schedules.* Gale Genealogy and Local History
Series, Vol. 6. Detroit: Gale Research Co., 1979, op.
  FHL US/CAN REF AREA 973 X22p.
  Reprint. Turlock, Calif.: Marietta Publishing Co., 1994.
  Microfiche. Turlock, Calif.: Marietta Publishing Co., 1990.
  The cities, towns, and townships in the 1850 schedules are not in
  alphabetical order in each county. This index has them in
  alphabetical order for the entire nation and provides the page
  numbers for the exact location of communities and townships on
  the microfilm of the census schedules, as well as the Family
  History Library and National Archives microfilm numbers.

Smith, Leonard H., Jr. *U.S. Census Key: 1850, 1860, 1870.*
Bountiful, Utah: American Genealogical Lending Library, 1986.
  FHL US/CAN REF AREA 973 X2s 1850-1870.
  For counties that have two or more reels of microfilm this work
  lists the townships in the order in which they appear in the
  schedules.

Family History Library. *A Key to the 1880 United States Federal Census*. 2d rev. and corr. Bowie Md.: Heritage Books, 1986. Bountiful, Utah: American Genealogical Lending Library, 199?
  FHL US/CAN REF AREA 973 X2ch.
    Lists the first and last enumeration district and all district numbers on each microfilm reel, as well as the National Archives and Family History Library microfilm numbers.

Accelerated Indexing Systems, U.S. Census Indexes (on Microfiche). Resource Guide. 3d ed. Ser. US No. 1. Salt Lake City: Family History Library, 1992. 4 pages.

SUMMARY:

Your American ancestors are probably recorded in some census schedules. The Family History Library has U.S. federal census schedules, as well as some state census schedules. It also has census schedules of many other countries. Because of the usefulness of census enumerations, particularly those from 1850 to 1920, you should look for your ancestors in them.

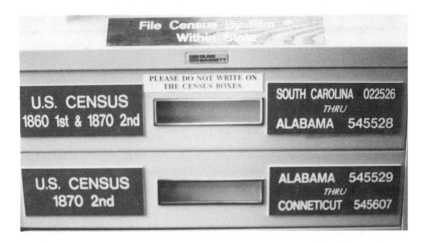

A UNITED STATES FEDERAL CENSUS SCHEDULES
MICROFILM CABINET

THE GRANITE MOUNTAIN RECORDS VAULT

Master Microform Storage, Not Open to the Public

Chapter 8

IS THERE A BIOGRAPHICAL SKETCH
ABOUT YOUR ANCESTOR?

Biographical sketches are an important secondary source for researchers
searching for ancestors who have lived in the United States. Like
family histories, they can provide missing clues to who, where, why,
and when. Of course, a state-wide index to biographical sketches in
city, county, regional, and state histories, and in biographical
directories is a very useful, time-saving research tool for finding
biographical sketches. By checking a name in *Michigan Biography
Index* (listed below) and consulting the biographical sketches cited for
that particular name, five earlier generations, including one
Revolutionary War ancestor, and an earlier New England immigrant
were discovered. The proliferation of biographical sketches in local,
county, regional, and state histories is a unique part of the American
life, mainly in the United States and some in Canada. Such a
phenomenon is not the case in other countries of the world.

If the indexes listed below that may relate to your research cannot be
located near your home, they should be consulted while you are at the
Family History Library. The Library locations and call numbers have
been provided in order to save you time looking them up while there.
Some are unpublished personal indexes that may be consulted free by
mail or for a small fee.

ALABAMA

Work Progress Administration. Alabama. Birmingham. "Alabama
Biography: An Index to Biographical Sketches of Individual Alabamians
in State, Local, and to Some Extent National Collections."
Birmingham, Ala.: Birmingham Public Library, in progress.
  Contains approximately 22,500 citations of biographical sketches
  from about eighty town, county, and state histories
  and biographical directories. For mail inquiries write the
  Librarian, Tutwiler Collection of Southern History, Birmingham

Public Library, 2100 Park Place, Birmingham, AL 35203; include self-addressed, stamped envelope.

The Library of Congress Index to Biographies in State and Local Histories. 31 reels of microfilm. Baltimore: Magna Carta Book Co., 1979. FHL US/CAN FILM AREA 1380344-1380373, 1528066. Indexes eight works relating to Alabama.

Aake - Bass	1380344	Long - McCr	1380359
Bast - Booz	1380345	McCu - Mezg	1380360
Bopp - Brow	1380346	Mial - Noon	1380361
Broy - Chappel	1380347	Nor - Pizt	1380362
Chappell - Cos	1380348	Plac - Rast	1380363
Coth - Dave	1380349	Ratc - Roby	1380364
Davi - Emsw	1380350	Rocc - Schl	1380365
Enda - Flyn	1380351	Schm - Shy	1380366
Foar - Garr	1528066	Siam - Sryg	1380367
Gars - Hanz	1380352	Staa - Szol	1380368
Haon - Hely	1380353	Taaf - Triv	1380369
Heme - Hods	1380354	Trob - Wall	1380370
Hoe - Huds	1380355	Walm - Whit	1380371
Hueb - Jones, J	1380356	Whitf - Wonn	1380372
Jones, K - Lazi	1380357	Wood - Zwaa	1380373
Lea - Lone	1380358		

ALASKA

Bradbury, Connie, David A. Hales, and Nancy Lesh. *Alaska People Index*. Alaska Historical Commission Studies in History, no. 203. 2 vols. Anchorage: Alaska Historical Commission, 1986 (also available on 9 microfiches).

A name index to obituaries and twenty-four other sources. This book is now part of the computer database *Ancestors* that includes additional names and will continue to grow. *Ancestors* may be searched by computer through (907) 474-7261. For mail inquiries write *Ancestors*, Alaska and Polar Regions Department, Elmer E. Rasmuson Library, University of Alaska Fairbanks, Fairbanks, AK 99775-1005; include self-addressed, stamped envelope.

Drazan, Joseph Gerald. *The Pacific Northwest: An Index to People and Places in Books*. Metuchen, N.J.: Scarecrow Press, 1979. op.
  Contains 6,830 entries in 320 local history titles for Alaska, British Columbia, Idaho, Montana, Oregon, Washington and the Yukon Territory. Fifty-one titles concerning the Northwest in general and forty-seven about Alaska. For availability see page 117 of *Going*.

ARIZONA

Wiggins, Marvin E., comp. *Mormons and Their Neighbors: An Index to Over 75,000 Biographical Sketches from 1820 to the Present*. 2 vols. Provo, Utah: Harold B. Lee Library, Brigham Young University, 1984.
  FHL US/CAN REG TABLE 979 D32w.
  Indexes 194 titles, eleven of which are for Arizona.

The Library of Congress Index to Biographies in State and Local Histories. 31 reels of microfilm. Baltimore: Magna Carta Book Co., 1979. FHL US/CAN FILM AREA 1380344-1380373, 1528066. See page 82 for contents of reels.
  Indexes six works relating to Arizona.

Parker, J. Carlyle, and Janet G. Parker. *Arizona Biographical and Genealogical Sketch Index*. Turlock, Calif.: Marietta Publishing Co., in progress.
  Contains 31,197 index entries to the biographees in biographical and genealogical sketches in ninety-two (112 volumes) state, county, and city histories and biographical directories of Arizona published between 1889 and 1993. The publisher will consult this index for researchers and provide them with bibliographic citations and page numbers, for a modest fee. Address correspondence to the Marietta Publishing Co., 2115 North Denair Avenue, Turlock CA 95382, and for this service include a self-addressed, stamped envelope.

ARKANSAS

"Arkansas Biographical Index." University of Arkansas.
  Contains 7,500 index cards to biographical sketches of persons in state, county, city, and church histories and biographical

directories, most of which were published from the 1880s to 1962. Address inquiries for only a few names at a time to Special Collections Department, University of Arkansas Libraries, Fayetteville, AR 72701. The Library charges a modest fee for making photocopies.

The Library of Congress Index to Biographies in State and Local Histories. 31 reels of microfilm. Baltimore: Magna Carta Book Co., 1979. FHL US/CAN FILM AREA 1380344-1380373, 1528066. See page 82 for contents of reels.
Indexes ten works relating to Arkansas.

CALIFORNIA

California State Library. *California Information File.* 550 microfiches. Bellevue, Wash.: Commercial Microfilm Service, 1986.
FHL US/CAN FICHE AREA 6333977 (550 microfiches). Contains approximately 721,000 cards with an estimated 1.4 million citations to periodicals, newspapers, manuscript collections, books, histories, theses, dissertations, government documents, biographical directories, and the Library's biographical files.

Parker, J. Carlyle. *An Index to the Biographees in 19th Century California County Histories.* Gale Genealogy and Local History Series, vol. 7. Detroit: Gale Research Co., 1979.
FHL US/CAN REF AREA 979.4 D32p.
Microfiche. Turlock, Calif.: Marietta Publishing Co., 1994. Contains approximately 16,500 entries from sixty-one county histories. Only four of the titles indexed in this work are not indexed in the *California Information File.*

COLORADO

Bromwell, Henriette Elizabeth. *Colorado Portrait and Biography Index.* 4 vols. plus a 2 vol. supp., on 2 reels of microfilm. Denver: n.p., 1935. Microfilmed by the Western History Department, Denver Public Library, 1979. FHL US/CAN FILM AREA 1688547 (A-Z)-1688548 (Appendix A-Z).

Contains about thirty-three thousand name entries from 170
histories, magazines, newspapers, land records, and other records.

CONNECTICUT

"Connecticut Biography and Portrait Index." Thomas J. Kemp, Editor,
410 Broxburn Avenue, Temple Terrace FL 33617, in progress.
  Contains 250,000 citations of biographical sketches from town,
  county, state, fraternal, etc., histories and photographs, sketches,
  silhouettes, and artistic portraits. The editor will search the index
  for a small fee and a self-addressed, stamped envelope.

Greenlaw, William Prescott. *The Greenlaw Index of the New England
Historic Genealogical Society.* 2 vols. Boston: G. K. Hall, 1979.
  FHL US/CAN BOOK AREA Q 974 D22g.
  Indexes many Connecticut and New England local histories and
  genealogies up to 1940.

Newberry Library, Chicago. *The Genealogical Index.* 4 Vols.
Boston: G. K. Hall, 1960. FHL US/CAN REF AREA Q 929 N424g.
Available from FHL through FHC: Microfilm 928135-928137.
  Contains 512,000 entries, including many for Connecticut, indexed
  between 1896 and 1917. However, the microfilm is difficult to read.

*The Library of Congress Index to Biographies in State and Local
Histories.* 31 reels of microfilm. Baltimore: Magna Carta Book Co.,
1979. FHL US/CAN FILM AREA 1380344-1380373, 1528066.
See page 82 for contents of reels.
  Indexes three works relating to Connecticut.

DELAWARE

"Surname File." Historical Society of Delaware Library.
  The Library has a 500,000 card index to church records, obituaries,
  research files and family history files. Will search the index for a
  fee. Write the Library at 505 Market Street Mall, Wilmington DE
  19801.

Chapter 8

"Genealogical Surname File." Delaware State Archives.
Index to surnames in genealogies and histories. Write the Delaware
State Archives, Hall of Records, Dover DE 19901 and include a self-
addressed, stamped envelope.

*The Library of Congress Index to Biographies in State and Local
Histories.* 31 reels of microfilm. Baltimore: Magna Carta Book Co.,
1979. FHL US/CAN FILM AREA 1380344-1380373, 1528066.
See page 82 for contents of reels.
Indexes three works relating to Delaware.

Newberry Library, Chicago. *The Genealogical Index.* 4 Vols.
Boston: G. K. Hall, 1960. FHL US/CAN REF AREA Q 929 N424g.
Available from FHL through FHC: Microfilm 928135-928137.
Contains 512,000 entries, including a few for Delaware, indexed
between 1896 and 1917. However, the microfilm is difficult to read.

DISTRICT OF COLUMBIA

*The Library of Congress Index to Biographies in State and Local
Histories.* 31 reels of microfilm. Baltimore: Magna Carta Book Co.,
1979. FHL US/CAN FILM AREA 1380344-1380373, 1528066.
See page 82 for contents of reels.
Indexes three works relating to District of Columbia.

Newberry Library, Chicago. *The Genealogical Index.* 4 Vols.
Boston: G. K. Hall, 1960. FHL US/CAN REF AREA Q 929 N424g.
Available from FHL through FHC: Microfilm 928135-928137.
Contains 512,000 entries, including a few for the District of
Columbia, indexed between 1896 and 1917. However, the
microfilm is difficult to read.

FLORIDA

"Florida Biography Index." State Library of Florida.
Contains approximately twenty-five thousand entries to biographical
sketches from town, county, and state histories; yearbooks and
directories of organizations; biographical dictionaries; newspapers,
and periodicals. Address inquiries to the Florida Collection, State

Library of Florida, R.A. Gray Building, Tallahassee FL 32399-0250.

GEORGIA

The Library of Congress Index to Biographies in State and Local Histories. 31 reels of microfilm. Baltimore: Magna Carta Book Co., 1979. FHL US/CAN FILM AREA 1380344-1380373, 1528066. See page 82 for contents of reels.
 Indexes thirty-six works relating to Georgia.

Newberry Library, Chicago. *The Genealogical Index.* 4 Vols. Boston: G. K. Hall, 1960. FHL US/CAN REF AREA Q 929 N424g. Available from FHL through FHC: Microfilm 928135-928137.
 Contains 512,000 entries, including a few for Georgia, indexed between 1896 and 1917. However, the microfilm is difficult to read.

HAWAII

The Library of Congress Index to Biographies in State and Local Histories. 31 reels of microfilm. Baltimore: Magna Carta Book Co., 1979. FHL US/CAN FILM AREA 1380344-1380373, 1528066. See page 82 for contents of reels.
 Indexes three works relating to Hawaii.

Parker, J. Carlyle, and Janet G. Parker. *Hawaii Biographical and Genealogical Sketch Index.* Turlock, Calif.: Marietta Publishing Co., in progress.
 Contains 4,096 index entries to the biographees in biographical and genealogical sketches in fourteen state, county, and city histories and biographical directories of Hawaii published between 1898 and 1988. The publisher will consult this index for researchers and provide them with bibliographic citations and page numbers, for a modest fee. Address correspondence to the Marietta Publishing Co., 2115 North Denair Avenue, Turlock CA 95382, and for this service include a self-addressed, stamped envelope.

Chapter 8

IDAHO

Drazan, Joseph Gerald. *The Pacific Northwest: An Index to People and Places in Books*. Metuchen, N.J.: Scarecrow Press, 1979. op.
Contains 6,830 entries in 320 local history titles for Alaska, British Columbia, Idaho, Montana, Oregon, Washington and the Yukon Territory. Fifty-one titles concerning the Northwest in general and thirty about Idaho. For availability see page 117 of *Going*.

Wiggins, Marvin E., comp. *Mormons and Their Neighbors: An Index to Over 75,000 Biographical Sketches from 1820 to the Present*. 2 vols. Provo, Utah: Harold B. Lee Library, Brigham Young University, 1984.
FHL US/CAN REG TABLE 979 D32w.
Indexes 194 titles, thirteen of which are for Idaho.

The Library of Congress Index to Biographies in State and Local Histories. 31 reels of microfilm. Baltimore: Magna Carta Book Co., 1979. FHL US/CAN FILM AREA 1380344-1380373, 1528066.
See page 82 for contents of reels.
Indexes twelve works relating to Idaho.

Parker, J. Carlyle, and Janet G. Parker. *Idaho Biographical and Genealogical Sketch Index*. Turlock, Calif.: Marietta Publishing Co., in progress.
Contains 24,681 index entries to the biographees in biographical and genealogical sketches in forty-four state, regional, county, and city histories and biographical directories of Idaho published between 1884 and 1982. The publisher will consult this index for researchers and provide them with bibliographic citations and page numbers, for a modest fee. Address correspondence to the Marietta Publishing Co., 2115 North Denair Avenue, Turlock CA 95382, and for this service include a self-addressed, stamped envelope.

ILLINOIS

"Illinois Biographical Sketch Index." Illinois State Historical Library.
Contains 135,000 index cards to biographical sketches of persons in two hundred state, county, and city histories and biographical

directories. Address inquiries to the Illinois State Historical Library, Old State Capitol, Springfield IL 62701.

Newberry Library, Chicago. *The Genealogical Index*. 4 Vols. Boston: G. K. Hall, 1960. FHL US/CAN REF AREA Q 929 N424g. Available from FHL through FHC: Microfilm 928135-928137.
Contains 512,000 entries, including many for Illinois, indexed between 1896 and 1917. However, the microfilm is difficult to read.

California. State Library, Sacramento. Sutro Branch, San Francisco. *The Surname Catalog*. 3d ed. Sacramento: California State Library Foundation, 1990. FHL US/CAN FICHE AREA 6334474 (1986 ed.).
Good for family histories, includes individuals, and is nationwide in coverage. Over fifty thousand entries, including some for Illinois, to 12,000 family histories and other books (also includes *State and Local History Catalog* and *Miscellaneous Catalog*).

INDIANA

Indiana Biographical Index. 16 microfiches. West Bountiful, Utah: Genealogical Indexing Associates, 1983.
FHL US/CAN FICHE AREA 6331353 (16 microfiches).
Contains 247,423 name entries from 537 state, county, city, and local histories.

IOWA

Morford, Charles. *Biographical Index to the County Histories of Iowa*. Baltimore: Gateway Press, 1979.
FHL US/CAN BOOK AREA 977.7 D32m.
Contains 40,540 entries of the biographees in 131 of the 251 county histories for all of Iowa's ninety-nine counties.

KANSAS

Newberry Library, Chicago. *The Genealogical Index*. 4 Vols. Boston: G. K. Hall, 1960. FHL US/CAN REF AREA Q 929 N424g. Available from FHL through FHC: Microfilm 928135-928137.

Contains 512,000 entries, including a few for Kansas, indexed between 1896 and 1917. However, the microfilm is difficult to read.

KENTUCKY

Cook, Michael Lewis. *Kentucky Index of Biographical Sketches in State, Regional, and County Histories*. Evansville, Ind.: Cook Publications, 1986. FHL US/CAN BOOK AREA 976.9 D32c.
   Contains nearly seventy thousand entries to sixty-five state, regional, and county histories.

The Library of Congress Index to Biographies in State and Local Histories. 31 reels of microfilm. Baltimore: Magna Carta Book Co., 1979. FHL US/CAN FILM AREA 1380344-1380373, 1528066. See page 82 for contents of reels.
   Indexes fifty works relating to Kentucky.

LOUISIANA

The Library of Congress Index to Biographies in State and Local Histories. 31 reels of microfilm. Baltimore: Magna Carta Book Co., 1979. FHL US/CAN FILM AREA 1380344-1380373, 1528066. See page 82 for contents of reels.
   Indexes twenty-one works relating to Louisiana.

Newberry Library, Chicago. *The Genealogical Index*. 4 Vols. Boston: G. K. Hall, 1960. FHL US/CAN REF AREA Q 929 N424g. Available from FHL through FHC: Microfilm 928135-928137.
   Contains 512,000 entries, including a few for Louisiana, indexed between 1896 and 1917. However, the microfilm is difficult to read.

MAINE

Estes, Marie. "Name Index to Maine Local Histories." Typescript. Portland: Maine Historical Society Library, 1985.
   This unpublished index was started in the 1940's and is added to occasionally. Contains approximately eleven thousand entries to several hundred local histories of Maine. May be consulted by mail for simple single requests with self-addressed, stamped envelope.

Mail inquiries to Maine Historical Society Library, 485 Congress Street, Portland, ME 04101.

Maine Genealogical Society. "Surname Index to Maine Town Histories." Bar Harbor: Maine Genealogical Society, in progress.
Contains approximately fourteen thousand entries for Maine families and settlers in Maine town histories. Write Dr. Thomas Roderick, 4 Seely Road, Bar Harbor, ME 04609 and include a self-addressed, stamped envelope.

Roderick, Thomas "Name Index to Maine Families in Periodicals." Bar Harbor: The Author, in progress.
Contains approximately thirteen thousand entries for Maine family groups in all Maine genealogical periodicals and selected titles in the other New England states. Write Dr. Thomas Roderick, 4 Seely Road, Bar Harbor, ME 04609 and include a self-addressed stamped envelope.

Newberry Library, Chicago. *The Genealogical Index.* 4 Vols. Boston: G. K. Hall, 1960. FHL US/CAN REF AREA Q 929 N424g. Available from FHL through FHC: Microfilm 928135-928137.
Contains 512,000 entries, including many for Maine, indexed between 1896 and 1917. However, the microfilm is difficult to read.

MARYLAND

Andrusko, Samuel M. *Maryland Biographical Sketch Index.* Silver Spring, Md.: S. M. Andrusko, 1983.
FHL US/CAN BOOK AREA 975.2 D3a.
Contains over 10,500 entries in thirty-three local histories.

Passano, Eleanor Phillips. *An Index of the Source Records of Maryland: Genealogical, Biographical, Historical.* Baltimore: Waverly Press, 1940. Reprint. Baltimore: Genealogical Publishing Co., 1967. Also printed in 1974 and both are the same.
FHL US/CAN BOOK AREA 975.2 D22p 1967.
Contains an estimated twenty-five thousand entries to an estimated 5,750 sources.

Chapter 8

MASSACHUSETTS

Longver, Phyllis O., and Pauline J. Oesterlin. *A Surname Guide to Massachusetts Town Histories*. Bowie, Md.: Heritage Books, 1993.
 FHL US/CAN BOOK AREA 974.4 H22Lp.
 56,000 citations to over fourteen thousand surnames in 128 volumes.

Greenlaw, William Prescott. *The Greenlaw Index of the New England Historic Genealogical Society*. 2 vols. Boston: G. K. Hall, 1979.
 FHL US/CAN BOOK AREA Q 974 D22g.

Newberry Library, Chicago. *The Genealogical Index*. 4 Vols.
Boston: G. K. Hall, 1960. FHL US/CAN REF AREA Q 929 N424g.
Available from FHL through FHC: Microfilm 928135-928137.
 Contains 512,000 entries, including a large number for
 Massachusetts, indexed between 1896 and 1917.
  Indexes many Massachusetts and New England local histories
 and genealogies up to 1940. However, the microfilm is difficult to
 read.

MICHIGAN

Loomis, Frances, comp. *Michigan Biography Index*. Detroit: Detroit Public Library, 1946. 4 reels of microfilm. Woodbridge, Conn.: Research Publications, 1973.
 FHL US/CAN FILM AREA 485331, Items 4-5, 1303166-1303168.
  Contains approximately seventy-three thousand names of the
  biographees in 361 biographical directories, city and county
  directories.

Aaga - Canf	485331, Items 4-5
Cani - Levy	1303166
Lewe - Shett	1303167
Shetz - Zynd	1303168

MINNESOTA

"Minnesota Biography Sketch Index." Minnesota Historical Society Reference Library.
 The Library has two indexes of approximately 103,000 total entries to

biographical sketches of persons in state, county, city and church histories; biographical directories; newspapers; and periodicals. Early index entries are primarily newspaper obituaries. Address inquiries to the Minnesota Historical Society Reference Library, 690 Cedar Street, St. Paul, MN 55101.

MISSISSIPPI

"Biographical Index." Mississippi State Department of Archives and History.
Contains approximately 200,000 index cards to biographical information on persons in an estimated fifty state and church histories, biographical directories, and newspapers. The index also includes entries from tax rolls, participants in the War of 1812 and Mexican War, and many state records. Address inquiries to the Mississippi State Dept. of Archives and History, P.O. Box 571, Jackson, MS 39205.

The Library of Congress Index to Biographies in State and Local Histories. 31 reels of microfilm. Baltimore: Magna Carta Book Co., 1979. FHL US/CAN FILM AREA 1380344-1380373, 1528066. See page 82 for contents of reels.
Indexes thirteen works relating to Mississippi.

MISSOURI

Newberry Library, Chicago. *The Genealogical Index.* 4 Vols. Boston: G. K. Hall, 1960. FHL US/CAN REF AREA Q 929 N424g. Available from FHL through FHC: Microfilm 928135-928137.
Contains 512,000 entries, including a few for Missouri, indexed between 1896 and 1917. However, the microfilm is difficult to read.

MONTANA

Parker, J. Carlyle, and Janet G. Parker. *Montana Biographical and Genealogical Sketch Index.* Turlock, Calif.: Marietta Publishing Co., in progress.
Contains 42,036 index entries to the biographees in biographical and

genealogical sketches in eighty-one state, regional, county, and city histories and biographical directories of Montana published between 1894 and 1983. The publisher will consult this index for researchers and provide them with bibliographic citations and page numbers, for a modest fee. Address correspondence to the Marietta Publishing Co., 2115 North Denair Avenue, Turlock CA 95382, and for this service include a self-addressed, stamped envelope.

Drazan, Joseph Gerald. *The Pacific Northwest: An Index to People and Places in Books*. Metuchen, N.J.: Scarecrow Press, 1979. op.
Contains 6,830 entries in 320 local history titles for Alaska, British Columbia, Idaho, Montana, Oregon, Washington and the Yukon Territory. Fifty-one titles concerning the Northwest in general and thirty-three about Montana. For availability see page 117 of *Going*.

NEBRASKA

Newberry Library, Chicago. *The Genealogical Index*. 4 Vols. Boston: G. K. Hall, 1960. FHL US/CAN REF AREA Q 929 N424g. Available from FHL through FHC: Microfilm 928135-928137.
Contains 512,000 entries, including a few for Nebraska, indexed between 1896 and 1917. However, the microfilm is difficult to read.

NEVADA

Parker, J. Carlyle, and Janet G. Parker. *Nevada Biographical and Genealogical Sketch Index*. Turlock, Calif.: Marietta Publishing Co., 1986. FHL US/CAN BOOK AREA 979.3 D32p.
Contains 7,230 index entries to the biographees in biographical and genealogical sketches in eighty-six state, regional, county, and city histories and biographical directories of Nevada published between 1870 and 1985.

The Library of Congress Index to Biographies in State and Local Histories. 31 reels of microfilm. Baltimore: Magna Carta Book Co., 1979. FHL US/CAN FILM AREA 1380344-1380373, 1528066.
See page 82 for contents of reels.
Indexes eleven works relating to Nevada.

NEW HAMPSHIRE

New Hampshire Notables Card File, 1600 to the Present. 8 reels of
microfilm. Salt Lake City, Utah: The Genealogical Society for the
New Hampshire Historical Society, Concord, N.H., 1988.
    FHL US/CAN FILM AREA 1570255-1570262.
    Contains approximately thirty-two thousand entries to collected
    biographies, histories, and selected New Hampshire periodicals.
        Abbo - Andrews, Elisha   1570255
        Andrews, Elisha - Chickering, J.B.   1570256
        Chickering, J.B. - Farrington, Jeremiah   1570257
        Farrington, Jeremiah - Hobart, James   1570258
        Hobart, James - Mean, Robert   1570259
        Mean, Robert - Richardson, Ellen Ruddick   1570260
        Richardson, Ellen R. - Treadwell, Thom   1570261
        Treadwell, Thom - Zwicker, Kenneth F.   1570262

Copeley, William. *Index to Genealogies in New Hampshire Town
Histories*. Concord: New Hampshire Historical Society, 1989.
    FHL US/CAN BOOK AREA 974.2 D22c.
    FHL US/CAN FICHE AREA 6010808 (2 microfiches)
    An index to 302 histories for 198 towns published up to 1986.
    Thirty-six towns have no published histories. Only indexes
    surnames of families who had three generations (male or female
    lines) in a history. Supersedes the following:

Hunt, Elmer M. "Family Names in New Hampshire Town Histories,"
Historical New Hampshire (December 1946): 2-78.
    FHL US/CAN BOOK AREA 974.2 A1 no.34.
    FHL US/CAN FILM AREA 1033754 Item 11
    FHL US/CAN FICHE AREA 6046831
    Contains three thousand entries to early families from eighty-five
    town histories.

Copeley, William. "Family Names in New Hampshire Town Histories,
1947-1980," *Historical New Hampshire* 35 (Winter 1980): 417-39.
    FHL US/CAN BOOK AREA 974.2 H25n.
    Supplement to Hunt's work above and indexes 180 additional town
    histories.

Chapter 8

Greenlaw, William Prescott. *The Greenlaw Index of the New England Historic Genealogical Society.* 2 vols. Boston: G. K. Hall, 1979.
   FHL US/CAN BOOK AREA Q 974 D22g.
   Indexes many New Hampshire and New England local histories and genealogies up to 1940.

Towle, Glenn C. *New Hampshire Genealogical Digest, 1623-1900.* Volume 1. Bowie, Md.: Heritage Books, 1986.
   FHL US/CAN BOOK AREA 974.2 D32t.
   Digests numerous New Hampshire histories.

Newberry Library, Chicago. *The Genealogical Index.* 4 Vols. Boston: G. K. Hall, 1960. FHL US/CAN REF AREA Q 929 N424g. Available from FHL through FHC: Microfilm 928135-928137.
   Contains 512,000 entries, including lots for New Hampshire, indexed between 1896 and 1917. However, the microfilm is difficult to read.

NEW JERSEY

Sinclair, Donald Arleigh. *A New Jersey Biographical Index: Covering Some 100,000 Biographies and Associated Portraits in 237 New Jersey Cyclopedias, Histories, Yearbooks, Periodicals, and Other Collective Biographical Sources Published to about 1980.* Baltimore, Md.: Genealogical Publishing, Co., Inc., 1993.
   FHL US/CAN BOOK AREA 974.9 D32s.
   Both of Sinclair's indexes are excellent and should be consulted.

Sinclair, Donald Arleigh. *New Jersey Biographical Index: A Guide to the Genealogical Sketches in New Jersey Collective Sources.* New Brunswick, N.J.: Genealogical Society of New Jersey, 1991.
   FHL US/CAN BOOK AREA 974.9 D22si.
   Contains about 4,900 names in the text and over five hundred names in the Appendix. Both should be checked. This work indexes seventy-seven titles, seventeen of which may only be duplicated in part in his 1993 index. Nevertheless, most of the names in this 1991 index are not indexed in his 1993 index.

NEW MEXICO

Parker, J. Carlyle, and Janet G. Parker. *New Mexico Biographical and Genealogical Sketch Index*. Turlock, Calif.: Marietta Publishing Co., in progress.

Contains 34,408 index entries to the biographees in biographical and genealogical sketches in twenty-two state, county, and city histories and biographical directories of New Mexico published between 1895 and 1994. The publisher will consult this index for researchers and provide them with bibliographic citations and page numbers, for a modest fee. Address correspondence to the Marietta Publishing Co., 2115 North Denair Avenue, Turlock CA 95382, and for this service include a self-addressed, stamped envelope.

NEW YORK

"The New York State Biographical, Genealogical and Portrait Index." Personal index of Gunther E. Pohl, 24 Walden Place, Great Neck, NY 11020.

Includes over 500,000 names from over six thousand volumes, giving brief and/or extended biographical accounts and portraits appearing in New York historical resources; for example, state, county, city and town histories; church, social, Masonic, political, and military unit histories; atlases; school histories; necrologies; biographical compendiums; periodical literature; etc. Mr. Pohl will consult this index for researchers and provide them with bibliographic citations and page numbers, for a modest fee. All correspondence to him must include a self-addressed, stamped envelope.

Newberry Library, Chicago. *The Genealogical Index*. 4 Vols. Boston: G. K. Hall, 1960. FHL US/CAN REF AREA Q 929 N424g. Available from FHL through FHC: Microfilm 928135-928137.

Contains 512,000 entries, including many for New York, indexed between 1896 and 1917. However, the microfilm is difficult to read.

Chapter 8

NORTH CAROLINA

The Library of Congress Index to Biographies in State and Local Histories. 31 reels of microfilm. Baltimore: Magna Carta Book Co., 1979. FHL US/CAN FILM AREA 1380344-1380373, 1528066. See page 82 for contents of reels.

Indexes ten works relating to North Carolina.

NORTH DAKOTA

Peterson, Allen. "North Dakota Biography Index." North Dakota State University Library, Fargo, N.D.

A twenty-seven thousand card file index to over one hundred thousand biographical sketches in 475 titles. Mail inquiries concerning the index to the North Dakota Institute for Regional Studies, North Dakota State University Library, SU Station, P.O. Box 5599, Fargo, ND 58105-5599.

The Library of Congress Index to Biographies in State and Local Histories. 31 reels of microfilm. Baltimore: Magna Carta Book Co., 1979. FHL US/CAN FILM AREA 1380344-1380373, 1528066. See page 82 for contents of reels.

Indexes three works relating to North Dakota.

OHIO

Ohio Historical Society. *Ohio County History Surname Index*. 64 reels of microfilm. Columbus, Ohio: 1984.

FHL US/CAN FILM AREA 398201-398264.

Contains over 450,000 names. Reels may be purchased or borrowed on interlibrary loan from the Ohio Historical Society, 1982 Velma Avenue, Columbus OH 43211-2497, for a prepaid fee.

Aare - Alki	398201	Boyd, M - Brown, Ab	398208
All - Ashc	398202	Brown, Ad - Burdg	398209
Ashe - Ballard O.	398203	Burdi - Campbell, M	398210
Ballard, P. - Bealm	398204	Campbell, N. - Chap	398211
Beals - Bennett, R.	398205	Chap - Coay	398212
Bennett, S. - Blew	398206	Coba - Cooli	398213
Blic - Boyd, L.	398207	Coolm - Creighton P	398214

Creighton, R - Dan	398215	McCracken, L - McNe	398240
Dar - Dennis	398216	McNi - Mathews, Joh	398241
Dennison - Doly	398217	Mathews, Jos - Miller	398242
Dom - Dych	398218	Miller, M.G. - Morra	398243
Dye - Emry	398219	Morre - Neuh	398244
Emso - Ferguson, L	398220	Neul - Overl	398245
Ferguson, M. - Flo	398221	Overm - Penni	398246
Floy - Frisb	398222	Penno - Postlew	398247
Frisc - Gear	398223	Postley - Reams	398248
Gearh - Goode, J.	398224	Reamy - Riley, N.	398249
Goode, K - Griswol	398225	Riley, N. - Row	398250
Griswold - Hammon	398226	Rowa - Schmitt, K.	398251
Hammond - Harter	398227	Schmitt, P. - Shaw, I	398252
Hartes - Henderson	398228	Shaw, J. - Sker	398253
Henderson - Hint	398229	Skid - Snyder, I.	398254
Hiny - Hoslet	398230	Snyder J - Stevens, I	398255
Hosely - Hunter, M	398231	Stevens, I - Sunderl	398256
Hunter N - Jennings	398232	Sunderm - Thompson	398257
Jennings - Kaufman	398233	Thompson - Tuller	398258
Kaufman - Kimbal	398234	Tulles - Wagner	398259
Kimbar - Koontz,	398235	Wagner - Weaver, Ha	398260
Koontz, Ma - Laym	398236	Weaver, He - White, P	398261
Laymas - Linke	398237	White, R - Wilson, F.	398262
Linkh - Lydo	398238	Wilson, Fa - Woolm	398263
Lync - McCracken,	398239	Woolr - Zwve	398264

"Historical and Biographical Index of North East, Mid East, Mid South, Mid West, U.S., 1880 thru early 1900." Allen County Public Library, Fort Wayne, Indiana. FHL US/CAN FILM AREA 20 reels of microfilm.

Many Ohio biographical sketch books are indexed in this work, some of which are not included in the Ohio Historical Society (OHS) index, above. The OHS index contains many more entries than this work and is almost exclusive to Ohio; however, its microfilm reels may not be borrowed for use in the Family History Centers. The following reels may be borrowed through the services of the FHCs.

Aainsworth, Harry - 1452209 Beatty, Harrison L. -1452250
Arthur, Charles W. - 1452210 Borst, George -1452251

Buetch, Ernest C. -	1452252	Long, R. W. -	1487775
Chapin family -	1452253	McLain, Peter -	1613064
Cooper, Wilford -	1452254	Miller, Emory F. -	1503784
Davis, Almon -	1452463	Neal, John L. -	1614043
Duff, James M. -	1452464	Parrett, George -	1614044
Faulk, Andrew -	1452465	Prutsman, Marshall -	1614291
Fulton, Warren L. -	1439676	Rising, A. M. -	1614292
Graham, Emmett A. -	1493044	Sawyer, Iredell -	1614293
contains Hackworth - Harter		Shoemaker, Andrew -	1614450
Griffith, J. J. -	1674418	Spilker, B. F. -	1614592
Harter, Charles B. -	1493045	Strine, John -	1614593
Hinkle, Uriah -	1493046	Tower, Charlemagne -	1643160
Hurd, Jonathan -	1493168	Wantz, Frederick -	1643161
Kear, Byron -	1493558	Williams, Amos A. -	1643507
Kunst, John H. -	1493559	Zimmerman, George -	1643508

OKLAHOMA

The Library of Congress Index to Biographies in State and Local Histories. 31 reels of microfilm. Baltimore: Magna Carta Book Co., 1979. FHL US/CAN FILM AREA 1380344-1380373, 1528066. See page 82 for contents of reels.
Indexes three works relating to Oklahoma.

OREGON

Drazan, Joseph Gerald. *The Pacific Northwest: An Index to People and Places in Books*. Metuchen, N.J.: Scarecrow Press, 1979. op.
Contains 6,830 entries in 320 local history titles for Alaska, British Columbia, Idaho, Montana, Oregon, Washington and the Yukon Territory. Fifty-one titles concerning the Northwest in general and fifty-one about Oregon. For availability see page 117 of *Going*.

Brandt, Patricia, and Nancy Guilford, eds. *Oregon Biography Index*. Oregon State University Bibliographic Series, no. 11. Corvallis: Oregon State University, 1976.
FHL US/CAN BOOK AREA 979.5 D3b Index
FHL US/CAN FILM AREA 1321470, Item 18

Contains over seventeen thousand names to biographees from forty-seven historical volumes.

PENNSYLVANIA

State Library of Pennsylvania. *Genealogical Surname Card Index.* 42 reels of microfilm. Salt Lake City, Utah: Genealogical Society, 1977.
FHL US/CAN FILM AREA 1002825 Item 2-1002840, 1004983; 1005107-1005116; 1205178-1205191; 1275523
Contains an estimated forty-three thousand entries to an undetermined number of books.

A - Allen, P.	1002825 Item 2	Jord - Kett	1005110
Allen, S - Bailies	1002826	Kitt - Lawrence, A	1005111
Balliet - Bedw	1002827	Lawrence J - Longc	1005112
Bee - Boden	1002828	Longc - McDorma	1005113
Boden - Brittian	1002829	McDormo - Marshall	1005114
Brittian - Calve	1002830	Marshall - Miller S	1005115
Calvi - Clark	1002831	Miller S - Musser	1005116
Clark - Cothran	1002832	Musser - Otis	1205178
Cothran - Daven	1002833	Otis - Pidd	1205179
Daven - Dobler	1002834	Pide - Rausch	1205180
Dobler - Edlebult	1002835	Rauschb - Rockwell	1205181
Edlebult - Felty	1002836	Rockwell - Schlep	1205182
Felty - Frey, D.	1275523	Schley - Shimp	1205183
Edleblute - Fenn	1002837	Shimp - Snyder JC	1205184
Frey, E. - Gils	1002838	Snyder JC - Stone	1205185
Gils - Groves	1002839	Stone - Thomas	1205186
Groves - Hartman	1002840	Thomas - Van Dyk	1205187
Hartman - Hazell	1004983	Van Dyke - Weave	1205188
Hazell - Hobbs	1005107	Weaver - Williams	1205189
Hobbs - Humer, G	1005108	Williams - Yost D	1205190
Humer, H. - Jaco	1005109	Yost, E. - Zwoe	1205191

"Index to Pennsylvania County Histories." Carnegie Library of Pittsburgh.
A seventy-five thousand card index to western Pennsylvanians. Two or three specific names will be searched free; with a fee if photocopies are requested. Mail inquiries to the Carnegie Library of

Pittsburgh, 4400 Forbes Avenue, Pittsburgh, PA 15213-4080.

"Pennsylvania Encyclopedia Biography Field Notes for American Guide Series." Pennsylvania Bureau of Archives and History, Harrisburg.
  FHL US/CAN FILM AREA 1015709-1015725.
  Approximately 18,870 abstracted biographical sketches from international, national, state, and local histories and biographical directories and encyclopedias. Prepared by a Federal Writer's Project, 1939-1942.

Hoenstine, Floyd G. *Guide to Genealogical and Historical Research in Pennsylvania.* Hollidaysburg, Pa.: F. G. Hoenstine, 1978. Supplements, 1985- .
  FHL US/CAN BOOK AREA 974.8 A3h 1978.
  Contains a surname index with some given names, with no page numbers, to an undetermined number of entries to 2,201 books.

RHODE ISLAND

Parker, J. Carlyle. *Rhode Island Biographical and Genealogical Sketch Index.* Turlock, Calif.: Marietta Publishing Co., 1991.
  FHL US/CAN BOOK AREA 974.5 D32p.
  Contains approximately thirty-five thousand index entries for about 19,500 biographees in 214 (364 volumes) state, regional, county, and city histories, periodical articles, newspaper articles, and histories and biographical directories of Rhode Island published between 1827 and 1989.

Greenlaw, William Prescott. *The Greenlaw Index of the New England Historic Genealogical Society.* 2 vols. Boston: G. K. Hall, 1979.
  FHL US/CAN BOOK AREA Q 974 D22g.
  Indexes many Rhode Island and New England local histories and genealogies up to 1940.

SOUTH CAROLINA

Cote, Richard N., and Patricia H. Williams. *Dictionary of South Carolina Biography.* Vol. 1. Easley, S.C.: Southern Historical Press,

1985. FHL US/CAN BOOK AREA 975.7 D36c.
Contains about 13,300 entries.

The Library of Congress Index to Biographies in State and Local Histories. 31 reels of microfilm. Baltimore: Magna Carta Book Co., 1979. FHL US/CAN FILM AREA 1380344-1380373, 1528066. See page 82 for contents of reels.
Indexes thirteen works relating to South Carolina.

SOUTH DAKOTA

Parker, J. Carlyle, and Janet G. Parker. *South Dakota Biographical and Genealogical Sketch Index.* Turlock, Calif.: Marietta Publishing Co., in progress.
Contains 19,920 index entries to the biographees in biographical and genealogical sketches in thirty-seven state, regional, county, and city histories and biographical directories of South Dakota published between 1898 and 1984. The publisher will consult this index for researchers and provide them with bibliographic citations and page numbers, for a modest fee. Address correspondence to the Marietta Publishing Co., 2115 North Denair Avenue, Turlock CA 95382, and for this service include a self-addressed, stamped envelope.

TENNESSEE

The Library of Congress Index to Biographies in State and Local Histories. 31 reels of microfilm. Baltimore: Magna Carta Book Co., 1979. FHL US/CAN FILM AREA 1380344-1380373, 1528066. See page 82 for contents of reels.
Indexes thirty-two works relating to Tennessee.

TEXAS

Ming, Virginia H., and William L. Ming. *Biographical Gazetteer of Texas: Publication of the Biographical Sketch File of the Texas Collection at Baylor University.* 6 vols. Austin, Texas: W. M. Morrison Books, 1985.
FHL US/CAN BOOK AREA 976.4 D3bgt.

Contains over seventy thousand entries to over fifty thousand
individuals in 202 historical works.

*The Library of Congress Index to Biographies in State and Local
Histories*. 31 reels of microfilm. Baltimore: Magna Carta Book Co.,
1979. FHL US/CAN FILM AREA 1380344-1380373, 1528066.
See page 82 for contents of reels.
Indexes twenty-seven works relating to Texas.

UTAH

Wiggins, Marvin E., comp. *Mormons and Their Neighbors: An Index
to Over 75,000 Biographical Sketches from 1820 to the Present*. 2 vols.
Provo, Utah: Harold B. Lee Library, Brigham Young University, 1984.
FHL US/CAN REG TABLE 979 D32w.
Index to over seventy-five thousand sketches from 1820 to 1984 in
194 titles, thirteen of which are for Idaho and eleven for Arizona.
The index also covers Latter-day Saints from Canada to Mexico,
New York, Ohio, Missouri, and the Pacific Islands.

VERMONT

Greenlaw, William Prescott. *The Greenlaw Index of the New England
Historic Genealogical Society*. 2 vols. Boston: G. K. Hall, 1979.
FHL US/CAN BOOK AREA Q 974 D22g.
Indexes many Vermont and New England local histories and
genealogies up to 1940.

VIRGINIA

Newberry Library, Chicago. *The Genealogical Index*. 4 Vols.
Boston: G. K. Hall, 1960. FHL US/CAN REF AREA Q 929 N424g.
Available from FHL through FHC: Microfilm 928135-928137.
Contains 512,000 entries, including some for Virginia, indexed
between 1896 and 1917. However, the microfilm is difficult to read.

WASHINGTON

"Regional Newspaper and Washington Periodical Index." University of Washington, Allen Library, Seattle.

Contains thousands of index cards to biographical sketches of persons in newspapers; periodicals; some obituaries; state, county, city, and church histories; and biographical directories, most of which were published from the 1860s to date. Address inquiries for only a few names at a time to Pacific Northwest Librarian, Special Collections Division, Allen Library FM-25, University of Washington, Seattle WA 98195. All correspondence to the Librarian should include a self-addressed, stamped envelope.

Drazan, Joseph Gerald. *The Pacific Northwest: An Index to People and Places in Books*. Metuchen, N.J.: Scarecrow Press, 1979. op.

Contains 6,830 entries in 320 local history titles for Alaska, British Columbia, Idaho, Montana, Oregon, Washington and the Yukon Territory. Fifty-one titles concerning the Northwest in general and eighty-three about Washington. For availability see page 117 of *Going*.

WEST VIRGINIA

Newberry Library, Chicago. *The Genealogical Index*. 4 Vols. Boston: G. K. Hall, 1960. FHL US/CAN REF AREA Q 929 N424g. Available from FHL through FHC: Microfilm 928135-928137.

Contains 512,000 entries, including a few for West Virginia, indexed between 1896 and 1917. However, the microfilm is difficult to read.

WISCONSIN

State Historical Society of Wisconsin. Library. *Subject Catalog; of the Library of the State Historical Society of Wisconsin, Madison, Wisconsin; Including the Pamphlet Subject Catalog Beginning in Volume 22*. 23 vols. Westport, Conn.: Greenwood Publishing Corp., 1971.

Contains approximately forty-five thousand index cards to biographical sketches of persons in state, county, city, and church histories and biographical directories. Researchers without access to this catalog or who may wish to have the fifteen thousand entries of sketches made since 1971 checked may write the Reference Librarian, The State Historical Society of Wisconsin, 816 State Street, Madison, WI 53706. Please give full name of person requested. Searches for all of a surname cannot be undertaken.

WYOMING

Parker, J. Carlyle, and Janet G. Parker. *Wyoming Biographical and Genealogical Sketch Index*. Turlock, Calif.: Marietta Publishing Co., in progress.
  Contains 8,582 index entries to the biographees in biographical and genealogical sketches in thirty state, regional, county, and city histories and biographical directories of Wyoming published between 1899 and 1984. The publisher will consult this index for researchers and provide them with bibliographic citations and page numbers, for a modest fee. Address correspondence to the Marietta Publishing Co., 2115 North Denair Avenue, Turlock CA 95382, and for this service include a self-addressed, stamped envelope.

CANADA

BRITISH COLUMBIA

Drazan, Joseph Gerald. *The Pacific Northwest: An Index to People and Places in Books*. Metuchen, N.J.: Scarecrow Press, 1979. op.
  Contains 6,830 entries in 320 local history titles for Alaska, British Columbia, Idaho, Montana, Oregon, Washington and the Yukon Territory. Fifty-one titles concerning the Northwest in general and forty-seven about British Columbia. For availability see page 117 of *Going*.

YUKON

Drazan, Joseph Gerald. *The Pacific Northwest: An Index to People and Places in Books*. Metuchen, N.J.: Scarecrow Press, 1979. op.
  Contains 6,830 entries in 320 local history titles for Alaska, British

Columbia, Idaho, Montana, Oregon, Washington and the Yukon
Territory. Fifty-one titles concerning the Northwest in general and
three about the Yukon. For availability see page 117 of *Going*.

I. FAMILY HISTORY CENTER USERS:

A few of the Family History Centers may have some of the above
indexes to help you find a biographical sketch of an ancestor. An
alternative for consulting any of the above indexes that are available in
the Family History Library but not available or obtainable through the
microform loan services of the Family History Center is to fill out and
submit a "Request for Photocopies--Census Records, Books, Microfilm
or Microfiche" available at a Family History Center. Obtain and
complete the request and mail it to the Family History Library along
with the required minimum nominal fee. However, the Library's
workload of correspondence is very heavy, so the answer may not be
immediate.

II. LOCAL PUBLIC LIBRARY USERS:

Some genealogical libraries and public libraries may have some of the
above titles. Any published sources not available or obtainable through
the interlibrary loan services of your local public library may possibly
be consulted through the reference service networks to which some
public libraries belong. If such services are not available at your
library, inquire if the librarian can tell you where the work may be
available in your locality, region, or state. Then write that library and
ask if they will check the source for you, one or two surnames at a
time. Such a correspondence service may not be free at the library to
which you write.

III. HOME LIBRARY USERS:

Look for newspaper obituaries and funeral programs; photocopied
sketches from biographical directories and printed histories; and

Chapter 8

typewritten or manuscript autobiographies and biographies among your
personal papers. Write or call relatives and ask that they check their
personal papers for the same. Some of the above unpublished personal
indexes can be consulted by mail.

SUMMARY:

Checking indexes mentioned in this chapter can reward you by adding
historical information about known ancestors and extending generations.
Prepare bibliographic cards for items of interest.

UNITED STATES & CANADA INFORMATION (REFERENCE) DESK

Chapter 9

IS AN ANCESTOR'S NAME IN NATIONAL
OR REGIONAL INDEXES?

PERIODICAL INDEXES

Genealogical and historical magazines and periodicals contain some
biographical information, and some periodicals are indexed in
genealogical periodical indexes. The following are a few titles that
relate to the United States, with Family History Library call numbers
included, that should be checked for names of interest:

Jacobus, Donald Lines. *Index to Genealogical Periodicals,
1932-1953*. Reprint. Baltimore, Genealogical Publishing Co., 1973.
3 Vols. in 1.
   FHL US/CAN BOOK AREA 973 B22j
   FHL US/CAN FILM AREA 161989

Genealogical Periodical Annual. Index. 1962-1965. Edited by Ellen
Stanley Rogers. Bladensburg, Md.: Genealogical Records, 1963-1967,
op.
   FHL US/CAN REF AREA 929.1 G286gpa.

Genealogical Periodical Annual. Index. 1966-1969. Edited by George
E. Russell. Bowie, Md.: The Author, 1966-1973, op.
   FHL US/CAN REF AREA 929.1 G286gpa.

Genealogical Periodical Annual. Index. 1974-   Edited by Laird C.
Towle, Bowie, Md.: The Heritage Books, 1976- .
   FHL US/CAN REF AREA 929.1 G286gpa.

Periodical Source Index (PERSI). 1847-1985. Prepared by the Staff of
the Allen County Public Library, Genealogy Department, Fort Wayne,
Indiana. Edited by Anne Dallas Budd, Michael Barren Clegg, and Curt
Bryan Witcher. Fort Wayne, Ind.: The Foundation, 1988.
   FHL US/CAN REF AREA 973 D25per & FHCs 6016863.

Chapter 9

Periodical Source Index (PERSI). 1986- Prepared by the Staff of
the Allen County Public Library, Genealogy Department, Fort
Wayne, Indiana. Fort Wayne, Ind.: Allen County Public Library
Foundation, 1987- .

FHL US/CAN REF AREA 973 D25per & FHCs 6016864.
Available at many libraries and Centers of the Family History
Library. If the Family History Library does not have any
periodical titles of interest, an easy way to obtain copies of articles
listed in the PERSI index is for the researcher to order photocopies
from the Allen County Public Library, P.O. Box 2270, Ft. Wayne,
IN 46801, as they hold all of the titles indexed. You should
provide the index entry from PERSI for not more than eight
articles at a time. The Allen County Public Library will bill
patrons several dollars for each letter, plus a few cents per page
photocopied. Because there are no page numbers given in the
index, it is impossible to estimate the cost of photocopying. You
should not request articles by telephone or FAX.

Additional titles of cumulative indexes to individual periodicals are
listed in Kip Sperry's *A Survey of American Genealogical
Periodicals and Periodical Indexes* (Detroit: Gale Research Co, 1978.
FHL US/CAN BOOK AREA 973 B23s).

If you find an article of interest in any of the above periodical indexes,
prepare a bibliographic card for it and consult the *Family History
Library Catalog: Author/Title Catalog* (on microfiche only) for that
periodical title. When you find the call number in the *Catalog*, add it
to your bibliographic card.

There are many periodicals that are not indexed, and it may be useful to
browse through such titles as time permits while at the Family History
Library. If you do not know the name of a genealogical or historical
periodical for a specific geographical location, you may find some in
the *Family History Library Catalog: Locality Catalog* by using the
following periodicals subject headings subdivisions for a state:

State-wide periodicals:
CALIFORNIA - ARCHIVES AND LIBRARIES - PERIODICALS
CALIFORNIA - GENEALOGY - PERIODICALS

CALIFORNIA - GENEALOGY - SOCIETIES - PERIODICALS
CALIFORNIA - HISTORY - PERIODICALS
CALIFORNIA - HISTORY - SOCIETIES - PERIODICALS
CALIFORNIA - MINORITIES - GENEALOGY - PERIODICALS
CALIFORNIA - NATIVE RACES - PERIODICALS
CALIFORNIA - PERIODICALS
CALIFORNIA - SOCIETIES - PERIODICALS

County periodicals:
CALIFORNIA, AMADOR - GENEALOGY - SOCIETIES -
    PERIODICALS
CALIFORNIA, EL DORADO - PERIODICALS
CALIFORNIA, STANISLAUS - HISTORY - SOCIETIES -
    PERIODICALS

City periodicals:
CALIFORNIA, FRESNO, REEDLEY - HISTORY -
    PERIODICALS

The above examples are taken from the California portion of the *Family
History Library Catalog: Locality Catalog*. There may be a few
additional subject headings used for other states and foreign countries.
However, the last subdivision will always be PERIODICALS.

Periodicals of nationwide interest and scope are found in the *Family
History Library Catalog: Subject Catalog* (on microfiche only) under
the subject heading GENEALOGY - PERIODICALS and also in the
Family History Library Catalog: Locality Catalog under the subject
headings:
    MEXICO - GENEALOGY - PERIODICALS
    UNITED STATES - GENEALOGY - PERIODICALS

U.S. NATIONWIDE INDEXES

The following nationwide indexes for the United States are listed in
order of importance according to the value judgment of the author:

Chapter 9

American Genealogical-Biographical Index to American Genealogical, Biographical and Local History Materials. Middletown, Conn.: Godfrey Memorial Library, 1952- in progress.
FHL US/CAN BOOK AREA 973 D22ag.

> Clark, Patricia I., and Dorothy Huntsman, eds. *Key Title Index to the American Genealogical-Biographical Index: Register of Family History Library Call Numbers.* Salt Lake City: FHL, 1990.
> FHL US/CAN BOOK AREA 973 D22am Index.
> Microfiche. Salt Lake City, Genealogical Society of Utah, 1992.
> FHL US/CAN FICHE AREA 6088377 (1 microfiche).
> Includes the book and microform numbers for the books indexed that are available in the Family History Library.

Newberry Library, Chicago. *The Genealogical Index.* 4 Vols. Boston: G. K. Hall, 1960. FHL US/CAN REF AREA Q 929 N424g. Available from FHL through FHC: Microfilm 928135-928137.
> Contains 512,000 entries, indexed between 1896 and 1917.
> However, the microfilm is difficult to read.

California. State Library, Sacramento. Sutro Branch, San Francisco. *The Surname Catalog.* 3d ed. Sacramento: California State Library Foundation, 1990. FHL US/CAN FICHE AREA 6334474 (1986 ed.).
> Good for family histories, includes individuals, and is nationwide in coverage. Over fifty thousand entries to twelve thousand family histories and other books (also includes *State and Local History Catalog* and *Miscellaneous Catalog*).

"Historical and Biographical Index of North East, Mid East, Mid South, Mid West, U.S., 1880 thru early 1900." Allen County Public Library, Fort Wayne, Indiana. FHL US/CAN FILM AREA 20 reels of microfilm.

Aainsworth, Harry -	1452209	Davis, Almon -	1452463
Arthur, Charles W. -	1452210	Duff, James M. -	1452464
Beatty, Harrison L. -	1452250	Faulk, Andrew -	1452465
Borst, George -	1452251	Fulton, Warren L. -	1439676
Buetch, Ernest C. -	1452252	Graham, Emmett A. -	1493044
Chapin family -	1452253	contains Hackworth - Harter	
Cooper, Wilford -	1452254	Griffith, J. J. -	1674418

Haab -	1493045	Prutsman, Marshall -	1614291
Hinkle, Uriah -	1493046	Rising, A. M. -	1614292
Hurd, Jonathan -	1493168	Sawyer, Iredell -	1614293
Kear, Byron -	1493558	Shoemaker, Andrew -	1614450
Kunst, John H. -	1493559	Spilker, B. F. -	1614592
Long, R. W. -	1487775	Strine, John -	1614593
McLain, Peter -	1613064	Tower, Charlemagne -	1643160
Miller, Emory F. -	1503784	Wantz, Frederick -	1643161
Neal, John L. -	1614043	Williams, Amos A. -	1643507
Parrett, George -	1614044	Zimmerman, George -	1643508

Brown, Stuart E., Jr., comp. *Virginia Genealogies, A Trial List of Printed Books and Pamphlets.* 3 vols. Berryville, Va.: Virginia Book Co., 1967-1989. FHL US/CAN BOOK AREA 975.5 D23b.

> Cites 1,962 family histories and gives numerous "see references" in its index in volume one. Volumes two and three cite many more.

Index to American Genealogies; and to Genealogical Material Contained in All Works as Town Histories, County Histories, Local Histories, Historical Society Publications, Biographies, Historical Periodical and Kindred Works. 5th ed. rev. Albany, N.Y.: Munsell, 1900, 1908. Reprint. Baltimore: Genealogical Publishing Co., 1967.
FHL US/CAN REF AREA 929.173 IN2a
FHL US/CAN FICHE AREA 6051301 (6 microfiches)
FHL US/CAN FILM AREA 599811

The American Genealogist, Being a Catalogue of Family Histories. A Bibliography of American Genealogy, or a List of the Title Pages of Books and Pamphlets on Family History, Published in America, from 1771 to Date. 5th ed. Albany: Munsell, 1900. Reprint. Detroit: Gale Research Co., 1975. Baltimore: Genealogical Publishing Co., 1967.
FHL US/CAN REF AREA 973 D23am 1900.

> This work and the *Index to American Genealogies* (see above) should be used together. The *American Genealogist* is, in part, a bibliography of the family histories indexed in the *Index to American Genealogies*.

Chapter 9

Kirkham, E. Kay. *An Index to Some of the Bibles and Family Records of the United States: (Excluding the Southern States); 45,000 References as Taken from the Microfilm at the Genealogical Society of Utah.* Volume II. Logan, Utah: Everton Publishers, Inc., 1984.
    FHL US/CAN BOOK AREA 973 D22kk v.2.

The Library of Congress Index to Biographies in State and Local Histories. 31 reels of microfilm. Baltimore: Magna Carta Book Co., 1979. FHL US/CAN FILM AREA 1380344-1380373, 1528066. See page 82 for contents of reels.
    Contains approximately 170,000 entries to biographees of some volumes in the Library of Congress. It indexes only 340 titles. Kentucky has the largest number of titles indexed, with 50; Georgia has 36; California, 34; Tennessee, 32; Texas, 27; Louisiana, 21; Mississippi, 13; South Carolina, 13; Idaho, 12; Nevada, 11; Arkansas, 10; North Carolina, 10; Alabama, 8; Arizona, 6; and all other states, 3 or less.

McMullin, Phillip W., ed. *Grassroots of America; A Computerized Index to the American State Papers: Land Grants and Claims (1789-1837) with Other Aids to Research.* Salt Lake City: Gendex Corp., 1972.
    FHL US/CAN REF AREA 973 R2m
    FHL & FHCs US/CAN FICHE AREA 6051323
    Reprint. Conway, Ark.: Arkansas Research, 1990.
    Reprint. Greenville, S.C.: Southern Historical Press, 1994.
    This index is simply a personal name index to the sections of public land and claims in the *American State Papers*. Index entries are to the *American State Papers*, volumes 1-9 which are available on FHL US/CAN FILM AREA 899878-85 or 908743-50. The following table converts the volume numbers into *American State Papers* Serial Set numbers:

	Index Entry no.	Serial Set	FHL no.
Public Lands	1	028	899878 or 908743
Public Lands	2	029	899879 or 908744

Public Lands	3	030	899880 or 908745
Public Lands	4	031	899881 or 908746
Public Lands	5	032	899882 or 908747
Public Lands	6	033	899883 or 908748
Public Lands	7	034	899884 or 908749
Public Lands	8	035	899885 or 908750
Claims	9	036	944495

In many cases the information found in the *American State Papers* is nothing more than a petition list or a list of landholders. However, the location and date are usually given; and these are useful for continued research, particularly if a county was previously unknown.

REGIONAL INDEXES

Southern States

Kirkham, E. Kay. *An Index to Some of the Family Records of the Southern States: 35,000 Microfilm References from the N.S.D.A.R. Files and Elsewhere.* Logan, Utah: Everton Publishers, Inc., 1979.
   FHL US/CAN BOOK AREA 973 D22kk v.1.
      Indexes Bibles, family records, and family histories. Entries refer to the microfilm reel numbers of the Family History Library.

Leon S. Hollingsworth Genealogical Card File.
   FHL US/CAN FILM AREA 1308005-1308007.
      Contains approximately 297,000 given names. Covers research concerning persons from throughout the Southeast, primarily Georgia, but also including North and South Carolina, Virginia, and Alabama.

Stewart, Robert Armistead. *Index to Printed Virginia Genealogies, Including Key and Bibliography.* Richmond, Va.: Old Dominion Press, 1930. Reprint. Baltimore: Genealogical Publishing Co., 1970.
   FHL US/CAN BOOK AREA 975.5 D22s

FHL US/CAN FILM AREA 962558, Item 2
FHL US/CAN FICHE AREA 6019375
   The author includes anyone from Virginia listed in any book he
   checked in his nationwide search for Virginians.

New England

Greenlaw, William Prescott. *The Greenlaw Index of the New England
Historic Genealogical Society.* 2 vols. Boston: G. K. Hall, 1979.
   FHL US/CAN REF Q AREA 974 D22g.
      Contains over thirty-five thousand entries. Indexes genealogical
      works; family histories; state, county, and city histories;
      biographical directories; and periodicals acquired by the society
      between 1900 and 1940. Entries are limited to families for which
      three or more generations are reported in a work.

Middle Atlantic States

Genealogical Society of Pennsylvania. Manuscript Card Catalog of the
Genealogical Society of Pennsylvania. Salt Lake City: Genealogical
Society of Utah, 1964.
   FHL US/CAN FILM AREA 377629-377637.
      The collections indexed in this source represent many of the
      Eastern Seaboard states, England and Nassau, but mainly the states
      of Pennsylvania and New Jersey. The guide that follows this entry
      must be used with this index in order to convert the call numbers
      of most of the large manuscript collections on the index cards to a
      Family History Library microfilm reel number. All of the
      microfilm for the above index and the materials indexed (over one
      thousand reels) may be borrowed through Family History Centers.

Index A-B	377629	Index L	377634
Index C	377630	Index M-P	377635
Index D	377631	Index Q-S	377636
Index E-G	377632	Index T-Z	377637
Index H-K	377633		

Manuscript Card Catalog is also known as the Manuscript
Material Index of the Historical Society of Pennsylvania
and as the Genealogical Material Index.

Parker, J. Carlyle. *Pennsylvania and Middle Atlantic States
Genealogical Manuscripts: A User's Guide to the Manuscript
Collections of the Genealogical Society of Pennsylvania as Indexed in
Its Manuscript Materials Index Microfilmed by the Genealogical
Department, Salt Lake City.* Turlock, Calif.: Marietta Publishing Co.,
1986.
  FHL US/CAN BOOK AREA 974.8 D27pp.
    It is essential that this guide be used with the above index. After
    this guide was prepared the Family History Library recataloged the
    index and renamed it Manuscript Card Catalog of the Genealogical
    Society of Pennsylvania, replacing the name Manuscript Materials
    Index.

Pacific Northwest

Drazan, Joseph Gerald. *The Pacific Northwest: An Index to People and
Places in Books.* Metuchen, N.J.: Scarecrow Press, 1979.
  Contains 6,830 entries in 320 local history titles for Alaska, British
  Columbia, Idaho, Montana, Oregon, Washington and the Yukon
  Territory. This title is not available at the Family History Library but
  is available in many North American libraries and should be
  available through the interlibrary loan services of your local public
  library. The Marietta Publishing Company, 2115 North Denair
  Avenue, Turlock CA 95382, will check their copy of Drazan for you
  by letter if a self-addressed, stamped envelope is enclosed. If your
  ancestor is indexed in Drazan they will send you free the
  bibliographic citations and page numbers of books indexed.

Prepare bibliographic cards for all books and articles found to be of
interest in the above sources.

Chapter 9

I. FAMILY HISTORY CENTER USERS:

Some of the titles in this chapter are available in some Family History Centers.

II. LOCAL PUBLIC LIBRARY USERS:

Some of the above titles may be available in local public libraries. Your library may also have some of the following indexes to national and international biographical directories:

Bio-Base: A Periodic Cumulative Master Index on Microfiche to Sketches Found in about 700 Current and Historical Biographical Dictionaries, 1995; Master Cumulation. Microfiche. Detroit: Gale Research Co., 1995, or *Biography and Genealogy Master Index* (Detroit: Gale Research Co., 1980- , or *Abridged Biography and Genealogy Master Index: A Consolidated Index to More Than 1,600,000 Biographical Dictionaries Indexed in Biography and Genealogy and Master Index Through 1987.* Detroit: Gale Research Co., 1988.
    FHL US/CAN REF AREA 016.92 G131 no.1.
    The 1995 cumulation contains over 9,700,000 names.

Hyamson, Albert Montefiore. *A Dictionary of Universal Biography of All Ages and of All Peoples.* 3d ed., entirely rewritten. New York: Dutton, 1951. Reprint. Detroit: Gale Research Co., 1980.
    Contains index entries to over 110,000 persons in twenty-four early twentieth century biographical dictionaries and encyclopedias.

Riches, Phyllis M. *An Analytical Bibliography of Universal Collected Biography, Comprising Books Published in the English Tongue in Great Britain and Ireland, America and the British Dominions.* London: The Library Association, 1934. Reprint. New York: Johnson Reprint Corp., 1973. Reprint. Detroit: Gale Research Co., 1980.
    Contains over fifty-six thousand index entries to biographical sketches in over three thousand biographies published through 1933.

Phillips, Lawrence Barnett. *The Dictionary of Biographical Reference; Containing Over One Hundred Thousand Names; Together with a Classed Index of the Biographical Literature of Europe and America.* New ed., rev., cor. and augm. with supplement to date, by Frank Weitenkampf. London: S. Low, Marston and Co., 1889. Reprint. Graz, Austria: Akade-mische, Druck-u Verlagsanstalt, 1966.
   An index to forty-two nineteenth century biographical dictionaries and encyclopedias.

III. HOME LIBRARY USERS:

Those indexes among the above titles that may be of interest to you should be checked for your surnames while you are researching at the Family History Library.

ADDITIONAL READING:

Parker, J. Carlyle. "Genealogical Name Indexes," chapter 9, pages 119-24; and "Genealogical Periodicals and Periodical Indexes," chapter 10, pages 125-29. In *Library Service for Genealogists.* Gale Genealogy and Local History Series, vol. 15. Detroit: Gale Research Co, 1981, op. FHL US/CAN REF AREA 026.9291 P226L. 2d edition in progress by Marietta Publishing Co.

SUMMARY:

As time permits, the appropriate national and regional indexes listed in this chapter can be helpful in your search for information concerning ancestors. Prepare bibliographic cards for sources that indexes indicate deal with ancestors of interest.

INTERNATIONAL INFORMATION (REFERENCE) DESK

Chapter 10

WHAT TO TAKE?

A reader responded to our survey on how to improve the second edition by asking for suggestions on what to take to Salt Lake City for research. Below is a list of what the author believes is essential.

Nevertheless, I once made a research trip abroad almost empty-handed. I had the opportunity to do a couple of days of research in the county archives of Surrey, in Guildford, and Hampshire, in Winchester, England. Long before going, I used the parish registers available at the Family History Library and through its Family History Centers, and determined that the Library did not have microfilm of all of the registers that were needed. Because baggage was limited in poundage and the trip involved four weeks of sedan travel in nine countries, research papers were limited to as few as needed. After some analysis the necessary research information was penned on eleven three by five cards and note paper was purchased in England. The end result was a very successful research trip which far exceeded the prepared research objectives and priorities.

The following is a prioritized list of what is recommended for a research trip to the Family History Library:

Checklist of research and personal items to be checked off as you pack
(example: pedigree sheets, paper clips, tooth brush, comb, etc.)
Your copy of *Going to Salt Lake City to Do Family History Research*
Cards or computer printouts of ancestral research needs, objectives, and priorities
Pedigree sheets related to needs, objectives, and priorities
Family group sheets related to needs, objectives, and priorities
Research logs (or equivalent) related to needs, objectives, and priorities
Correspondence logs related to needs, objectives, and priorities
Note paper, 3"x5" cards and 3"x5" pad of note paper (free 8½"x11" scratch paper is available in limited quantities at the Library)

Chapter 10

Return address stickers or a rubber stamp for marking ownership of
   research notes and photocopies
Sticky notes (self-stick removable notes): Caution, they leave residue.
   Please do not place them in books or on microforms, on your
   original documents, photographs, or leave on any papers for an
   extended length of time.
Pencils and pens
Extra manila file folders or ring binder dividers for families,
   persons, or places
Paper clips
Rubber bands
Case (not a box) for 3"x5" cards (a bank passbook case works for some
   researchers)
Sweater for cold spots in the Library both summer and winter
Briefcase or canvas bag
Magnifying glass
Stapler and staples
Hand held paper punch, if binders are used for research notes
Coin purse with strap or waist pack for women without pockets
Ear plugs for those unfortunate occasions when you are reading near
   other researchers who make too much noise

Leave at home:

Original documents, certificates, licenses
Research papers that do not relate to research objectives

SUMMARY

Travel as light and as comfortably as possible. Please don't take your
two-drawer file cabinet; it is hard on other patrons' shins.

PART II

WHEN YOU'RE THERE

Chapter 11

AT THE FAMILY HISTORY LIBRARY

It is very important that you read all of this chapter and chapter 12 before going to the Family History Library. The information covered in both chapters is essential for your efficient use of the Library.

The Library is located at 35 North West Temple Street, next to JB's Restaurant and the Howard Johnson Hotel on the south, the Salt Lake valley's first log cabin and the Church History Museum on the north, and Temple Square on the East. The Library is shown as number 3 on the attractions map on the inside back cover of this work.

Some researchers advocate that an orientation to the Library is helpful. Orientation is offered to the left of the main entrance lobby.

If you have decided to orient yourself, find the floor on which your books, microfilm, and microfiche are located (see list below). If you have already used the *Family History Library Catalog* in a Family History Center, upon arrival at your floor of research interest, take out your prioritized bibliographic cards or computer printouts and find the first item in the collection. If you still need to consult the *Family History Library Catalog*, take your geographical, individual, family surname cards, and cards of ancestral research needs in priority order and look up the call numbers for the research materials needed as explained in chapters 5 and 6.

You will need to approach the Library's collection geographically, except for family histories, which are alphabetical, and microforms which are filed by number. Books, microfilm, and family histories are located together on their respective floors, except for Canada and the United States. The organization of the collection, including Dewey Decimal Classification Scheme numbers, is by the following areas of research, which are located on the indicated floors of the Family History Library:

Africa	960-968	Basement 1
Asia	950-959	Basement 1

British Isles	941-942	Basement 2
Canada Books	971	Main Floor
Canada Family		
History Books	929.271	Main Floor
Canada Microforms		Second Floor
European	943-949	Basement 1
Latin America	972-980	Basement 1
Middle East	955-956	Basement 1
Oceania	969 990	Basement 1
Scandinavia	948	Basement 1
United States Books	973-979	Main Floor
United States Family		
History Books	929.273	Main Floor
Newsletters	929.27305	Main Floor
United States Microforms		Second Floor

If it is difficult to find a microfilm reader or table space on the U.S. and Canada floors of the Library, there are usually microfilm readers and table space available on the lower levels of the Library, and you are allowed to take your books and microfilm there. Please do not take more than five books or microforms at one time, and, when you are finished with them, return them to the floor where you found them. Books should be returned to the red shelves at the end of the range of shelving from which you removed them. Make sure that you refile your microfilms and that they are refiled in the correct place. Microfiche are refiled by library attendants. Please place microfiche in the baskets on top of the microfiche cabinets.

When leaving microfilm readers for lunch, dinner, or anytime for more than thirty minutes, the Library staff requests that researchers remove their materials in order for others to use the readers. Library attendants may remove unattended materials left by a microfilm reader for longer than thirty minutes.

Reference books are shelved near the Information (Reference) Desk on each floor and include the most-often-used titles, such as gazetteers, atlases, how-to-do-it books, indexes, and bibliographies. Bound state-wide United States federal census schedule indexes are shelved on reference tables on the second floor near the reference desk, where they are most useful.

The oversize or folio collection consists of larger or taller-than-average books not shelved with the general collection. Oversize book call numbers are preceded with a capital letter "Q." U.S. oversize books are shelved in a compact "High Density" shelving area closed to the public. They may be requested at the main floor library assistants' station. The British oversize book collection in basement 2 is shelved at the end of the British general book collection. Oversize books for other foreign countries are also usually shelved at the end of other foreign countries' general collections.

Also shelved in an area closed to the public are many pamphlets with the second line of the library's call number reading "A1," example:

> 979.1
> A1
> no. 25

Request them at the library assistants' stations.

While doing research at the Family History Library, review research needs. Review may help you keep your sights on your research objectives. Remember to ask yourself: "Is this part of my research really necessary at this time?"

BROWSING

Browsing may distract from your research objectives and you should not overindulge in it; but it can be a useful part of using a library. The Family History Library facilitates easy browsing in its book collection through the use of its library subject classification scheme. The second line of the call number on the spine of the book identifies the subject contents of the book. The letter and the digit, "V2," on the second line of the call number, for example, means that the book contains vital records. This means that some vital records of Shelby County, Ohio abstracted, published, and added to the Library's collection, have the following call number:

> 977.145
> V2ab

Similarly, "K2" is used for church records of births, christenings, marriages, and deaths. Church records of Bloomfield Township, Bedford County, Pennsylvania abstracted and published, would be assigned the following call number:

> 974.871/B1
> K2b

"P2" is used for wills and probate records. The wills and probate records of Jefferson County, Iowa, abstracted and published, are labeled with the following call number:

> 977.794
> P2j

The above and additional selected subject classification scheme numbers that may be of interest are listed below by both subject and number:

Biography	D3
Cemetery records	V3
Church histories	K2
Church records	K2
City directories	E4
City histories	H2
County histories	H2
Court records	P2
Genealogical periodicals	B2 or D25*
Genealogies	D2
Guardianships	P2
Minority histories	F2
Land and property	R2
Military records	M2
Naturalization	P4
Obituaries	V4
Parish registers	K2
Probate records	P2
Racial group histories	F2
School records	J2
Ship passenger lists	W3
Genealogical, societies	C4
State histories	H2

Tax records	R4
Vital records	V2
Voting records	N4
Wills	P2

B3 or D25	Genealogical periodicals*
C4	Societies
D2	Genealogies
D3	Biography
E4	City directories
F2	Minority histories (national, racial or religious groups)
H2	City, county, and/or state histories
J2	School records
K2	Church histories, records and parish registers
M2	Military records
N4	Voting records
P2	Court, guardianship, and probate records, and wills
P4	Naturalization
R2	Land and property
R4	Tax records
V2	Vital records (Church records and parish registers)
V3	Cemetery records
V4	Obituaries
W3	Ship passenger lists
X2	Census schedules

* The B2 category is for general periodicals but was also used for genealogical periodicals for many years. The D25 category is now used for genealogical periodicals, but many genealogical periodicals still remain under the B2 category.

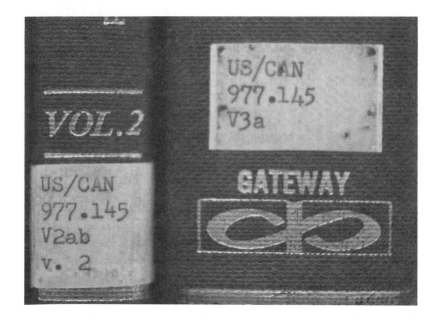

GENEALOGY BOOK CALL NUMBERS

CENSUS SCHEDULES

It is not necessary to look up the microfilm numbers for the census schedules and soundexes for the United States and the census schedules for Canada that you will use at the Family History Library, as they are arranged in their cabinets by census year, state, and province; and boxes are labeled just like the catalogs listed in part II, "Local Public Library Users," of Chapter 7. The microfilm cabinets for these censuses are located to the left of the rest rooms on the second floor.

It is important to pay attention to the following note that appears on some reel box labels:

LISTINGS CONTINUED
ON THE SIDE OF BOX -->

The census cabinets contain two filmings of the 1860 and 1870 U.S. federal census schedules. In both cases read first the second microfilming. If the second microfilming is difficult to read then you should consult the first microfilming. The first microfilming has two sheets (leaves) of the schedules per microfilm frame, the second microfilming has one sheet per frame.

Census schedules for other countries are filed by number in the regular microfilm cabinets on their respective floors in the Library. Their microfilm numbers may be looked up in the *Family History Library Catalog: Locality Catalog* on microfiche or *FamilySearch* at your local Family History Center before traveling to Salt Lake City. Usually the microfilm numbers for the census schedules of most foreign countries are found under the subject heading "(name of country) - Census - (year)."

DEWEY DECIMAL CLASSIFICATION SCHEME

The Family History Library utilizes the Dewey Decimal Classification Scheme, which does not arrange states on the library shelves in alphabetical order, Alabama through Wyoming, but places the books geographically by state, starting with Maine westward to Hawaii.

The following is a numerical list of beginning numbers of the arrangement of states in the Dewey Decimal Classification Scheme:

974.1	Maine	975.3	District of Columbia
974.2	New Hampshire	975.4	West Virginia
974.3	Vermont	975.5	Virginia
974.4	Massachusetts	975.6	North Carolina
974.5	Rhode Island	975.7	South Carolina
974.6	Connecticut	975.8	Georgia
974.7	New York	975.9	Florida
974.8	Pennsylvania	976.1	Alabama
974.9	New Jersey	976.2	Mississippi
975.1	Delaware	976.3	Louisiana
975.2	Maryland	976.4	Texas

976.6 Oklahoma	978.4 North Dakota
976.7 Arkansas	978.6 Montana
976.8 Tennessee	978.7 Wyoming
976.9 Kentucky	978.8 Colorado
977.1 Ohio	978.9 New Mexico
977.2 Indiana	979.1 Arizona
977.3 Illinois	979.2 Utah
977.4 Michigan	979.3 Nevada
977.5 Wisconsin	979.4 California
977.6 Minnesota	979.5 Oregon
977.7 Iowa	979.6 Idaho
977.8 Missouri	979.7 Washington
978.1 Kansas	979.8 Alaska
978.2 Nebraska	996.9 Hawaii
978.3 South Dakota	

In general, the arrangement of states begins in the Northeast with Maine and works south down the Atlantic Coast, and then with variations of south to north and north to south, westward to the Pacific Coast and Hawaii.

For researchers who would prefer a list with an alphabetical approach, here is a list of the Dewey Decimal Classification Scheme in alphabetical order by state:

Alabama	976.1	Idaho	979.6
Alaska	979.8	Illinois	977.3
Arizona	979.1	Indiana	977.2
Arkansas	976.7	Iowa	977.7
California	979.4	Kansas	978.1
Colorado	978.8	Kentucky	976.9
Connecticut	974.6	Louisiana	976.3
Delaware	975.1	Maine	974.1
District of		Maryland	975.2
Columbia	975.3	Massachusetts	974.4
Florida	975.9	Michigan	977.4
Georgia	975.8	Minnesota	977.6
Hawaii	996.9	Mississippi	976.2

Missouri	977.8	Pennsylvania	974.8
Montana	978.6	Rhode Island	974.5
Nebraska	978.2	South Carolina	975.7
Nevada	979.3	South Dakota	978.3
New Hampshire	974.2	Tennessee	976.8
New Jersey	974.9	Texas	976.4
New Mexico	978.9	Utah	979.2
New York	974.7	Vermont	974.3
North Carolina	975.6	Virginia	975.5
North Dakota	978.4	Washington	979.7
Ohio	977.1	West Virginia	975.4
Oklahoma	976.6	Wisconsin	977.5
Oregon	979.5	Wyoming	978.7

The Dewey Decimal Classification Scheme for counties within a state is not only not in alphabetical order but it does not conform to the historical growth of a state nor to the chronological creation of the counties. Counties are arranged by geographical regions. The Family History Library has created for patrons who wish to browse books on the shelves an alphabetical list of all the counties of the United States by state with their Dewey Decimal Classification Scheme call numbers. Several copies of this county call number list are provided in three ring binders; one is at the United States and Canada Information (Reference) Desk on the main floor. At present it is on the corner of the desk nearest to the book shelves and the restrooms. There are additional copies on the shelves around the building column located between the Information (Reference) Desk and *FamilySearch*.

Some researchers have condemned Melvil Dewey and the Library of Congress for not putting their classification scheme in alphabetical order by state. When Dewey and the Library of Congress were preparing their schemes, many states did not exist, nor were they created in alphabetical order.

Chapter 11

ETIQUETTE FOR THE LIBRARY

There are numerous rules of etiquette and principles of common sense that should be followed in the Library. Both underlining and check-marking with pens on microform reading machine screens and surfaces are a nuisance to others. When using library materials special care should be taken not to mark, mutilate, dog-ear corners, deface, finger lick (to turn pages), nor to place note paper on book pages while taking notes. When photocopying books be careful not to push down so hard on the spines that the bindings break. When other researchers are waiting in line for photocopying, please limit yourself to five copies at a time, then move to the end of the line if you have additional copies to make.

Research materials should be limited to five items removed from shelves or microform drawers at a time. Rewind the microfilm back onto the reel that was in the box. Spreading papers across a table into the area where others may need to work can be as annoying and inconsiderate as talking loudly or constantly to others or oneself. Helping to maintain a quiet library atmosphere is the responsibility of all researchers. On a recent visit to the Library one gentleman was wearing ear plugs. Not a bad idea when others nearby are making too much noise.

Please be careful of pet phrases or oaths which may be offensive to researchers seated next to you. Modest dress is also a courtesy in any library. Family History Library policy requires that children under twelve be kept under control. The Library does not have a children's collection and children may find the Library boring.

FAMILY GROUP RECORDS COLLECTION

Another project that should not be overlooked while at the Family History Library is to search for your ancestors in the Family Group Records Collection (FGRC). This collection contains approximately eight million family group sheets representing research submitted by LDS Church members from 1942 to 1969. Its contents cover twentieth century families back to the sixteenth century. Some group sheets contain errors; nevertheless, the search should be made.

The collection is arranged in alphabetical order by the surname and given names of the father of each family and further sub-arranged by the birth date of the fathers, for names that are the same. The cards or computer lists for individuals which you prepared as a part of chapter 1 can be used to check the Family Group Records Collection.

The Family Group Records Collection is available on microfilm and is located in the east wing of the fourth floor of the Joseph Smith Memorial Building, South Temple and Main Streets (number 8 on the attractions map on the inside back cover of this work). It consists of many parts, the largest of which is the Family Group Records Collection: Archive Section, which was collected from members of the Church of Jesus Christ of Latter-day Saints from 1942-1969, but represents families from about 1500-1969.

There are two microfilm sets of this collection. While at the Family History Library it is best to read the 35mm microfilm copy (1060000-1063691). The 16mm microfilm (1273501-1275491) may circulate to Family History Centers and is available on the fourth floor of the Joseph Smith Memorial Building. The original records are still also available in the east wing. However, they are not as complete as the microfilm, as over the years some records have been removed from them.

FAMILYSEARCH

FamilySearch has been explained in numerous earlier chapters. However, the following are some suggestions concerning variations on its use in Salt Lake City.

FamilySearch computers are available on all floors of the Family History Library, in the Joseph Smith Memorial Building *FamilySearch* Center, and in the west wing of the fourth floor of the Joseph Smith Memorial Building. For short time use of *FamilySearch* there are computer waist-high stand-up stations limited to a few minutes of use on all floors. There are several stations with secretarial chairs on all floors, some limited for shorter use, others that access some different CD-ROM programs, and some with wheelchair access. Computer stations in the Automated Resource Center, discussed on the first page of chapter 12, are limited to one hour's use.

The *FamilySearch* stations in the Joseph Smith Memorial Building *FamilySearch* Center have more space than most of the stations in the Family History Library. The west wing of the Joseph Smith Memorial Building *FamilySearch* stations have even more space than *FamilySearch* Center stations. The *FamilySearch* stations in the Joseph Smith Memorial Building are supplied with laser printers, while most of the stations in the Family History Library have not so sophisticated printers.

The *FamilySearch* computer terminals available in the Family History Library and in the Joseph Smith Memorial Building, South Temple and Main Streets, are on a computer network mainframe (not online) that does not require the use of CD-ROM diskettes. These networked terminals for *FamilySearch* run much faster than the computers in the Family History Centers.

HELP - FIXING AND OPERATING MACHINES - LOCATING BOOKS AND MICROFORMS

If equipment fails, documents are not understandable, or a different size lens is needed for a microform reading machine or printer, ask for help at the Library Attendants Window or Station adjacent to the Copy Center on each floor. Examples of other problems that should be brought to the attention to the Library Attendants are difficulties finding books or microforms, burned out reader bulbs, and mechanical problems with readers or copy machines. They may also be able to locate duplicate copies of microfilm that may be lost or misplaced.

Library Attendants will help you with everything but research questions. If the Library Attendants Stations personnel or librarians or volunteers at the Information (Reference) Desk are too busy at the

moment and you must wait in line, pick up some work to do while
waiting in line.

HELP - REFERENCE AND/OR RESEARCH

Go to the Information (Reference) Desk for research help. Write down
the suggestions that the librarian makes concerning research problems.

If a particular book is confusing, check the introduction or preface for
an explanation of how it is organized or how to use it. After having
read and studied the introduction and preface, if you are still confused,
consult a librarian at the Information (Reference) Desk. In the front of
most books there is usually also a list of abbreviations used that you
may find helpful.

Also read "Reference Questions: How to Ask Them" and "Reference
Service" in this chapter.

JOSEPH SMITH MEMORIAL BUILDING

The *FamilySearch* Center, on the lower level in the historic Joseph
Smith Memorial Building, South Temple and Main Streets, provides
computers containing *FamilySearch*. There are also *FamilySearch*
computers in the west wing of the fourth floor of the Joseph Smith
Memorial Building. In the east wing of the fourth floor are housed
microfilm copies of the 1920 federal census schedules, and its Soundex;
the Family Group Records Collection in legal size binders; and also
16mm microfilm copies of it. If a family is not found in the binders
you should also check the microfilm of the Family Group Records
Collection.

Both wings of the fourth floor have spacious work areas and are quieter
than the Family History Library. The *FamilySearch* computer
terminals in the Joseph Smith Memorial Building are on a computer
network mainframe (not online) and operate fast without using CD-
ROM diskettes.

Chapter 11

MAPS

If you need to consult some maps while at the Family History Library, check the *Family History Library Catalog: Locality Catalog* under your geographical place of interest with the subject heading subdivision, "MAPS:"

OHIO, ROSS, CHILLICOTHE - MAPS

The United States and Canada maps are shelved in locked cases to the right of the Automated Resource Center on the main floor. Provide the Library Attendants in their Station adjacent to the Copy Center with the call number and title of the map. The attendant will open the cases and locate the map for you. Foreign maps are on their respective floors. Sample call numbers are as follows:

US/CAN	BRITISH	EUROPE
MAP CASE	MAP CASE	MAP CASE
970	942.85	946
E7cm	E7c	E7mc

MICROFORMS AND READING MACHINES

Microform collections are shelved near their reading machines. Microforms include microfiche and 35mm and 16mm reel microfilm. Microfiche catalogs and indexes are located near the Information (Reference) Desk on each floor.

The basic parts of microfilm reading machines are the loading apparatus, focus device, hand crank or motor switch, and the margin device. The margin device, sometimes called a scanning device, moves the microfilm from side to side under the lens and thereby moves the image on the reading surface.

If, after experimenting with the machine, you are unable to discover these parts or how they work, make sure that you ask someone for assistance. A fellow researcher may be able to help and save the time that it might take to find a Library Attendant to help you. If a microform is difficult to read, it may be a little easier to read on a different reading machine. Often the lens sizes are not standard on reading machines, the brightness of the lamps differ, lamps grow dim with age, and the clarity of microfilm readers also differs because of dust and scratches on the glass plates.

Microfilm in a one inch box is 16mm. Microfilm in an 1 5/8" thick box is 35mm. Usually, both 16mm and 35mm may be used on a regular reader. However, if the reader you are using is incapable of enlarging the film's image enough for your reading comfort, move to a reader with zoom or a higher magnification. Some of these readers are labeled "Adjustable Magnification," "High Magnification," "Zoom Lens," "42X," or "65X." If a reader or table space is not available on the floor where your materials are located, you may take the material to another floor for use. There is usually space available on the 1st and 2d basement floors.

There are left handed microfilm readers in reader row 26 on the U.S. and Canada floor. There are also other left handed microfilm readers on the basement floors and some wheelchair access microfilm readers, motorized microfilm readers, and *FamilySearch* computers throughout the Library.

PEDIGREE FILE

Family History Library Catalog includes entries for materials identified as in the "PEDIGREE FILE," which is located in locked cases to the right and left of the Automated Resource Center on the main floor.

REFERENCE QUESTIONS: HOW TO ASK THEM

Some researchers have difficulty asking the right questions for the help that they need. The successful reference question is specific, to the point, and is a short explanation of what is really needed. Genealogical reference questions are usually best accompanied by a pedigree, along with supporting family group sheets for each couple on the pedigree, that can be shown to a reference librarian as needed. Quantities of unorganized notes, letters, certificates, etc., piled upon the Information (Reference) Desk create confusion.

Don't hesitate to ask a question, but try to ask for the right thing. Often asking for a specific book or type of material, such as, "Do you have a history of Queen Annes County, Maryland?" may meet with a negative answer or with a referral to the *Family History Library Catalog: Locality Catalog.* On the other hand, a question with a short explanation that you need to find the names of the father and mother of an ancestor born in Barclay, Queen Annes County, Maryland in 1789, may bring a reference to a source that may answer the question. These comments are offered to assist you, not to intimidate you from asking questions.

Please do not tell the librarian your complete family history or ask at one time all of the questions that relate to your research needs. Another good point to remember is that librarians, being human, need time to ponder and think about a problem. They may even need quiet time to analyze a difficult problem. Please remember how distracting a talkative child can be when you need time to concentrate on a problem.

Librarians have limited time to help each patron and cannot go through the details of all of your research. Learn to research as independently as possible. Try to think through all problems alone; then if you cannot solve them, ask for help.

Another distracting factor, though it may not appear so to a researcher, is the continuous stating of your relationship to the person for whom you are searching, such as, "my maternal great, great grandmother." Usually librarians do not find that helpful, and often much time is spent by researchers simply trying to keep the relationships straight. It is more efficient just to use the name and show where the ancestor is on a pedigree.

REFERENCE SERVICE

The reference desks at the Family History Library, as well as at many libraries, are called Information (Reference) Desks. Usually there is a full-time genealogist or genealogical librarian on duty at all times, assisted by volunteers. If you are not satisfied with an answer to your question, ask if there is someone to whom you may be referred concerning your question. There are many additional specialists who are working in their offices, who may be called upon, when necessary, to address difficult questions. There is also an Information Desk (not a reference desk) in the lobby of the Library entrance on the main floor.

Please remember to take some work along, just in case you have to stand in line and wait for assistance.

RESEARCH NOTES

Research notes should include the author, title, date of publication, publisher, book call number or microform number, and page of the book or microform where information was found. The date and the library where the data was found are also helpful to add to research notes. Don't forget to write on your photocopies the author, title, date of publication and publisher of the book and the name of the library and the date when photocopied; or photocopy the title page and add any of the above information that is not on it. The title pages of Family History Library books have the Library's call numbers written thereon, which can be a help at a future time to identify your source.

Single sheets of paper or cards are best for research notes. Bound note books, backs of utility bills, used envelopes or cash register receipts are not good for note taking. If you are short of paper, there is usually extra paper on top of the computer stations in the Library.

All notes, notebooks, and other personal research materials should contain the name and address of the researcher. A return address sticker is a quick way to handle this. Librarians in all types of libraries discard reams of lost notes and notebooks annually because there is no

141

identification on the material (see also "Lost and Found" in the next
chapter). The Family History Library encourages the protection of
your records and would like a telephone number included with your
name and address.

RESEARCH OUTLINES

The Library staff has written very instructive "Research Outlines" for
each state of the United States and many foreign countries. If you have
not already read the "Research Outlines" of the geographical area of
research that you are pursuing, it should be read soon after you arrive
in Salt Lake City. Even if you had read it beforehand you should
review it again and again while in Salt Lake City. They are on display
near each general Information (Reference) Desk and available for
purchase in the Copy Centers.

RULES

FAMILY HISTORY LIBRARY RULES

1. Please maintain a quiet atmosphere for research study.

2. There is a **5 MICROFILM LIMIT** that you may use at one time.

3. **REFILE EACH MICROFILM YOU USE.**

4. Use extra care when handling books and other research material.

5. There is a **5 BOOK OR BINDER LIMIT** that you have away from
   the shelves at one time. Return books to the red shelves at the end
   of the row where they were found.

6. Children under twelve must be supervised by their parents.

7. When using photocopy equipment and there are others waiting
   LIMIT YOURSELF TO 5 COPIES.

8. Food and drinks are not permitted in the library.

9. Smoking is not permitted in the building or on the grounds.

10. Keep personal belongings with you at all time. The Library is not responsible for items that are lost or stolen.

SPECIAL COLLECTIONS ROOM

Nearly all of the materials in the Special Collections Room relate to LDS temple records, including the *Temple Records Index Bureau.* They are limited to use by LDS members who have either a temple recommend or a bishop's letter for their use. There are a few other non-LDS collections housed therein that have special use requirements, such as close relationships. The Special Collections Room is located on the second floor, room 218.

TEMPLE RECORDS INDEX BUREAU

Another index that may be useful to have checked is the *Temple Records Index Bureau (TIB)*. It contains approximately thirty million names for research done between 1927 and 1970. It is the predecessor of the *International Genealogical Index*. However, it is not as productive for researchers as the *IGI*. Researchers who have exhausted many other sources or who had ancestors who were members of the Church of Jesus Christ of Latter-days Saints should definitely consult this index for ancestors not found in the *IGI* or the Family Group Records Collection.

The *TIB* is an unpublished card file of the Family History Library and includes the names of individuals born between 1501 and 1970. It is international in scope and is arranged first by country of birth and

143

subarranged in alphabetical order. The pamphlet listed under "Additional Reading" below provides details concerning its contents and use.

In order to protect the rights of privacy of the individuals listed in the *TIB* that are still living, it is not open for use by the general public. However, it may be consulted by mail for a small fee through the use of a request form that is available from the Family History Library or at its Family History Centers. The *TIB* may also be checked in the Special Collections Room, 218, second floor, by accredited genealogists and active members of the LDS Church who have temple recommends or letters of recommendation from their Bishop. Search requests are limited to direct line ancestors of the researcher or client of an accredited genealogist who has either a temple or bishop's recommend.

The name and address of the person who submitted the data is not provided on the *TIB*, and for many cards, the information on the *TIB* card is taken from the Family Group Records Collection form. The information on the *TIB* may eventually be available on *FamilySearch*.

I. FAMILY HISTORY CENTER USERS:

If you have already used the *Family History Library Catalog* in a Family History Center, upon arrival at your floor of research interest, take out your prioritized bibliographic cards and find the first item in the collection.

II. LOCAL PUBLIC LIBRARY USERS:

If you haven't had an opportunity to use the *Family History Library Catalog*, find the floor on which your books, microfilm, and microfiche will be located and select a microfiche reader that is located next to the *Family History Library Catalog* or a *FamilySearch* computer station. Select the microfiche or search the *FamilySearch* for the state and county or family name on your prioritized bibliographic cards and look up the Family History Library call number for your first item, following the directions for use of the *Family History Library Catalog* in chapters 5 and 6.

You should also consult the *Family History Library Catalog* for your geographical, individual or family surname cards and look up the call numbers for the research materials needed.

III. HOME LIBRARY USERS:

Find the floor on which the materials for your country of interest are located and select a microfiche reader by the *Family History Library Catalog* or a *FamilySearch* computer station. Follow the directions for use of the *Family History Library Catalog* in chapter 6. Find the microfiche for the state and county or family name of your prioritized research cards and look for materials that may be of use in your research.

Please remember to read the locality part of the *Catalog* on microfiche and/or on *FamilySearch* backwards, starting with the "Vital Records" of city, county, or state and moving towards the front of the catalog through "Probate Records," "Land Records," "Church Records," "Census Records," and "Biography." Following this backwards reading method, the records are arranged generally in order of importance. It is more economical to use the microfilmed vital records of a county that may be available in the Family History Library, rather than writing for, and paying for, individual certificates.

SUMMARY:

All research is time-consuming. However, adequate preparation can make your research time in Salt Lake more efficient, enjoyable, and productive.

AUTOMATED RESOURCE CENTER

Chapter 12

LIBRARY MISCELLANEOUS SERVICES AND ODDS AND ENDS

AUTOMATED RESOURCE CENTER

The entrance to the Automated Resource Center is located between the map cases to the right of the main floor Library Attendants Station. There are many IBM compatible computers that contain *FamilySearch* and other computers for online and CD-ROM products. Use of the computers is limited to one hour. The Center has no Macintosh or Apple computers, but they report that they have programs for the conversion of data to the Macintosh.

The *AIS* (Accelerated Indexing Systems) consolidated indexes for the 1790 through 1850 federal census schedules, including some earlier and later census schedules are available on CD-ROM in the Automated Resource Center. The Center also provides free access for research patrons to the genealogy files of *Genie*, *Prodigy*, or *CompuServe*.

BOOKSTORES FOR GENEALOGICAL BOOKS

Heritage Quest Genealogy Resource Center, 122 West South Temple Street, is next door to the Library in the Howard Johnson Hotel Lobby; turn left at the front desk. The Center is near the end of the hall and on the right hand side (801) 359-9353.

Deseret Book is in the ZCMI Center (mall) right behind the Park Food Court at the South Temple entrance (Number 14 on the attractions map on the inside back cover of this work). The genealogy section is along the back wall of the store (801) 328-8191.

Chapter 12

BULLETIN BOARDS

There is a bulletin board in the Library's main floor entrance which lists classes being offered. Additional bulletin boards are on the other floors, and most of them also list classes, as well as post announcements and floor plans. A bulletin board next to the security desk in the main floor lobby has space for researchers to leave messages for friends.

CHANGE MACHINES

All photocopy machines and vending machines make change for quarters and dimes and some for five dollar bills. Please do not use any foreign coins in them (including Canadian coins; they jam the machines). There are bill changers in the Copy Centers and one just outside the Snack Room. Also the Library Attendants Stations adjacent to the Copy Centers have some change for larger bills.

CLASSES

The Library offers free lectures or classes in family history research and use of the Family History Library, including the use of some of its most important research resources. Lectures cover a great variety of subjects on how-to-do research, the major research tools in the Library, *FamilySearch* and its parts, and the *Personal Ancestral File*. A free copy of the schedule of lectures may be obtained by writing the Family History Library, 35 North West Temple Street, Salt Lake City, UT 84150 or by telephoning (801) 240-3702. Lectures are held in classrooms 134 and 136 on the main floor and B120 on the basement first floor.

COMPUTERS

Most of the computers contain *FamilySearch* and its files: "Using The Computer, *Ancestral File*, *International Genealogical Index*, *U.S. Social Security Death Index*, *Military Index*, portions of the *Family*

History Library Catalog, and *TempleReady*. *TempleReady* is used for submitting names for ordinances of baptism, endowment, and sealing to be done, by proxy, in the temples of the LDS Church. In order to use a computer more than a few minutes you need to sign up for those that may be used for an hour at a time in the Automated Resource Center.

There are some computers that contain the *Personal Ancestral File*. If you plan to use these *PAF* computers or download to diskettes from *FamilySearch* files, you may supply your own formatted diskettes or you can buy formatted 5¼" and 3½" diskettes at the Library Attendants Stations.

COPY MACHINES

Copy Centers with photocopy machines for books, microfilm, and microfiche are located on the east side of each floor (to your left as you enter the reading room of each floor). Typewriters, paper cutters, staplers, pencils, genealogical supplies, hole punches, and bill change machines are also available in or near the Copy Centers. At present copy cost for microforms is 20¢ and books 5¢ per copy.

Some microfilm copiers are set on a slow winding speed in order to cut down on damage to microfilm. When you wish to copy from a microfilm it saves time to select the page or pages you wish to copy on a reader in the microfilm reading area, remove both reels from the reader, and take them to the microfilm reader printer. You may have to try several reader printers to determine which lens size, 12X, 19X, etc., will be best for the microfilm you wish to copy.

After the completion of copying from a reel, please do not waste time rewinding it on a reader printer or a reader in the reading area, unless you wish to continue to read that microfilm. Please rewind on the special "Film Rewinder" constructed by the Library and located near the exit to the microform copying room.

Chapter 12

Recently the author witnessed a bifocaled researcher standing on a step stool in front of one of the high positioned reader printers in order to save a cricked neck. Not a bad idea, as long one remembers that one's standing on a stool before walking off.

When photocopying books please be careful not to push down so hard on the spines that the bindings break. When other researchers are waiting in line for photocopying, please limit yourself to five copies at a time, then move to the end of the line if you have additional copies to make. Don't forget to take something with you to read while you are waiting in line. If you have a lot you wish to copy, it can become a real "ring around the copy machines." Sorry! It could be helpful to move to a Copy Center on a different floor.

DIRECTORIES

Building directories are located between the two main elevators on each floor, inside the entrance to each floor's reference area, and in each elevator.

FAMILYSEARCH CENTER

The *FamilySearch* Center in the historic Joseph Smith Memorial Building, South Temple and Main Streets, provides computers containing *FamilySearch*. There are also *FamilySearch* computers in the west wing of the fourth floor of the Joseph Smith Memorial Building, and microfilm copies of the 1920 federal census schedules, plus the Family Group Records Collection, both in legal size binders and on microfilm in the east wing of the fourth floor.

FOOD

Patrons are requested not to bring food and drinks into reading and computer areas of the Library outside of the Snack Room. See the paragraph under the heading "Snack Room" in this chapter and the list of eating places in the first part of chapter 13. The Snack Room is on

the main floor, room 132. Bags of lunch brought into the Library are
permissible for storage in lockers and in the storage bins at microfilm
reading stations. Please do not eat lunches, drink, or snack outside of
the Snack Room or at drinking fountains.

FOREIGN LANGUAGE TRANSLATION

Brief translation assistance is usually available for some foreign
languages as time and staff are available at reference desks in the
foreign language departments of the Library. Also, there have been
many word lists published that may still be available for purchase at the
Library Attendants windows on the foreign research floors: Danish,
Dutch, French, German, Latin, Norwegian, Polish, Portuguese,
Spanish, and Swedish. Draft copies of other language word lists may
be available at the Information (Reference) Desks.

GIFTS

The Library welcomes your gifts of manuscripts and printed records of
or about your family. The Acquisitions Unit of the Library is on the
third floor of the Library. Please call their office to arrange to present
your gift in person or by mail, (801) 240-2337, 35 North West Temple
Street, Salt Lake City, UT 84150. Your gift will be more useful to
other researchers if you, the holder of the copyright, also give the
Library written permission to microfilm your gift for world-wide use
through the Library's Family History Centers.

GROUP USE OF THE LIBRARY

Groups of ten or more researchers are requested to register in advance
to use the Library by writing the Family History Library, 35 North
West Temple Street, Salt Lake City, UT 84150, or by telephoning
(801) 240-3702. Advance registration helps the Library staff better
prepare to help researchers during a group visit.

Chapter 12

HOLIDAYS

The Library is closed on the following holidays:
> New Year's Day
> 4th of July
> 24th of July, Pioneer Day, a Utah State holiday
> Thanksgiving Day
> Christmas Day

The Library is open shortened hours on the following holidays:
> The day before Thanksgiving Day, 7:30 a.m. -5:00 p.m.
> Christmas Eve, 7:30 a.m. - 5:00 p.m.
> New Year's Eve, 7:30 a.m. - 5:00 p.m.
> Memorial Day, 7:30 a.m. - 6:00 p.m.
> Labor Day, 7:30 a.m. - 6:00 p.m.

The Family History Library occasionally has unplanned days when it may be closed for a few hours or the entire day for the funeral services of prominent leaders of the LDS Church. On rare occasions, a severe winter storm or power outage may cause the Family History Library to close early.

If you are in Salt Lake City for research and are, unfortunately, faced with these problems, you could spend the hours profitably by reviewing your research problems, objectives, and notes. However, another comprehensive collection that could be used is the genealogical collection at the Utah Valley Regional Family History Center at the Harold B. Lee Library of Brigham Young University, Provo, Utah. Provo is forty-four miles south of Salt Lake City and is accessible via inexpensive public bus transportation. Visitor parking is available east of the Wilkinson Center which is next to and east of the Library and has a fast food center (CougarEat), a cafeteria, and Skyroom Restaurant (top floor with a fine view). The author's favorite off-campus eatery is the Brick Oven, 200 East and 700 North (801) 374-8800, with homemade pasta and the West's best root beer.

HOURS

The hours of the Family History Library are as follows:

Monday	7:30 a.m. to 6:00 p.m.
Tuesday through Saturday	7:30 a.m. to 10:00 p.m.

The Library closes at 6:00 on Monday in order to permit its employees to participate in Family Home Evening, a program encouraging Latter-day Saints to reserve Monday evening for family gospel study and family recreation. There is a religious saying, "The family that prays together stays together." The LDS have added: "The family that prays, studies, and plays together stays together."

Because the *FamilySearch* Center is primarily staffed by young women missionaries of the Church who are away from their homes and families for eighteen months, the Center is able to be open from 8:00 a.m. to 10:00 p.m., Monday through Saturday in the summer, Memorial Day through Labor Day. For the rest of year the hours are 9:00 a.m. - 8:00 p.m.

The fourth floor hours are, Monday through Saturday, summer: 8:00 a.m. to 10:00 p.m.; winter: 9:00 a.m. to 9:00 p.m. This floor is basically staffed by couple missionaries, also away from their homes and families. All of these missionaries are volunteering their services, primarily at their own expense. Some of the young missionaries who are not able to support themselves are helped by their parents or may be assisted by their local congregations or by funds donated for this service by Church members throughout the world.

INFORMATION (REFERENCE) DESKS

The desk in the main entrance lobby is a general information desk, not a library type reference desk. The volunteers there will assist you with directions to the different facilities of the Library, research floors, city sights and services, as well as parking tokens and guest passes for the cafeteria in the Church Office Building, 50 East North Temple Street.

Chapter 12

The Information Desks in the reading rooms of each floor are reference desks where you ask for assistance concerning research.

LOCKERS

Lockers are available for day use only on all floors, usually near the Copy Centers, and in the *FamilySearch* Center and on the fourth floor in the historic Joseph Smith Memorial Building, South Temple and Main Streets.

LOST AND FOUND

Lost materials are taken by the staff to the Library Attendant window on each floor. After one week they are taken to the Library Attendant window (room 112) on the main floor. The Library keeps lost items for eight weeks and does not accept responsibility for lost items. It is a good idea to have a name, address, and phone number on all personal research materials, notes, and papers in order to assist in returning them to you. Gummed address labels or rubber stamps can assist with this problem.

The same advice goes for this book. Please put your name, address, and telephone number in it. One happy owner recently told us of having lost her copy of *Going* in the Family History Library. Checked the Lost and Found to no avail. Returned home lamenting her loss. After a week it was mailed to her by, we hope, another happy reader.

MESSAGES AND MAIL

Have mail sent to the hotel or motel where you are planning to stay. Please do not have people call or send mail for you to the Library. There is a message board in the main floor lobby to aid you in contacting others in the Library. Paging patrons via the Library loudspeakers is available only for "life and death" matters and must be approved by the Library security staff. The bulletin board next to the security desk has space for researchers to leave messages for friends.

NEW ADDITIONS TO THE LIBRARY COLLECTIONS

The *UGA News* (a quarterly publication of the Utah Genealogical Association) reports new major acquisitions to the Library collections. On the main floor there is a list of new major additions to the United States and Canada collection provided in three-ring binders located on the shelves around the building column located between the Information (Reference) Desk and the *FamilySearch* computer terminals.

NEWSPAPERS

The below information is included as a result of a *Going* owner's suggestion in her response to the author's survey of several owners.

The Family History Library has not collected large numbers of microfilm of newspapers. Usually the best collections of newspapers are in the communities in which they were published. The union catalogs report where some of the various newspapers are available (none of these catalogs is complete):

U.S. Library of Congress. Catalog Publication Division. *Newspapers in Microform: Foreign Countries, 1948-1983*. Washington, D.C.: Library of Congress, 1984.
    FHL US/CAN BOOK AREA 011.35 N479f 1983.
    FHL US/CAN FICHE AREA 6085887 (7 microfiches).

U.S. Library of Congress. Catalog Publication Division. *Newspapers in Microform: United States, 1948-1983*. 2 vols. Washington, D.C.: Library of Congress, 1984.
    FHL US/CAN REF AREA 011.35 N479 1984.
    FHL US/CAN FILM AREA 1145942.

United States Newspaper Program National Union List. 4th ed. Dublin, Ohio: OCLC Online Computer Library Center, 1993. 70 microfiche. FHL US/CAN FICHE AREA 6332710-6332714 (3d ed., 1989 microfiche and 1989 booklet US/CAN BOOK AREA 973 B32u 1989).

Gregory, Winifred. *American Newspapers, 1821-1936.* New York:
1937. Reprint. New York: Kraus, 1967. Ultra-microfiche. Library
of American Civilization, LAC 16878. Chicago: Library Resources,
Inc., 1970. 2 ultra-microfiche.
    FHL US/CAN FILM AREA 430291 or 483713 Item 1.

Brigham, Clarence S. *History and Bibliography of American
Newspapers, 1690-1820.* Worcester, Mass.: The American Antiquarian
Society, 1947. Reprint. Westport, Conn.: Greenwood Publishing
Corp., 1976.
    FHL US/CAN REF AREA 973 A3bc.

"State Union Lists." In *Library Service for Genealogists*, pp. 208-212.
By J. Carlyle Parker. Gale Genealogy and Local History Series, vol.
15. Detroit: Gale Research Co., 1981. op. 2d edition in progress by
Marietta Publishing Co.
    FHL US/CAN REF AREA 026.9291 P226L.

Many of the above catalogs are available in larger public libraries, and
in college and university libraries.

ORIENTATION

To the left of the Information Desk opposite the main entrance is an
Orientation Center where you can receive brief explanations of how to
do family history research and how to use the Library. You will also
find out why Latter-day Saints do genealogical research and what they
do in their temples. Orientations are presented every 30 minutes for
from 15 to 20 minutes. A how-to-use-it Library guide is provided free.

PERSONAL ANCESTRAL FILE

Personal Ancestral File (PAF), the genealogical computer program for organizing your personal genealogical information, is available for use in the Automated Resource Center on the main floor of the Library, the *FamilySearch* Center, and in the west wing of the fourth floor in the Joseph Smith Memorial Building, South Temple and Main Streets. All of these locations have volunteers who provide tutorage. The west wing of the fourth floor in the Joseph Smith Memorial Building is the quietest place to compute for longer hours without interruptions by hourly reservations. The *PAF* is written for MS-DOS and Macintosh computers; however, the Library has no Macintosh computers for public use. While in Salt Lake City, *PAF* may be easily purchased at the Distribution Center in the basement of the Joseph Smith Memorial Building.

REFERENCE BOOKS

The Library's most often used reference tools are shelved near the Information (Reference) Desk on each floor. Be sure to browse them for works of interest.

RESEARCHERS FOR HIRE

If you want to hire a professional genealogist to help you, ask at any Information (Reference) Desk for the Library's list of Accredited Researchers and purchase at one of Attendants Stations the following very inexpensive publication:

Hiring a Professional Genealogist. Resource Guide. Salt Lake City: Church of Jesus Christ of Latter-day Saints, 1993. 4 pages.

You may also wish to consult the following additional lists of professional genealogists:

Chapter 12

Roster of Persons Certified. Falmouth, Va.: Board for Certification of Genealogists, (P.O. Box 5816, Falmouth, VA 22403) 1993.
    FHL US/CAN REF AREA 973 A1 no. 209.

"Directory of Professional Genealogical Researchers." *Genealogical Helper*, September-October issue of each year.
    FHL GENERAL BOOK AREA 929.05 G286.

Directory of Professional Genealogists. Salt Lake City: Association of Professional Genealogists, 1993.
    FHL GENERAL REF AREA 929.1 D628 1993.

Additional professional genealogists are listed in the telephone yellow pages under the subject heading, "Genealogists." A recent edition of the US West Communications Yellow Pages for Salt Lake City contained twenty-one entries.

There are many professional genealogists doing research daily in the Library. Observe the genealogists to see who, by their methods of research, appear to be the most knowledgeable. Ask them if they are acquainted with professional genealogists, and you may be able to make direct contact right in the Library. However, they are restricted by Library policy from soliciting.

RESTROOMS

Restrooms are located on the north side of each floor (to your right as you enter the reading room of each floor).

SECURITY

There is a security control at the door to check, if necessary, briefcases, bags, and purses of exiting researchers. A plainclothes security officer is usually in the lobby of the main floor. You should keep your valuables with you at all times. Some women find small purses with shoulder straps or waist packs are useful for keeping their change and keys. Lockers are available for day use only on all floors, near the

Copy Centers, for items that you do not need with you for research.
The Library does not accept responsibility for items stolen or lost.

SMOKING

Smokers are asked not to smoke in the Library, the restrooms, or on
the grounds, which includes the planter box ledges in front of and along
the side the Library and the Museum of Church History and Art.

SNACK ROOM

A Snack Room (132) is available on the north end of the main floor (to
the left of the rest rooms) for eating bag lunches brought into the
Library. A microwave oven; straws; plastic forks, spoons, and knives;
and paper napkins are provided free of charge. Vending machines
include choices of cold soft drinks, milk, juice, sandwiches, bagels, hot
dogs, corn dogs, burritos, pizza slices, salads, apples, oranges, chips,
cookies, donuts, cakes, muffins, Danish pastries, pudding, fruit pies,
yogurt, ice cream bars, ice cream sandwiches, and candies. A bill
change machine is available just outside the Snack Room. Please do
not eat lunches, drink, or snack outside of the Snack Room or at
drinking fountains.

SPECIAL NEEDS PATRON SERVICES

Wheelchair access entrance doors, microfilm readers, and
FamilySearch computers are available and some assistance for the
hearing-impaired and sight-impaired is provided in the Library.
Wheelchairs are available for Library use by request at the lobby
Information Desk. Visualtak and Secturm Jr. readers (for books) are
available on the main floor for sight-impaired.

There are left handed microfilm readers in reader row 26 on the U.S.
and Canada floor. There are also other left handed microfilm readers
on the basement floors and some motorized microfilm readers
throughout the Library.

Chapter 12

The *FamilySearch* Center in the Joseph Smith Memorial Building has two *FamilySearch* computers for the visually impaired. The Center also has two *FamilySearch* computers for hearing-impaired that provide for increased volume of the voice orientation to *FamilySearch*.

Wheelchair and ease-of-walking access to the *FamilySearch* Center is by elevator at the east end of the hall that provides a stairway down to the Center. Once in the elevator press the button for "LR Parking." Exit the elevator on the LR Parking level and proceed beyond the door to the parking garage to the "*FamilySearch* CALL FOR ACCESS" door that has a telephone to its left. By lifting the receiver you are directly connected to the *FamilySearch* Center information desk. Inform them that you would like entry and ask them to please open the door. The volunteers at the information desk will also unlock the door for you to exit the Center.

There is also a reading machine for visually impaired in the east wing of the fourth floor of the Joseph Smith Memorial Building for use of the paper copies of the Family Group Records Collection. Wheelchairs are available for use in the Joseph Smith Memorial Building by request at the volunteer office in the South Temple Street lobby.

Telephone (801) 240-4428 concerning details of Special Needs Patron Services for the Library.

STAMPS

A full value Postal Products machine is located by the elevators on the Main Floor. A mail box is near the crosswalk in front of the Library. A post office substation is three blocks from the Library at 230 West 200 South Street.

SUPPLIES

Some researchers have found that printed research forms are time-saving and efficient. Forms for recording data from the U.S. federal census schedules, and the Canadian and British censuses are helpful, as

160

are Research Logs. These forms and others, along with research papers, are available for sale in the Copy Centers. Pencils, pens, envelopes, and formatted computer diskettes are also available for sale. Forms which pertain to geographical areas are available only on the floors relating to their research.

The closest source for genealogical books and supplies and office supplies is the Heritage Quest Genealogy Resource Center, 122 West South Temple Street, next door to the Library in the Howard Johnson Hotel Lobby; turn left at the front desk. The Center is near the end of the hall and on the right hand side (801) 359-9353.

The next nearest office supply store is the Quick Connections in the Crossroads Plaza (Mall) on the lower level in the South hall, 328-1099. It is the second store on the left at the 100 South Street level entrance. Also provides photo developing, gift wrapping, packing and shipping, Western Union, Fax service, and private mail boxes, (801) 328-1099, FAX (801) 364-6573.

The next closest office supply store with a larger selection of supplies, Office and Things, is in the ZCMI Mall on the second floor in its south hall, 36 South State Street, Suite 238, 533-8070. The ZCMI Mall has entrances on Main, South Temple, State, and First South Streets.

Genealogical books and some supplies are also available at Deseret Book in the ZCMI Center (mall) right behind the Park Food Court at the South Temple entrance, 328-8191. The genealogy section is along the back wall of the store.

TELEPHONES

There are telephones near the elevators on each floor. Local calls are twenty-five cents.

Family History Library telephone numbers:
   (Gifts) Book Acquisitions   (801) 240-2337

Information (Reference) Desks

Asian (Catalog Dept.)	(801) 240-3796
Australia	(801) 240-2623
Automated Resource Center	(801) 240-1159
British	(801) 240-2367
Chinese (Catalog Dept.)	(801) 240-3796
Europe	(801) 240-2881
International	(801) 240-3433
Japanese (Catalog Dept.)	(801) 240-3796
Latin America	(801) 240-1738
Library Information Desk	(801) 240-3702
Library Information (recording)	(801) 240-2331
New Zealand	(801) 240-2090
Scandinavia	(801) 240-2198
Spanish	(801) 240-1738
Special Needs Patron Services	(801) 240-4428
U.S.-Canada (Books)	(801) 240-2720
U.S.-Canada (Microform)	(801) 240-2364

Joseph Smith Memorial Building

FamilySearch Center (Main Floor)	(801) 240-4085
Fourth Floor	
Family Group Records Collection	
(4th Floor, East Wing)	(801) 240-3574
FamilySearch (4th Floor, West Wing)	(801) 240-4673

TEMPERATURES

In the Library temperatures are usually comfortable; however, microfilm readers generate some heat and can overheat some areas of the Library. Lots of eager researchers also generate extra heat. Therefore, it is wise to wear layered clothes that can be peeled off when the Library warms and put on again when it cools.

Outside the Library, temperatures can vary, and preparedness is always better than unnecessary exposure to the elements. Researchers who stay until the 10:00 p.m. closing hour should be aware that temperatures drop nearly every evening in Salt Lake City.

TYPEWRITERS

The free use of typewriters is available in most of the Copy Centers.

SUMMARY:

The Library may appear somewhat overwhelming. However, it is
really not too complicated, and the staff and volunteers are very
helpful. Try to find things yourself, but don't hesitate to ask for
assistance at the Information (Reference) Desk or Library Attendants'
Stations when you can't do it on your own. Work hard and enjoy your
research at the world's largest genealogical library.

Shortly after the festive wedding of Prince Charles to Diana, a lady
came into the Family History Center and declared that she wanted to
prove her relationship to the Queen of England, because: "My niece
looks just like the Queen Mother, and my family descends from
Prince George who came over on the Mayflower."

-- Modesto California Family History Center, 1981

MAIN FLOOR PLAN: UNITED STATES AND CANADA INFORMATION AND BOOKS

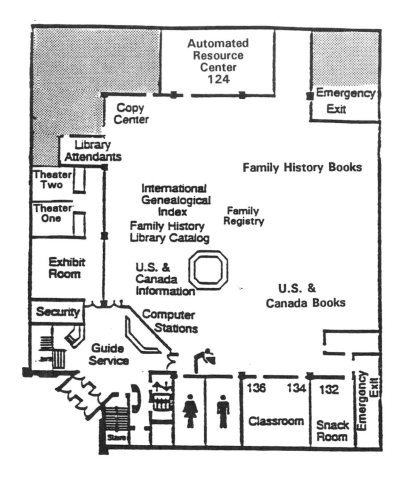

Automated Resource Center 124

Copy Center

Emergency Exit

Library Attendants

Theater Two

Theater One

Family History Books

International Genealogical Index

Family History Library Catalog

Family Registry

Exhibit Room

U.S. & Canada Information

U.S. & Canada Books

Security

Computer Stations

Guide Service

136   134   132

Classroom

Snack Room

Emergency Exit

Stairs

SECOND FLOOR PLAN: UNITED STATES AND CANADA MICROFORMS

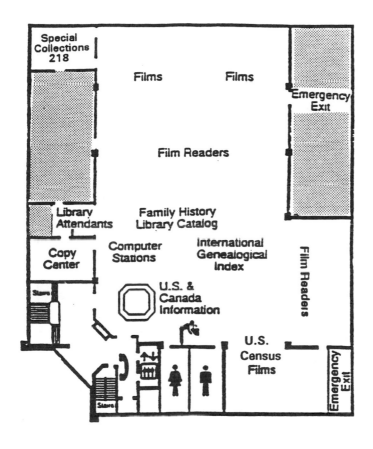

BASEMENT 1 FLOOR PLAN: EUROPE, SCANDINAVIA, LATIN AMERICA, AND INTERNATIONAL

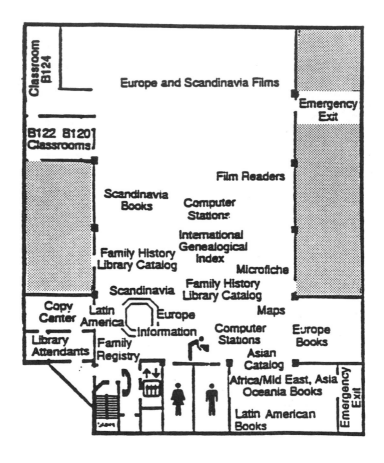

BASEMENT 2 FLOOR PLAN: BRITISH ISLES

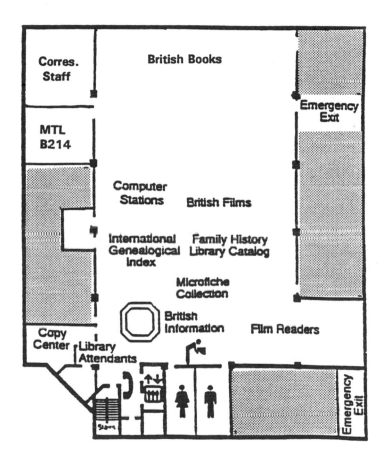

LIBRARY ATTENDANT -- MICROFILM CABINETS

Chapter 13

DINING, LODGING, AND HEALTH CARE IN SALT LAKE CITY

STREET NUMBERING ORIENTATION

BEWARE! Visitors are often surprised at the generous length of a Salt Lake City block:

Salt Lake City was laid out on a grid, the center of which was the Brigham Young statue in its original location in the center of the intersection of Main and South Temple. Its present location is in the middle of Main Street north of South Temple Street. When you stand on the northeast corner of that intersection, please don't be confused by the historic street name inscription on the corner of the Joseph Smith Memorial Building that reads, "East Temple." At one time Main Street was East Temple. A map of downtown Salt Lake City is provided on the inside of the back cover of this book. The following table may help you to understand the arrangement of the City's streets:

> Main Street is the north-south base street or "0."
> South Temple is the east-west base street or "0."
> West Temple Street could have been First or 100 West Street
> North Temple Street could have been First or 100 North Street
> State Street could have been First or 100 East Street
> There are no First or 100 East, 100 West, or 100 North Streets
> There is a First or 100 South Street
> 300 South Street is also called Broadway

You should also be aware that most Salt Lakers do not use "Street" when speaking of their streets. It's simply, "On the corner of 5th East and 3rd South."

Chapter 13

RESTAURANTS AND FAST FOOD ESTABLISHMENTS NOT AFFILIATED WITH HOTELS

The Family History Library **Snack Room** has been explained in chapter 12, under "Snack Room." The following is a list of nearby restaurants and fast food eateries listed in order of proximity to the Library:

Within one block of the Library

Before going to any of these places it would be wise to call to see if they are open, as hours are subject to change. One *Going* owner inquired if any of the restaurants, hotels, etc., pay to be listed in *Going*. No, but most of them have been visited, if not eaten in, slept in, or been a patient in, etc. A great deal of time has been spent to try to have all the information correct at the time of publication. However, no guarantee is given as to accuracy, quality or comfort.

JB's Restaurant, on the northwest corner of South Temple and West Temple Streets, next to the Library, 122 West South Temple Street, lunch under $6, dinner under $10, 328-8344.

Carriage Court Restaurant, The Inn at Temple Square on the southeast corner of South Temple and West Temple Streets, 75 West South Temple Street, 84101, lunch under $11, dinner under $19.50, 536-7200. One dining critic has praised it as having better cuisine than a cruise ship.

JB's Restaurant, Crossroads Plaza Mall at the South Temple Street entrance, lunch under $6, dinner under $10, 355-2100. The Crossroads Plaza Mall is shown as number 15 on the attractions map on the inside back cover of this work.

There are several fast food stands in the **"Richards Street Marketplace"** in the basement of the Crossroads Plaza Mall, including such favorites as **A & W, Arby's,** and **McDonalds.** Among the author's favorites are the daily specials at **Lotsa Hotsa** pasta. Their pizza slices are very popular. "Richards Street Marketplace" is easily reached via the escalator just to the left as you enter Crossroads from the South Temple Street entrance.

Terrace of Mervyns, Crossroads Plaza, 3rd floor next to Mervyns at the South Temple Street entrance; Monday-Saturday, 9:30 a.m.-5:00 p.m., 521-8716.

Windows on the Square, Crossroads Plaza, 3rd Floor next to Mervyns at the South Temple Street entrance, lunch under $7.50 and dinner under $10; Monday & Tuesday, 11:30 a.m.-3:00 p.m.; Wednesday-Saturday, 11:30 a.m.-9:00 p.m., 521-2165. Overlooking Temple Square, "A Scenic Dining Experience." -- Mervyns ad.

Nordstrom's Cafe, Crossroads Plaza, 3rd floor east concourse, under $6, 322-4200, ext. 1611.

Dee's Family Restaurant, 143 West North Temple Street, 359-4414.

Pizza Hut Express, 75 South West Temple Street in the southwest corner of the Marriott Hotel.

Within two blocks of the Library

The Garden Restaurant, 10th floor, 15 East South Temple Street, Monday-Saturday, 11:00 a.m.-10:00 p.m., lunch under $12 and dinner under $15, 536-7277.

The Roof Restaurant, 10th floor, 15 East South Temple Street, Wednesday-Saturday, 5:00 p.m.-10:00 p.m., gourmet dinner buffet, $21.95, 539-1911.

Both of the above restaurants are located in the Joseph Smith Memorial Building, on the northeast corner of South Temple Street and Main Street, and number 8 on the attractions map on the inside back cover of this work. They offer some good views of the city, Temple Square, and sunsets.

Chapter 13

The Lion House, 63 East South Temple Street, provides a membership fee cafeteria in its basement and permits the general public to buy lunch at a very small extra cost. It is worth the little extra walk, 363-5466. One of the *Going* owners reported in her returned survey that "the Lion House now has a special Friday night buffet [$15.95] that is outstanding." Take the sidewalk along the West or left side of the House to the entrance near the back of the building (number 9 on the attractions map on the inside back cover of this work). National Register of Historic Places, built 1856.

> "...Johnson professed to have enjoyed a sociable breakfast in the Lion House. He gave a preposterous account of the 'calling of the roll,' and other preliminaries, and the carnage that ensued when the buckwheat-cakes came in. But he embellished rather too much."
> -- Mark Twain, *Roughing It* (New York: Grosset & Dunlap, 1913), page 70. Originally published : New York: American Publishing Co., 1871. Twain visited Salt Lake City in 1861.

Patrons of the Library are welcome to eat at **the Cafeteria** at The Church of Jesus Christ of Latter-day Saints Office Building, First Lower Level, 50 East North Temple Street, hours 7:00 a.m. - 7:45 a.m.; 9:00 a.m. - 10:30 a.m.; and 11:30 a.m. - 1:45 p.m. A guest pass is required and may be obtained free at the Information (Reference) Desk in the lobby on the Main Floor of the Library. No tea or coffee is served and smoking is not permitted. The Church Office Building is shown as number 6 on the attractions map on the inside back cover of this work.

The Park Food Court in the ZCMI Center on the south side of South Temple east of Main Street. A **Burger King, McDonalds, TCBY Yogurt,** and other fast food stands are located in the Park Food Court. The ZCMI Center is shown as number 14 on the attractions map on the inside back cover of this work.

ZCMI Snack Bar, located in the basement of the ZCMI store.

Tiffin Room, ZCMI 4th floor on the Main Street or west side of the store, lunch under $7 and dinner under $8.25, 579-6116. One of the surveyed owners of *Going* liked its good food, service, and its "very reasonable prices."

Skool Lunch (deli and bakery), 60 East South Temple Street, #105, in the Eagle Plaza on the south side of the street nearly to State Street, 532-5269.

Subway Sandwiches, 18 West 100 South Street, 364-6229.

Within three blocks of the Library

Board Walk Sandwich Shop, Restaurant Row, 60 West 200 South Street, #100, under $5, will deliver, 532-7034.

Lamb's Restaurant, 169 South Main Street, lunch under $8 and dinner under $17, 364-7166, closed Sunday. The dedicatee of this book overheard some researchers in the Library raving about Utah's oldest restaurant, Lamb's (established in 1919).

Simply Delicious, 136 East South Temple Street, University Club Building, Main Floor, behind lobby, has espresso, cappuccino, and one vegetarian deli sandwich, prices under $6, will deliver, 596-9251.

Chart House Restaurant, 334 West South Temple Street, dinner only, under $23, 596-0990. In the Devereaux House near the Delta Center. The Devereaux House is on the National Register of Historic Places, built 1857, and is shown as number 31 on the attractions map on the inside back cover of this work. Complimentary parking is available on South Temple near 400 West Street.

Shenanigans Restaurant, 274 South West Temple, lunch under $7 and dinner under $14.50, 364-3663.

RESTAURANTS, LISTED BY CUISINE (Listed in order of proximity to the Library under type of cuisine. Many of these restaurants are beyond walking distance)

Chapter 13

AFGHAN

Baba Afghan Restaurant, 55 East 400 South, lunch under $12, dinner from 5-11 p.m., seven vegetarian selections, 596-0786.

CHINESE

Kwan's Downtown Chinese Restaurant, 139 East South Temple Street, lunch under $5 and dinner under $9, 328-8369.

Hunan Restaurant, Mandarin-Szechuan cuisine, 165 South West Temple Street, No. 2, lunch under $4.25 and dinner under $10.50, 531-6677, entrance on right side of the building.

FRENCH-ITALIAN

Le Parisien, 417 South 300 East Street, lunch and dinner under $23, 364-5223.

GERMAN

Siegfried's Delicatessen, 69 West 300 South Street, lunch under $5, not open for dinner, 355-3891.

INDIA

Royal Taj, 165 South West Temple, lunch buffet $5.50 and dinner under $20, 355-3617.

The Star of India Restaurant, 177 East 200 South Street, lunch and dinner under $16, ten vegetarian entries under $8, 363-7555.

ITALIAN

Cafe Molise, 55 West 100 South Street, lunch under $8 and dinner under $12, 364-8833.

The Olive Garden, 77 West 200 South Street, lunch under $12 and dinner under $14, 537-6202.

Baci Trattoria, 134 West Pierport Avenue (between West Temple and 100 West Streets; between Second South and Third South Streets), lunch under $18 and dinner under $25, 328-1500. One of our surveyed *Going* owners recommended it, "delicious Italian food."

Tavola, 330 West South Temple Street, to the right rear of the Carriage House, in the Triad Center, complimentary parking on South Temple near 400 West Street; lunch under $13 and dinner under $15, 355-8014.

Ninos, 136 East South Temple Street, 24th floor - University Club Building, dinners only, under $27, 359-0506.

Firenze, 358 South West Temple Street, closed Sunday, under $14, 532-1055.

JAPANESE

Benihana of Tokyo, 165 South West Temple Street, lunch under $7.50 and dinner under $27, 322-2421. From West Temple Street walk southeast through the mini park south of 165 South West Temple Street. It may be easier for some to find Benihana from Second South Street where their sign is located, just a few steps east of West Temple Street. The walkway into Benihana is signed, Restaurant Row.

Mikado Restaurant, 67 West 100 South, lunch under $13 and dinner under $20, 328-0929.

MEXICAN

Cafe Pierpont, 122 West Pierpont Avenue (between West Temple and 100 West Streets; between Second South and Third South Streets), lunch and dinner under $15, 364-1222.

Sophie Garcia's Fine Mexican Restaurant, 154 West 600 South Street, lunch under $6.50 and dinner under $10, 355-2081.

Chapter 13

MIDDLE EASTERN

The Cedars of Lebanon Restaurant, 152 East 200 South Street, lunch under $7 and dinner under $16, 364-4096.

Robert's Deli-Middle Eastern Cuisine, 1071 East 900 South Street, a deli meal under $5, 355-8141.

RUSSIAN

St Petersburg Cafe, 35 North 300 West Street in the Triad Center, complimentary parking entrance on South Temple near 400 West Street, breakfast and lunch under $5, dinner Friday and Saturday night under $11, 596-7746.

SEAFOOD

Chart House, 334 West South Temple Street, 596-0990.

VEGETARIAN

Simply Delicious, 136 East South Temple Street, University Club Building, Main Floor, behind lobby, has espresso, cappuccino, and one vegetarian deli sandwich, prices under $6, will deliver, 596-9251.

The Star of India Restaurant, 177 East 200 South Street, lunch and dinner under $16, ten vegetarian entries under $8, 363-7555.

Baba Afghan Restaurant, 55 East 400 South, lunch under $12, dinner from 5-11 p.m., seven vegetarian selections, 596-0786.

Park Ivy Garden Cafe, 878 South 900 East Street, lunch and dinner under $7, 328-1313.

ESPRESSO

Espresso Bar, 165 South West Temple Street, 328-2927.

Coffee Direct, offers espresso on their menu. Located in the center aisle of the lower level on the Richards Street Market, just past the North Concourse of the Crossroads Plaza Mall.

Nordstrom's Espresso Bar, 1st floor, south concourse next to elevator.

BREWERY

Squatter's Pub Brewery, 147 West 300 South Street, lunch and dinner under $8, 363-2739. Squatter's was recommended by the husband of one of *Going*'s readers, for good beer and food. A Salt Lake City restaurant reviewer claims that Squatter's chicken wings are among the best in the city.

IS UTAH WET OR DRY?

One of the readers of the first edition of *Going* suggested that something be included in the second edition about Utah's liquor laws:

LIQUOR LAWS
Utah's liquor laws are easy to understand. Alcoholic beverages are served with your meal in most restaurants and hotels. Liquor may be purchased in state liquor stores throughout Salt Lake. Mixed drinks are served in Utah's non-exclusive private clubs (visitors are welcome at these clubs, and temporary memberships are available for a nominal fee). The only difference between private clubs and public restaurants is the time of day the drinks may be served; private clubs may serve alcoholic drinks throughout the day and in restaurants, only after 1 p.m.

STATE LIQUOR STORES
State Liquor Stores sell packaged liquors and wines in various sized bottles. Utah also has several

177

innovative "Wine Stores" that provide a wide variety
and selection of wines from around the world. In all
State Stores, you must pay cash; checks or credit
cards are not accepted. State Liquor Stores are not
open on Sundays and holidays.

DRINKING AND DRIVING
It's not a good idea to drive under the influence of
alcohol anywhere; Utah is no exception. Utah laws,
similar to many Western states, are stringent. 0.08%
or more alcohol to blood content is considered drunk
and constitutes "Driving Under the Influence."
-- Salt Lake Convention & Visitors Bureau
Salt Lake Visitors Guide

FOOD STORES

Albertson's Food Center, 370 East 200 South Street, 364-5594.

Smith's Food and Drug Center, 402 6th Avenue, 328-1683, open 24
hours.

HEALTH FOOD MARKETS

New Frontiers Natural Foods Market and Cafe, 800 East 200 South,
355-7401 and 2454 South 700 East, 359-7913, hours of both, Monday-
Saturday 9:00 a.m. - 9:00 p.m., Sunday 10:00 a.m. - 6:00 p.m.

MINI MARTS

Rainbo Mart (Amoco), 163 West North Temple Street, 328-4433.

Circle K Food Stores, 210 West Temple Street, 364-6716.

Neighbors Market, 40 North State Street, 355-8061.

WATER

Salt Lake City has some of the finest drinking water in the world. However, in the downtown area the water is highly chlorinated and should not be consumed by people with chlorine intolerance. During a research trip to Salt Lake City and staying in a downtown motel, the author's wife, Janet, came down with some of the symptoms of the flu. She had also had the same problem in another Utah community, in an upstate New York community, and in a Nevada city. Recalling that a friend had had a similar experience in Maryland and upon consulting a doctor was instructed to stop drinking the local water, we changed Janet's drinking water to distilled water and have not had such an experience since.

Crossroads Drug, 355-5823, near the 100 South Street entrance has water (distilled and filtered) in gallon containers.

The Rainbo Mart (Amoco), 163 West North Street, 328-4433 and Circle K, 210 West North Street, 364-6716, both have only one liter or smaller bottles of spring water.

The Neighbors Market, 40 North State Street, 355-8061, has 2.5 gallon and smaller bottles of spring water and gallon bottles of distilled water.

NEAREST HOTELS AND MOTELS (Listed in order of proximity to the Library)

Within one block of the Library

Howard Johnson, next door to the Library at 122 West South Temple Street, 84101, (801) 521-0130, (800) 366-3684, or (800) 654-2000, FAX (801) 322-5057. Has a JB's Big Boy Family Restaurant adjacent, courtesy airport shuttle, and exercise room (number 5 on the accommodations map on page 259 of this work).

The Inn at Temple Square, 71 West South Temple Street, 84101, (801) 531-1000, (800) 843-4668, FAX (801) 536-7272. Totally nonsmoking, courtesy airport shuttle, and continental breakfast buffet.

Chapter 13

One dining critic has praised its elegant Carriage Court Restaurant as having better cuisine than a cruise ship (number 7 on the accommodations map on page 259 of this work).

Marriott Hotel, 75 South West Temple Street, 84101, (801) 531-0800 (800) 228-9290, (801) 532-3978. Courtesy airport shuttle, full breakfast on Friday and Saturday, indoor pool, recreational program, weight room, exercise room, tennis courts, and racquetball courts (number 10 on the accommodations map on page 259 of this work).

Salt Lake TraveLodge at Temple Square, 144 West North Temple Street, 84103, (801) 533-8200, (800) 578-7878 or (800) 367-2250, FAX (801) 596-0332 (number 2 on the accommodations map on page 259 of this work).

Within two blocks of the Library

Doubletree Hotel, 215 West South Temple Street, 84101, (801) 531-7500, (800) 222-8733, FAX (801) 328-1289. Courtesy airport shuttle, full breakfast, elegant restaurant on first floor, indoor pool, and exercise room (number 6 on the accommodations map on page 259 of this work).

The Kimball, 150 North Main Street, 84103, (801) 363-4000. A time share with some shares available for purchase. A Resort Condominiums International and Interval International Resort Directory participant. No overnight guests accommodated without membership or exchange (number 3 on the accommodations map on page 259 of this work).

Within three blocks of the Library

Royal Executive Inn, 121 North 300 West Street, 84103, (801) 521-3450, (800) 541-7639, FAX (801) 521-3452. Courtesy airport shuttle (number 1 on the accommodations map on page 259 of this work).

Carlton Hotel, 140 East South Temple Street, 84111, (801) 355-3418.
Courtesy Family History Library and airport shuttle, (number 8 on the
accommodations map on page 259 of this work).

Shilo Inn, 206 South West Temple Street, 84101-1994, (801) 521-
9500, (800) 222-2244, FAX (801) 359-6527. Restaurant and exercise
room (number 13 on the accommodations map on page 259 of this
work).

Peery Hotel, 110 West 300 South Street, 84101, (801) 521-4300, (800)
331-0073, FAX (801) 575-5014. Courtesy airport shuttle, continental
breakfast, restaurants, and exercise room (number 15 on the
accommodations map on page 259 of this work). National Register of
Historic Places, built 1910.

Red Lion Hotel, 255 South West Temple Street, 84101, (801) 328-
2000, (800) 547-8010, FAX (801) 522-1953. Courtesy airport shuttle,
restaurants, indoor pool, and exercise room (number 14 on the
accommodations map on page 259 of this work).

SELECTED ECONOMY MOTELS IN THE CITY AND AREA
(Listed in order of proximity to the Library)

Motel 6, 176 West 600 South Street, 84101, (801) 531-1252,
nationwide reservations (505) 891-6161 or FAX (505) 892-8667.

Super 8 Motel, 616 South 200 West Street, 84101, (801) 534-0808
(800) 843-1991 or (800) 800-8000, FAX (801) 355-7735 (number 27 on
the accommodations map on page 259 of this work).

Econo Lodge, 715 West North Temple Street, 84116, (801) 363-0062,
FAX (801) 359-3926. Courtesy airport shuttle. Right by I15 without
an on or off ramp. Frontier Pies Restaurant next door.

Chapter 13

SELECTED NATIONAL CHAIN HOTELS AND MOTELS IN THE CITY AND AREA (Listed in order of proximity to the Library)

Courtyard by Marriott, 150 West 400 South Street, 84101, (801) 531-6000, (800) 321-2211, FAX (801) 531-1273. Restaurant (number 16 on the accommodations map on page 259 of this work).

Deseret Inn, 50 West 500 South Street, 84101, (801) 532-2900. Restaurants (number 20 on the accommodations map on page 259 of this work).

Hilton Hotel, 150 West 500 South Street, 84101, (801) 532-3344, (800) 421-7602 or (800) 445-8667, FAX (801) 532-3344. Courtesy airport shuttle, but the hotel asks that you tip the driver. Restaurants and exercise room (number 19 on the accommodations map on page 259 of this work).

Little America Hotel and Towers, 500 South Main Street, 84101, (801) 363-6781, (800) 453-9450, FAX (801) 322-1610. Courtesy airport shuttle, restaurants, indoor pool, and exercise room (number 23 on the accommodations map on page 259 of this work).

Salt Lake City Center TraveLodge, 524 South West Temple Street, 84101, (801) 531-7100, (800) 578-7878, FAX (801) 359-3814 (number 22 on the accommodations map on page 259 of this work).

Quality Inn - City Center, 154 West 600 South Street, 84101, (801) 521-2930, (800) 521-9997, (800) 288-5151, or (800) 424-6423, FAX (801) 355-0733. Courtesy airport shuttle, continental breakfast, and restaurants (number 25 on the accommodations map on page 259 of this work).

Best Western Olympus Hotel, 161 West 600 South Street, 84101, (801) 521-7373, (800) 426-0722 or (800) 528-1234, FAX (801) 524-0354. Non-smoking floors. Courtesy shuttle to airport and to other downtown hotels, 24 hour restaurant, and exercise room (number 28 on the accommodations map on page 259 of this work).

Embassy Suites Hotel, 600 South West Temple Street, 84101, (801) 359-7800, (800) 362-2779 or (800) 825-7643, FAX (801) 359-3753. Courtesy airport shuttle, full breakfast, indoor pool, and exercise room (number 26 on the accommodations map on page 259 of this work).

Crystal Inn, 230 West 500 South Street, 84101,(801) 328-4666, (800) 366-4466. Courtesy airport shuttle, microwaves and refrigerators in every room (number 18 on the accommodations map on page 259 of this work).

Ramada Inn, 230 West 600 South Street, 84101, (801) 364-5200, (800) 272-6232 or (800) 228-2828, FAX (801) 364-0974. Courtesy 24 hour airport shuttle, restaurant, and indoor pool (number 24 on the accommodations map on page 259 of this work).

Holiday Inn - Downtown, 999 South Main Street, 84111, (801) 359-8600, (800) 933-9678, or (800) 465-4329, FAX (801) 353-7186. Courtesy airport shuttle, restaurant, pool enclosed in winter, tennis courts, and exercise room.

Residence Inn by Marriott, 765 East 400 South, 84102, (801) 532-5511 (800) 228-9290, FAX (801) 531-0416. Courtesy airport shuttle, continental breakfast, and sports court (number 17 on the accommodations map on page 259 of this work).

Holiday Inn Airport, 1659 West North Temple, 84116, (801) 533-9000, (800) 465-4329 or (800) 999-3736, FAX (801) 364-0614. Courtesy airport shuttle. Restaurant. Denny's Restaurant across the street and four fast food restaurants nearby.

Days Inn, 1900 West North Temple Street, 84116, (801) 539-8538, (800) 325-2525 or (800) 329-3466, FAX (801) 539-8538. Courtesy airport shuttle and continental breakfast.

Motel 6, 1990 West Temple Street, 84116, (801) 364-1053, renovated in 1995, nationwide reservations (505) 891-6161 or FAX (505) 892-8667.

Nendels Inn Airport. 2080 West North Temple, 84116, (801) 355-0088, (800) 626-2824 or (800) 547-0106, FAX (801) 355-0099. Courtesy 24 hour airport shuttle, continental breakfast, and restaurant next door.

Radisson Airport Inn, 2177 West North Temple Street, 84116, (801) 364-5800, (800) 333-3333, FAX (801) 364-5823. Courtesy airport shuttle, restaurant, and exercise room.

Comfort Inn-Salt Lake City Airport, 200 North Admiral Byrd Road, 84116, (801) 537-7444, (800) 535-8742, (800) 228-5150, or (800) 424-6423, FAX (801) 532-4721. Courtesy shuttle to airport and to other downtown hotels. Continental breakfast. Restaurant.

Quality Inn Airport and International Center, 5575 West Amelia Earhart Drive, 84116, (801) 537-7020, (800) 522-5575 or (800) 424-6423, FAX (801) 537-7701. Courtesy shuttle to airport and to other downtown hotels. Restaurant.

Airport Hilton, 5151 Wiley Post Way, 84116, (801) 539-1515, (800) 999-3736, FAX (801) 539-1113. Courtesy 24 hour airport shuttle, restaurant, indoor pool, sports court, and exercise room.

Motel 6, 2433 South 800 West Street, Woods Cross, 84087, (801) 298-0289, nationwide reservations (505) 891-6161 or FAX (505) 892-8667.

Motel 6, 496 North Catalpa Drive, Midvale, 84047, (801) 561-0058, nationwide reservations 505 891-6161 or FAX (505) 892-8667.

La Quinta Motor Inn, 530 North Catalpa Road, Midvale, 84047, (801) 566-3291, (800) 531-5900 or (800) 221-4731, FAX (801) 562-5943. Courtesy airport shuttle.

Comfort Inn, 8955 South 255 West Street, Sandy, 84070, (12 miles south) (801) 255-4919, (800) 221-2222, (800) 424-6423 or (800) 228-5150 , FAX (801) 255-4998. Continental breakfast and indoor pool.

BED AND BREAKFASTS (Listed in order of proximity to the Library)

Anniversary Inn, 678 East South Temple Street, 84102, (801) 363-4900 (number 9 on the accommodations map on page 259 of this work).

Anton Boxrud Bed & Breakfast, 57 South 600 East Street, 84102, (801) 363-8035, (800) 524-5511. National Register of Historic Places, built 1900. Full breakfast, and no smoking indoors (number 11 on the accommodations map on page 259 of this work).

Armstrong Mansion Bed and Breakfast, 667 East 100 South Street, (801) 531-1333, gourmet breakfast (number 12 on the accommodations map on page 259 of this work).

Brigham Street Inn, 1135 East South Temple Street, 84102, (801) 364-4461, FAX (801) 521-3201. National Register of Historic Places, built 1898. Continental breakfast.

Wildflowers Bed and Breakfast, 936 East 1700 South, 84105, (801) 466-0600, FAX (801) 484-7832. National Register of Historic Places, built 1891. Gourmet breakfast.

Pinecrest Bed and Breakfast Inn, 6211 Emigration Canyon Road, 84108, (801) 583-6663. National Register of Historic Places, built 1915. Continental breakfast and no smoking indoors.

CONDOMINIUMS (Listed in order of proximity to the Library)

The Kimball, 150 North Main Street, 84103, (801) 363-4000. A time share with some shares available for purchase. A Resort Condominiums International (RCI) and Interval International Resort Directory (II) participant. No overnight guests accommodated without membership or exchange (number 3 on the accommodations map on page 259 of this work). Within two blocks of the Library.

Chapter 13

Circle J Club at Jeremy Ranch, 4065 Jeremy Woods Road, Park City, 84060, (801) 649-0370, 25 miles from the Library, an RCI participant. Park City is at an elevation of 6,911 compared to Salt Lake City's 4,390 feet.

Iron Blosam Lodge-Snowbird, Snowbird, 84092, (801) 742-2222, 26 miles from the Library, an RCI and II participant. Snowbird is at an elevation of 8,100 feet, rising nearly 3,500 feet in the last eight miles.

Park Avenue Condominiums, 1650 Park Avenue, Park City, 84060, (801) 649-4500, 30 miles from the Library, an RCI participant.

Park Hotel Condominiums, 605 Main Street, Park City, 84060, (801) 649-3200, 30 miles from the Library, an RCI participant.

Park Plaza, 2060 Sidewinder Drive, Park City, 84060, (801) 649-0870, 35 miles from the Library, an RCI and II participant.

Sweetwater at Park City, 1255 Empire Avenue, Park City, 84060, (801) 649-9651, 35 miles from the Library, an RCI participant.

Skiers Lodge, 1235 Norfolk Avenue, Park City, 84060, (801) 649-6094, 37 miles from the Library, an RCI participant.

RENTALS

Some researchers may wish to try to find furnished apartments in order to research for extended periods of time. The following businesses try to provide assistance for such needs:

The Rental List, 3331 South 900 East Street, 84106, (801) 466-4848, in business since 1956.

Express Rental, 124 East 3900 South Street, 84107, (801) 261-4433, in business since 1992.

Reliable Rentals, 4901 South State Street, 84107, (801) 268-0099, in business since 1994.

CAMPGROUNDS (Listed in order of proximity to the Library)

Camp VIP RV Park, 1400 West North Temple Street, 84116, (801) 328-0224 or (801) 355-1214, (800) 226-7752, FAX (801) 355-1055.

Mountain Shadows RV Park, 13275 South Minuteman Drive, Draper, (801) 571-4024, 16 miles from the Library.

Lagoon's RV Park and Campground, 375 North Lagoon Lane, Farmington, 84025-0696, (801) 451-8100, ext. 3100, (800) 748-5246, ext. 5035, FAX (801) 451-8016, 17 miles from the Library. Lagoon amusement park is next door - take the Lagoon exit from I-15.

Cherry Hill Camping Resort, 1325 South Main Street, Kaysville, 84037, (801) 451-5379, 19 miles from the Library (may be the quietest location of the commercial campgrounds).

Wasatch National Forest campsites (without showers) in Big Cottonwood Canyon (SR-152), 19 miles from the Library and Little Cottonwood Canyon (SR-210) southeast of the city, 23 miles from the Library.

Hidden Haven Campground, east of the city on I-80, 2200 West Rasmussen Road, Park City, 84060, (801) 649-8935, 35 miles from the Library.

There are also other beautiful campsites (without showers) in the Wasatch National Forest; however, most of them are quite distant from the Library.

Laws governing the occupied overnight parking of RVs in Salt Lake City, Salt Lake County, and Davis County (the county north of Salt Lake City) require RVs used for overnight sleeping to be parked in RV parks or campgrounds.

Chapter 13

HEALTH CARE

Unfortunately, researchers sometimes need medical attention while traveling. Salt Lake City has some of the West's best health care facilities and physicians. However, the following medical facilities and professionals are listed because of their locations, without any personal recommendation of the author:

Hospitals (Listed in order of proximity to the Library)

Holy Cross Hospital, 1050 East South Temple Street, 84102, (801) 350-4111; 24-Hour Emergency 350-4631; Physician Referral 486-9338.

LDS Hospital, 8th Avenue & C Street, (801) 321-1100; 24-Hour Emergency 321-1180.

University Hospital & Clinics, 50 North Medical Drive, 84132, (801) 581-2121; 24-Hour Emergency 581-2291; Physician Referral (801) 581-2897, (800) 662-0052.

Physicians - Family Practice (Listed in order of proximity to the Library)

Northeast Family Health Center, 70 South Ninth East Street, Suit 1 (801) 238-6650.

Dr. John M. Tudor, Jr., 1060 East 100 South Street, (801) 531-8634.

Dr. J. Darrell Thueson, Salt Lake Clinic, 333 South 900 East Street, (801) 535-8398.

Utah Medical Association, State-wide referral, (801) 355-7477.

ASK-A-NURSE, free 24-hour health care hotline staffed by registered nurses, (801) 972-8488.

Dentists (Listed in order of proximity to the Library)

Dr. Donald A. Brooks, 40 East South Temple Street, (801) 364-7943.

Dr. F. Richard Austin, 60 East South Temple, Suite 610, (801) 321-7600.

Dr. Bengt J. Jonsson, 370 East South Temple Street, (801) 322-5252.

Dr. Mark James Callan, 370 East South Temple Street, Suite 220, (801) 355-8287.

(800) - DENTIST (336-8478).

Chiropractic Physicians (Listed in order of proximity to the Library)

Dr. Joseph Nicolich, Avenues Chiropractic Center, 382 4th Avenue, (801) 355-2024.

Dr. Richard K. Madsen, 490 South 400 East Street, (801) 521-0800.

Dr. Micael Lane, Downtown Chiropractic Office, 871 East 1st South Street, (801) 322-3067.

Dr. Orson P. Kesler, Midvale Chiropractic Office, Locust and Center, Midvale, 84047, (801) 255-3871, seven miles from Library.
An excellent chiropractor; ask his secretary for directions to his office. Recommended by a Salt Lake City resident, friend of the author.

Utah Association of Chiropractic Physicians, Doctor Referral Hot Line, (801) 486-3747, (800) 456-3820.

Opticians (Listed in order of proximity to the Library)

Knighton Optical, 60 East South Temple Street, Eagle Gate Plaza, nearly to State Street on the south side of South Temple, 364-2228.

Chapter 13

Standard Optical, 155 South Main Street, (801) 363-0835.

Afton, 34 South 500 East Street, Suite 105, (801) 359-7646.

Gardner Optical, 34 South 500 East Street, (801) 355-8340.

Optical Services (Listed in order of proximity to the Library)

Lenscrafters, Crossroad Plaza Mall, near the South Temple Street on the second level, 355-8945.

Pearle Vision Express, ZCMI Center, 36 South State Street, Suite 250, 359-5140, FAX (801) 532-3469. The ZCMI Center may be entered from Main, South Temple, and State Streets.

Eye Care Utah, 508 East South Temple Street, Suite 102, 532-1121.

Pharmacies (Listed in order of proximity to the Library)

Crossroads Drug, Crossroads Plaza, first store on the left at the 100 South Street level entrance, 322-1754 (pharmacy), 355-5823 (store).

Pay Less Drug Store, 72 South Main Street, (801) 531-0583 (pharmacy), (801) 531-0581 (information).

Broadway Pharmacy, 242 East 300 South, (801) 363-3939.

Medical Plaza Pharmacy, 508 East Temple Street, (801) 539-0231.

Fred Meyer (Prescriptions), 64 East 900 South, (801) 328-0356.

SPIRITUAL CARE

The following list includes houses of worship within six blocks of the Family History Library, listed in alphabetical order. Denominations not listed below may be located by checking the Salt Lake City

telephone book's yellow pages under, "Churches" and "Synagogues."
There are fifty-nine denominations listed there.

Cathedral Church of St. Mark, 231 East 100 South Street, 322-3400.
Catholic Cathedral of the Madeleine, 331 East Temple Street, 328-
8941.
Catholic Center - St. Paul's Chapel, 226 South Main Street, 328-8941.
Chavurah B'Yachad, 161 East Second Avenue, 359-1506.
First Presbyterian Church, 350 East South Temple Street, 363-3889.
First United Methodist Church, 203 South 200 East Street, 328-8726.
Holy Trinity Greek Orthodox Church, 279 South 300 West Street, 328-
9681.
LDS Chapels: 142 West 200 North, 578-6605, 578-6606.
375 East 100 South, 578-6623.
Salt Lake Valley Deaf Ward, 760 East 700 South, 760 East 700
South, 578-6716.
Non-denominational Sunday services are also provided by the Church
of Jesus Christ of Latter-day Saints in the Assembly Hall most
Sunday mornings following the Tabernacle Choir broadcast. No
offering.
Rock of The Foursquare Gospel Church, 45 East 400 South Street, 532-
6370.
Salt Lake Buddhist Church, 211 West 100 South Street, 363-4742.
Sts Peter & Paul Orthodox Christian Church, 355 South 300 East
Street, 532-5456.

GENEALOGICAL BOOKSTORES

Genealogy Resource Center, 122 West South Temple (Howard
Johnson's 1st floor), 359-9353.

Deseret Book, ZCMI Center (Street level, South Temple entrance),
328-8191.

Chapter 13

OFFICE SUPPLIES

Quick Connections, Crossroads Plaza (Mall) on the lower level in the South hall, 328-1099, the second store on the left at the 100 South Street level entrance. Also provides photo developing, gift wrapping, packing and shipping, Western Union, Fax service, and private mail boxes. 328-1099, FAX (801) 364-6573.

Office and Things, ZCMI Mall on the second floor in its south hall (36 South State Street, Suite 238, 533-8070. The ZCMI Mall has entrances on Main, South Temple, State, and First South Streets.
This store has a larger selection of supplies.

ADDITIONAL READING:

Salt Lake Restaurant Guide. Salt Lake City: Salt Lake Valley Convention & Visitors Bureau, 1989. Free. 180 South West Temple, Salt Lake City, Utah 84101-1493, (801) 521-2822.

American Automobile Association's *Colorado/Utah.* Heathrow, Fla.: American Automobile Association, 1994.

SUMMARY:

Please eat three square meals a day. You'll need all the energy you can get. Make sure that you get enough sleep to have a good, clear head on your shoulders for doing research.

> "Salt Lake City was healthy--an extremely healthy city.
> They declared that there was only one physician in the
> place and he was arrested every week regularly and held
> to answer under the vagrant act for having 'no visible
> means of support.'"
> > -- Mark Twain, *Roughing It* (New York: Grosset
> > & Dunlap, 1913), page 64. Originally published:
> > New York: American Publishing Co., 1871.
> > Twain visited Salt Lake City in 1861.

Chapter 14

TRANSPORTATION AND PARKING

BUSES

Greyhound Bus Lines, 160 West Temple Street, 84101, (801) 355-9581, (800) 231-2222. The bus depot is just around the corner from the Library.

Local buses are operated by the Utah Transit Authority (UTA), 3600 South 700 West Street, 84119, (801) 287-4636 (bus information). The UTA provides a "Free Zone" of free transportation on any of their buses within the area bounded by West Temple, Second East, Fourth South Streets, and the Utah State Capital.

AIRLINES

Many major airlines have routes to or through Salt Lake City. Airlines and their reservations telephone numbers for Salt Lake City are as follows:

Alaska	(800) 426-0333
America West	(800) 235-9292
American	(800) 433-7300
Continental	(801) 359-9800
Delta	(800) 221-1212
	(801) 532-7123
Northwest	(800) 225-2525
Skywest/Delta Connection	(800) 453-9417
Southwest	(801) 466-7747
	(800) 135-9792,
	(800) 435-9792
United	(800) 241-6522

Chapter 14

AIRPORT TRANSPORTATION

From the airport the *Utah Transit Authority* bus #50 runs:

Monday - Friday	6:32 a.m. - 6:52 p.m. (21 trips)
Saturday	6:34 a.m. - 6:44 p.m. (13 trips)
Sunday	6:34 a.m. - 5:34 p.m. (5 trips)

To the airport bus #50 leaves the East side of Temple Square:

Monday - Friday	5:48 a.m. - 6:10 p.m. (19 trips)
Saturday	6:00 a.m. - 6:00 p.m. (13 trips)
Sunday	6:00 a.m. - 5:00 p.m. (5 trips)

The airport is four miles west of the Library. For the latest stop locations and schedules, call Utah Transit Authority, (801) 287-4636.

RAILROADS

Amtrak, 320 South Rio Grande (400 West) Street, (801) 364-8562, (800) 872-7245. Very early morning arrival and late night departure. Amtrak is shown as number 34 on the attractions map on the inside back cover of this work.

TAXICABS

City Cab (801) 363-5550 or 363-5014.

Ute Cab (801) 359-7788.

Yellow Cab (801) 521-2100.

PARKING (Listed in order of proximity to the Library)

There is a parking lot with a three-hour limit on the northwest corner of West Temple Street and North Temple Street; free with token from the Library during working hours. Exit can also be managed with $5.00 in quarters. No recreational vehicles or trailers permitted.

Temple Square Parking, 30 West North Temple Street, (801) 322-2169. $3 for 0 - 12 hours. Space for recreational vehicles or trailers permitted, no in-and-outs for all vehicles. Zion Securities Corp.

Beehive Parking, Second West Street behind the Library, (801) 359-1152, $2.00 for all day. Coins or paper money needed.

The Parking Place, 240 West South Temple Street, a very large lot across from the Doubletree Hotel. $2 for all day; recreational vehicles or trailers are welcome.

Free all-day street parking is available within three blocks northwest of the Library, on Third North and West Temple and beyond.

CAUTION! Parking meters near the Library are free on Saturdays, but the signs on parking meters are not clear concerning the enforcement of the two hour parking limit. The two hour parking limit is enforced!

AUTOMOBILE RENTING - DOWNTOWN LOCATIONS (Listed in order of proximity to the Library)

Hertz, Marriott Hotel, 75 South West Temple Street, 84101, (801) 355-8427; Red Lion Hotel, 255 South West Temple Street, 84101, (801) 328-8915, (800) 654-3131, Airport (801) 575-2683.

Chapter 14

Agency Rent-A-Car, 307 West 200 South Street, 84101, (801) 534-1622, (800) 321-1972.

Alamo, 37 North 2400 West Street, (801) 575-2211, (800) 327-9633.

Avis Rent A Car, Embassy Suite Hotel, 600 South West Temple Street, 84101, (801) 359-2177, (800) 331-1212.

Budget, 750 South Main Street, 84101, (801) 298-1460, (800) 527-0700, Airport (801) 575-2830.

Dollar Rent A Car, (800) 800-4000, Airport (801) 575-2580

National Car Rental, (800) 227-7368, Airport (801) 575-2277.

Sears, 750 South Main Street, 84101, (801) 298-1777, (800) 527-0700.

Thrifty Car Rental, 958 South State Street, 84111, (801) 355-7368, (800) 367-2277, Airport (801) 595-6677.

ROAD SERVICE:

AAA Automobile Club of Utah, 560 East 500 South, (801) 364-5615, (800) 541-9902.

A-1 National Towing, 140 South 500 West Street, (801) 363-2233.

AUTOMOBILE REPAIR - DOWNTOWN LOCATIONS (Listed in order of proximity to the Library)

Firestone Mastercare Car Service, 204 East 300 South Street, (801) 363-6741.

Goodyear Tire & Automotive Service Center, 378 South West Temple Street, (801) 328-8473.

Garff Dealerships (GM Goodwrench - Honda - Hyundai - Jaguar - Mercedes-Benz - Oldsmobile - Saab - Volvo), 531 South State Street, (801) 521-6111.

Hamstead Motor Imports, 633 South Main Street, (801) 359-2266.

Super Ford Store, 730 South West Temple Street, (801) 578-1050.

Mark Miller Toyota, 84 West 700 South Street, (801) 268-3734.

Rick Warner GM-Mazda-Nissan-Pontiac, 702 South Main Street, (801) 364-1991.

Rick Warner Auto Dealerships (Chrysler-Plymouth), 777 South West Temple Street, (801) 328-4931.

Goodyear Tire & Automotive Service Center, 420 South 500 East Street, (801) 355-8473.

Brigham Street Service, 662 South 200 West, (801) 363-5721.

David Early Tires & Service Center, 332 East 400 South, (801) 363-4556.

Sears Tire and Auto Center, 754 South State Street, (801) 523-0913.

SUMMARY:

Make sure that your travel plans include enough sleep in order to arrive in Salt Lake City rested and with enough energy to fly into sound research.

"The city lies in the edge of a level plain as broad as the
state of Connecticut, and crouches close down to the
ground under a curving wall of mighty mountains whose
heads are hidden in the clouds, and whose shoulders
bear relics of the snows of winter all the summer long.
Seen from one of these dizzy heights, twelve or fifteen
miles off, Great Salt Lake City is toned down and
diminished till it is suggestive of a child's toy village
reposing under the majestic protection of the Chinese
wall."

> -- Mark Twain, *Roughing It* (New York: Grosset
> & Dunlap, 1913), page 63. Originally published:
> New York: American Publishing Co., 1871.
> Twain visited Salt Lake City in 1861.

Chapter 15

SIGHTSEEING AND ENTERTAINMENT

Most researchers are reluctant to take time from their precious research at the Family History Library for sightseeing, shopping, or sporting.

For those who need a break or who have a family along that needs entertaining, the Salt Lake Convention & Visitors Bureau publishes an excellent free *Salt Lake Visitors Guide*. Pick one up upon arrival in Salt Lake City at Terminal 2 at the airport or at their South West Temple Street office, or write or call for one beforehand. The Bureau's address is 180 South West Temple Street, Salt Lake City, Utah 84101-1493, phone (801) 521-2822 (number 1 on the attractions map on the inside back cover of this work).

Various additional guides to events, tours, and sights, etc., are available from:

Utah Travel Council, Council Hall/Capitol Hill, Salt Lake City, UT 84114. (801) 538-1030. Their best publication is the *Tour Guide to Utah*.

Salt Lake Area Chamber of Commerce, 175 East 400 South Street, Salt Lake City, UT 84101. (801) 364-3631.

There are, of course, other guides to Salt Lake City and Utah's recreation:

Angus, Mark. *Salt Lake City Underfoot: Self-Guided Tours of Historic Neighborhoods.* Signature Books, 1994.

American Automobile Association. *Colorado/Utah.* Heathrow, Fla.: American Automobile Association, 1994.
  A very practical guide to historic sites and entertainment, hotels, motels, and restaurants.

199

Chapter 15

Weir, Bill. *Utah Handbook*. 4th ed. Chico, Calif.: Moon
Publications, 1995 (P.O. Box 3040, 95927). (800) 345-5473. $16.95
paper. 458 pages.

SIGHTS

The following are the author's favorite sights:

Temple Square, 240-2534, across West Temple Street from the Library
(number 5 on the attractions map on the inside back cover of this
work). The Square is on the National Register of Historic Places, built
1855. Free. The Temple is also on the Register, built 1853-1893.

The Museum of Church History and Art, 45 North West Temple Street,
next door to the Library (number 4 on the attractions map on the inside
back cover of this work), 240-3310. Free

The Tabernacle Choir's 9:15 a.m. Sunday morning CBS broadcast
(usually no seats are available for tourists for the broadcast that
precedes the Church's General Conference the first Sunday of April and
October). Free.

Trolley Square at Sixth South and Ninth East, (801) 521-9877. A fee
trolley to the Square stops in front of the Library and a schedule is
posted at the stop.

The Tracy Aviary in Liberty Park at 859 East 1300 South. Admission
charge.

The Alpine Scenic Loop, a spectacular seventy-four mile round trip
drive from downtown Salt Lake City, climbing to an altitude of over
9,000 feet behind 11,750 Mt. Timpanogos and descending through
American Fork Canyon back to the 4,500 elevation of Utah Valley.
Take I-15 south of the city to Utah SR-52 (8th North Street in Orem).
Take SR-52 east up Provo Canyon on Highway 189 to SR-92 and
follow the signs back to I-15. Summer only. Free.

Sunset over the Great Salt Lake from the foothills of Bountiful; take I-15 north of town and turn off on Bountiful's Fifth South off ramp. Drive high up the hill, park, and drink in a glorious Utah treat. A shorter drive, but not as nice as Bountiful, is up North Main Street toward the State Capitol and right on either Third or Fifth North Street to East Capitol Boulevard; then left (or up) the hill to Seventh North, turn left and look for a place to park with a good view at the end of Seventh North on Cortez Street. Free.

If you want to get into the Tabernacle, take the free guided tour or attend a concert, an organ recital, or the free Tabernacle Choir broadcast on Sunday from 9:15-10:00 a.m., or the Choir rehearsal on Thursday night, 8:00-9:30 p.m. Organ recitals are presented free Monday through Saturday, 12:00-12:30 p.m. and Sunday, 2:00 p.m. During the months of June through September additional organ recitals are presented Monday through Friday, 4:00-4:30 p.m. The Tabernacle is on the National Register of Historic Places, built 1862-1867. Persons who depend on air conditioning should be aware that the Tabernacle is not air conditioned and can be hot on some days and for some occasions. Also its seats are pioneer wooden pews.

There are free concerts, "Temple Square Concert Series," in the air-conditioned Assembly Hall on the southwest corner of the Square. They begin at 7:30 p.m. and last approximately one hour. Ask for schedules at any of the visitor center desks or write Temple Square Visitor's Center, 50 North Temple Street, Salt Lake City UT 84050 or call (801) 240-4872.

Non-denominational Sunday services are also provided by the Church of Jesus Christ of Latter-day Saints in the Assembly Hall most Sunday mornings following the Tabernacle Choir broadcast. No offering.

"This is the Place" Monument in the Pioneer Trail State Park at the mouth of Emigration Canyon offers some historical background to the settlement of the Great Salt Lake Valley, as well as a fine view. Take South Temple Street east to 1300 East Street, turn right to 500 South Street, then left and east. 500 South Street becomes Foothill Drive. Turn left and east on Sunnyside Avenue to the park. Free.

Chapter 15

Kennecott's Bingham Canyon Mine, (801) 569-6000, is one of the largest open pit mines in the world and an interesting place to visit in summer. Take I-15 south to exit 301 (7200 South Street), then west to SR-48. The mine is at the end of SR-48, twenty-three miles southwest of the City. A small fee is charged for autos. National Register of Historic Places, started in 1904.

For researchers who love to visit lovely hotel lobbies, the architects, contractors, and construction workers preserved the grand Hotel Utah Lobby in the Joseph Smith Memorial Building when they remodeled the hotel into many Family History Department and Library functions, a chapel, meeting rooms, offices, restaurants, a theater, and public viewing areas on the east and west sides of the tenth floor. The lobby and views from the viewing areas are well worth the one block walk through Temple Square from the Library. On the National Register of Historic Places, built 1911. Free.

One of *Going*'s surveyed owners suggested that information concerning the fifty-five minute motion picture film, "Legacy" be added to the third edition. The "Legacy" portrays a segment of the early history of the Church of Jesus Christ of Latter-day Saints. Free tickets to the "Legacy" may be obtained at the west entrance of the hallway to the *FamilySearch* Center in the Joseph Smith Memorial Building as you enter the building from the east gate of Temple Square. Tickets may also be obtained at the information desks of the North and South Visitors' Centers on Temple Square.

SIGHTSEEING TOURS

Innsbrook Tours, 57 West South Temple Street, #400, 84101, (801) 534-1001. City tours that include tours of grounds, buildings, and sites outside of a bus.

Gray Line Motor Tours, 553 West 100 South Street, 84101, (801) 521-7060, (800) 309-2052, FAX (801) 521-7060. City tours and tours of national parks.

Old Salty Tour Train, 549 West 500 South Street, 84101, (801) 359-8677. City lecture-tours in an open-air, rubber tire vehicle, three times a day from the Temple Square South gate, 11:00 a.m., 1:00 p.m., and 3:00 p.m.

CINEMA:

Crossroads Cinema, Crossroads Plaza, Richards Street level, near the South Temple entrance, 355-3883.

CULTURAL EVENTS AND EDUCATIONAL CENTERS (Listed in order of proximity to the Library)

Maurice Abravanel Concert Hall, formerly Symphony Hall, home of the Utah Symphony, 123 West South Temple Street, 84111, (801) 533-5626 (number 2 on the attractions map on the inside back cover of this work).

Salt Lake Art Center, 20 South West Temple, (801) 328-4201 (number 2 on the attractions map on the inside back cover of this work).

LDS Church Office Building, 50 East North Temple Street, 240-3789 provides a very high-rise view of the city from the top floor observation deck, and an inviting lobby graced by a mural. You may exit the lobby into a spacious court yard filled with lovely fountains, sculptures, and flower beds (number 6 on the attractions map on the inside back cover of this work). Free.

Garden Tours, April through September, from thirty minutes to one hour and a half, 240-5916. Begins in the southwest lobby of the Church Office Building, 50 East North Temple Street. Free.

Beehive House, 67 East South Temple Street, 240-2671 (number 10 on the attractions map on the inside back cover of this work). Brigham Young's official family residence. On the National Register of Historic Places, built 1853. Hours: Monday-Saturday, 9:30 a.m. - 4:30 p.m.; Sunday, 10:00 a.m. - 1:00 p.m. Free.

Chapter 15

Capitol Theatre, home of the Utah Opera Company, (801) 534-0888; and Ballet West, (801) 363-9318; 50 West 200 South Street, 84101. National Register of Historic Places (number 17 on the attractions map on the inside back cover of this work).

Hansen Planetarium, 15 South State Street, (801) 538-2098 (Number 12 on the attractions map on the inside back cover of this work).

Promised Valley Playhouse, 132 South State Street, 84111 , (801) 364-5696.

Utah State Historical Society Museum, 300 Rio Grande Avenue (400 West), 84101-1182, (801) 533-3500 (number 34 on the attractions map on the inside back cover of this work). National Register of Historic Places. Free.

City and County Building, between Fourth and Fifth South State Street, 533-0858 is a classic building that merits a visit (number 36 on the attractions map on the inside back cover of this work). National Register of Historic Places, built 1891-1894. Free.

Utah State Capitol, Capitol Hill, 538-3000 is another building worth a visit (number 22 on the attractions map on the inside back cover of this work). National Register of Historic Places. Free.

Children's Museum of Utah, 840 North 300 West Street, 328-3383.

Red Butte Garden and Arboretum, University of Utah, 18A de Trobriand Street, 585-5227, recorded information: 581-4747. Take 400 South to Foothill Boulevard, left on Wakara Way to Visitor's Center.

Old Deseret, near the "This is the Place" Monument in the Pioneer Trail State Park at the mouth of Emigration Canyon, listed above. Period cabins, homes, stores and costumes of 1847-1869 with furnishings and demonstrations offered daily, noon to 5:00 p.m. Memorial Day through Labor Day. Admission is a modest fee.

Wheeler Historic Farm, 6351 South 900 East, Murray, 264-2212, Dial-A-Story 268-6253, National Register of Historic Places.

ENTERTAINMENT

Cyberspace Virtual Reality Entertainment Center, 165 South West Temple Street, 264-9989.

Hogle Zoo, 2600 East Sunnyside Avenue, (801) 582-1631.

The 49th Street Galleria has indoor miniature golf, a bowling center, roller skating rink, batting cages, rides for small children, arcade, and eateries. Take the 53rd South Street off ramp from I-80, drive west to 700 West Street and turn right or north. 700 West Street becomes Murray Blvd. Just after it crosses Vine Street turn right on the first street, which becomes the freeway frontage road in front of the Galleria, 4998 South 360 West Street, Murray 84118, (801) 265-3866.

Lagoon is a well-landscaped summer amusement park with rides, water slides, swimming pools, and a pioneer village, 375 North Highway 91, P.O. Box 696, Farmington 84025-0696, (801) 451-8000, (800)748-5246, ext. 5035.

Raging Waters (20 water slides, 11 swimming pools, waves, etc.), 1200 West 1700 South Street, 84104, (801) 973-9900.

Classic Skating Center and Waterslides (roller skating, water slides, etc., 9151 South 255 West Street, Sandy, (801) 561-1791.

Classic Roller Skating, 2774 South 625 West Street, Bountiful (801) 295-8301.

The Sports Park (batting cages, mini-golf, video arcade, and race cars), 8695 South Sandy Parkway (west of I-15 on 90th South, (801) 562-4444.

SPECTATOR SPORTS

The Winter Olympics, 2002, information line, (801) 322-2002.

Chapter 15

Utah Jazz (Basketball Team) Ticket Office, (801) 355-3865. Games are played in the Delta Center, 300 West South Temple Street (number 33 on the attractions map on the inside back cover of this work).

Utah Grizzles (Hockey Club) Ticket Office, (801) 535-7825, Administration, (801) 530-7166. Games for the 1995/96 and 1996/97 seasons played in the Delta Center, 300 West South Temple Street, thereafter in a new ice rink in West Valley City.

Salt Lake Buzz Baseball Club Ticket Office (801) 485-3800. Franklin Quest Field located at 1300 South West Temple Street.

GOLF COURSES - PUBLIC (Listed in order of proximity to the Library)

Nibley Park Golf Course, 2780 South 700 East Street, 84106, (801) 483-5418. Nine holes and driving range.

Rose Park Golf Course, 1386 North Redwood Road, 84116, (801) 596-5030. Eighteen holes and driving range.

Glendale Golf Course, 1630 West 2100 South, 84119, (801) 974-2403. Eighteen holes and driving range.

Mountain Dell Golf Course, Parleys Canyon, 84106, (801) 582-3812. Thirty-six holes and driving range.

GYMNASIUMS (Listed in order of proximity to the Library)

Deseret Gymnasium, 161 North Main Street, (801) 359-3911. Basketball, handball, racquetball and squash courts; climbing wall; exercise and weight rooms; and indoor pools.

SKI RESORTS (Listed in order of proximity to the Library). Utah's license plates read, "The Greatest Snow on Earth":

Solitude Ski Resort (Big Cottonwood Canyon SR-190), P.O. Box 21350, Salt Lake City, UT 84121-0350, (801) 534-1000, FAX (801) 649-5276, 23 miles from the Library.

Brighton Ski Resort (Big Cottonwood Canyon SR-190), Star Route, Brighton, UT 84121, (801) 943-8309, FAX (801) 649-1787, 25 miles from the Library.

Snowbird Ski and Summer Resort (Little Cottonwood Canyon SR-210), Snowbird, UT 84092-6019, (801) 742-2222, (800) 453-3000, FAX (801) 742-3300, 26 miles from the Library.

Alta Ski Lifts (Little Cottonwood Canyon SR-210), Alta, UT 84092, (801) 742-3333, Snow Report (801) 572-3939, 27 miles from the Library.

Park City Ski Area, P.O. Box 39, Park City, UT 84060, (801) 649-8111, Snow Report (801) 649-9571, FAX (801) 649-5964, 30 miles from the Library.

Deer Valley, P.O. Box 1525, Park City, UT 84060, (801) 649-1000, FAX (801) 649-1910, 38 miles from the Library.

Bus transportation to all resorts is available seven days a week for skiers via Lewis Bros. Stages, (801) 359-8677, (800) 826-5844; Ski Bus Express, (801) 975-0202; Ski Bus (801) 262-5626.

MALLS (Listed in order of proximity to the Library)

Crossroads Plaza Mall, 50 South Main Street, (801) 363-1558. The Crossroads Plaza Mall is shown as number 15 on the attractions map on the inside back cover of this work.

ZCMI Center, 36 South State Street, (801) 321-8743 (number 14 on the attractions map on the inside back cover of this work). The cornice and cast iron facade, 15 South Main Street, dating from the earlier 1901 building, is on the National Register of Historic Places.

Chapter 15

Trolley Square, 602 East 500 South Street, (801) 521-9877.

Valley Fair Mall, 3601 South 2700 West Street, West Valley City, (801) 969-6211.

Cottonwood Mall, 4835 South Highland Drive 84117, (801) 278-0416.

Fashion Place, 6191 South State Street, Murray (801) 265-0504.

South Towne Mall, 10450 South State Street, Sandy (801) 571-5492.

Factory Stores of America, 12101 South Factory Outlet Drive, Draper, 84020, On I-15, take Exit 294, (801) 572-6440, (808) 772-8336.

SUMMARY:

A little relaxation is good for clearing the mind, lifting the soul and refreshing the body.

"The accustomed coach life began again, now, and by midnight it almost seemed as if we never had been out of our snuggery among the mail-sacks at all. We had made one alteration, however. We had provided enough bread, boiled ham, and hard-boiled eggs to last double the six hundred miles of staging we had still to do.

"And it was comfort in those succeeding days to sit up and contemplate the majestic panorama of mountains and valleys spread out below us and eat ham and hard-boiled eggs while our spiritual natures reveled alternately in rainbows, thunder-storms, and peerless sunsets."

-- Mark Twain, *Roughing It* (New York: Grosset & Dunlap, 1913), page 85. Originally published: New York: American Publishing Co., 1871.
Twain visited Salt Lake City in 1861.

Chapter 16

SIGHTS ALONG THE HIGHWAYS
TO SALT LAKE CITY

INTERSTATE 15 FROM LOS ANGELES AND LAS VEGAS

A colorful, scenic side loop trip of twenty-two extra miles is through
the fee-free **Valley of Fire State Park** east off of I-15. Thirty-six miles
northeast of Las Vegas turn east to the Park. After driving through the
Park you join SR-169 (state route) near Lake Mead south of Overton
and rejoin I-15 three miles northeast of the Moapa I-15 exit. An
enjoyable side trip in the cool months of the year.

The buffet at the **Peppermill Resort Hotel & Casino**, Mesquite,
Nevada, (702) 346-5232, (800) 621-0187, is one of the finest and very
reasonable; even cheaper nice meals are available from its menu.

Don't miss taking a little closer look at the grandeur of the **Virgin
River Narrows** as you leave Littlefield, Arizona traveling I-15 to St.
George, Utah.

A very short but memorable side trip is to drive west out of St. George
through Santa Clara to **Snow Canyon State Park** and return to St.
George from the north on SR-18. Next to Snow Canyon is the open air
Tuacahn Amphitheater, (800) 746-9882, where the drama, "Utah," is
presented late June to September.

No one should miss seeing **Zion Canyon** in Zion National Park. Years
ago when I worked as a desk clerk at the Lodge, an eastern tourist
exclaimed as he registered, "It's beautiful. Zion is Yosemite in color!"
Zion is particularly beautiful and interesting in a rain storm, as the
moisture changes the canyon walls into darker colors, and dry rivulets
above the cliffs come alive and spill colored waterfalls into the canyon.
It is a sixty-four mile round trip off the interstate on SR-9, open all
year. If you can't spare the time to see the main canyon, at least take
the fourteen-mile round trip into **Kolob Canyon**, near New Harmony
and Kanarraville. Kolob Canyon is open in the summer months.

Chapter 16

There is no fee to see the spectacular scenery of Kolob Canyon, just off I-15 at exit 40, thirty-two miles northeast of St. George and seventeen miles south of Cedar City. The seven-mile drive rises from 5,054 feet at the visitors center just off I-15 to 6,401 feet at the last, and highest, Kolob Canyon Viewpoint.

The **Shakespearean Festival,** which also includes contemporary plays, is held on the campus of Southern Utah State College at Cedar City and is a worthwhile mid-July through August stop. For their schedule write The Utah Shakespearean Festival, 351 West Center, Cedar City, Utah 84720, (801) 586-7878.

Colorful **Cedar Breaks National Monument,** with its magnificent vista overlooking Kolob Terrace and Zion National Park, is a scenic twenty-three mile summer loop trip via SR-14 from Cedar City and SR-143 to Parowan. You climb from an elevation of 5,840 at Cedar City to 9,900 in about fifteen miles.

Alpine Scenic Loop, SR-92, off US-189 in Provo Canyon, is a spectacular twenty-nine mile summer loop trip that climbs to an altitude of over 9,000 feet behind 11,750 foot Mt. Timpanogos, then descends through American Fork Canyon back to the 4,500 foot elevation of Utah Valley.

Timpanogos Cave National Monument is an adventurous summer excursion for amateur spelunkers, without ropes or flashlights. However, it is a strenuous three-mile round trip hike up the side of American Fork Canyon to the cave. Early weekday morning visits are the coolest and best, as waiting lists are created because tours can only accommodate a limited number of people.

Historical sites along I-15 include the **Brigham Young Winter Home** in St. George; **Old Silver Reef** mining town at Leeds; **Old Cove Fort;** and Utah's **first territorial capitol** in Fillmore.

Southern Californians and Nevadans might sometime extend their research trip to the Family History Library with a lengthy return sightseeing trip to **Dinosaur National Monument** via US-40, Split Rock and Harpers Point in Colorado for a spectacular view of the

210

confluence of the Green and Yampa Rivers. Then on to Rangely, Colorado on SR-64 and to Grand Junction on SR-139. Just out of Grand Junction is **Colorado National Monument** that is a worthwhile short side trip. Westward bound on I-70 turn off at Cisco and follow the Colorado River down its beautiful canyon to Moab. Take side trips from Moab sixteen miles to **Arches National Park** and another sixty miles to **Dead Horse Point State Park.** Continue south from Moab on US-191 with a sixty-eight mile round trip into Squaw Flat of **Canyon Lands National Park.** The road passes through **Newspaper Rock State Historical Monument.** At Blanding take SR-95 to **Natural Bridges National Monument** and on to Hanksville, with a side trip up to **Goblin Valley State Reserve** on SR-24. West out of Hanksville on SR-24 tour **Capitol Reef National Park.** Turn south on SR-12 at Torrey to Boulder, Escalante, Tropic, and Ruby's Inn. Take an awesome side trip into **Bryce Canyon National Park.** From Bryce drive to Panguitch and turn south and southwest into the Dixie National Forest and on to **Cedar Breaks National Monument.** Since you stopped at **Kolob Canyon** on the way to Salt Lake City, drive east out of **Cedar Breaks** to US-89 south to the Mount Carmel Junction and on into **Zion National Park,** up to the Narrows and a cool, very easy two-mile round trip hike along the Virgin River into the depths of one of the nation's wonders. The last sight to see would be **Snow Canyon State Park,** page 163, if you didn't see it on the way to Salt Lake City. A total of thirteen western wonders in just a few days, a glorious trip. A nice way to unwind from a heavy research trip to the Family History Library.

US-89 FROM PHOENIX AND FLAGSTAFF

Grand Canyon's South and North rims are notable side trips on this route to Salt Lake City. At least one of the rim trips is a must. The South rim can be visited by an eighty-eight mile loop trip via scenic US-180 and SR-64, all year. The North Rim is open in the summer and is an eighty-three mile partial loop trip.

Zion National Park is a forty-six mile round trip on SR-9 from the Mount Carmel Junction and, as explained above, is well worth the trip.

Chapter 16

The Mount Carmel entrance to the Park is considered by many visitors to be more spectacular than the valley entrance via St. George.

Bryce Canyon National Park is a thirty-four mile round trip off the route and is an unforgettable experience. It is open all year.

The Big Rock Candy Mountain merits learning the folk song about it (before you leave home) and a stop to look, see, and sing.

STATE ROUTE 44 AND US HIGHWAYS 64, 550, 160, 666, 191, AND 6, FROM ALBUQUERQUE

Southwest Colorado offers many wonderful scenic places to visit on two different routes to Salt Lake City. The **San Juan Mountains** provide a beautiful summer drive up US-550 to US-50 and on to I-70 at Grand Junction, Colorado. The second starts on SR-44 at Bloomfield, New Mexico. Then on to Aztec, Durango, Silverton, and over 11,018 foot Red Mountain Pass to Ouray, Montrose, and Grand Junction.

Mesa Verde National Park is a sixty-two mile round trip east off of US-666 east of Cortez, Colorado, a unique summer day trip.

Arches National Park's visitors center is right next to US-666, eight miles north of Moab. This beautiful park is open all year. A lot of the park may be seen from park roads, but a little hiking is required to see its better natural arches.

INTERSTATE 70 FROM DENVER

Colorado National Monument is only a few extra miles loop trip from Grand Junction to Fruita, Colorado, and well worth the time.

Arches National Park is a fifty-four mile round trip south of the interstate. It is an interesting park, open all year.

Goblin Valley State Reserve is further off the interstate. It is less well known, but very interesting for a summer visit because of its unique

formations. A few miles of the route into the park is dirt. For desert
lovers the dirt road drive from there northwest rejoining the interstate
via the **San Rafael Swell** is a very exciting and colorful dry weather
trip. However, you should return to Green River, as the shortest route
to Salt Lake City is via US-6 and US-191.

US-40 FROM DENVER

Dinosaur National Monument, near Vernal, offers two spectacular
sights. One, in Colorado, requires a moderate two-mile hike to
Harpers Corner Overlook to view the confluence of the Yampa and
Green Rivers. The other is Split Mountain on the Green River in Utah
at the Split Mountain campground. Of course, the open-all-year
Dinosaur Quarry Visitor Center is a must for everyone.

INTERSTATE 80 FROM ROCK SPRINGS AND CHEYENNE

History abounds on this route. It was the **Mormon Trail** and the route
of the Donner Party from **Fort Bridger** west. The scenery down the
canyons to the Salt Lake Valley is also super.

Sometime while driving from the east on I-80 all researchers should
take time to leave I-80 at Ogallala, Nebraska and travel along the North
Platte River, the **Oregon and Mormon Trails** via US-26 past
**Courthouse and Jail Rocks, Chimney Rock, Scottsbluff, and Fort
Laramie.** Continue on near the trail route on I-25 to Casper, then on
SR-220 past **Independence Rock and Devils Gate** and on US-287 to
SR-20 through **South Pass.** Please stop and read the **Whitman
monument.** At Farson turn south to Rock Springs and rejoin I-80.
You meet the **California and Mormon Trails** at Fort Bridger.

The following narrative histories and trail guides are recommended for
background reading for the above tour:

Chapter 16

Parkman, Francis. *The Oregon Trail.* New York: Penguin Books, 1982. Paper $4.95. Penguin Books, P.O. Box 120, Bergenfield, NJ 07621-0120, (201) 387-0600, (800) 526-0275.
 Originally published as *The California and Oregon Trail.* New York: Putnam, 1849.

Stewart, George Rippey. *The California Trail: An Epic with Many Heroes.* Lincoln: University of Nebraska Press, 1983. Paper $9.95. University of Nebraska Press, 901 North 17th Street, Room 327, Lincoln, NE 68588-0520, (800) 755-1105.
 Originally published: New York: McGraw-Hill, 1962.

Hafen, Le Roy Reuben, and Ann W. Hafen. *Handcarts to Zion: The Story of a Unique Western Migration, 1856-1860: With Contemporary Journals, Accounts, Reports, and Rosters of Members of the Ten Handcart Companies.* Lincoln: University of Nebraska Press in Association with the A. H. Clarke Co., 1992. Paper $9.95. University of Nebraska Press, 901 North 17th Street, Room 327, Lincoln, NE 68588-0520, (800) 755-1105.
 Originally published: Glendale, Calif.: A. H. Clarke Co., 1960.

Franzwa, Gregory M. *The Oregon Trail Revisited.* 4th ed. St. Louis, Mo.: Patrice Press, 1988. $14.95, paper $7.95. Patrice Press, 1701 South Eight Street, St. Louis, MO 63104, (800) 367-9242.

INTERSTATE 80 FROM WENDOVER AND RENO

Lots of people dislike this route to Salt Lake City. However, others find the mountains of Nevada and the salt flats of Utah interesting and even picturesque.

As the **Ruby Mountains** east of Elko come into view you are looking at some of the most beautiful mountains in Nevada. Nestled high on their eastern slope is a quiet little lake, **Angel Lake**. A good two lane paved road can take you on a scenic twenty-four mile round trip to Angel Lake out of Wells. You climb from an elevation of 5,625 at Wells to 8,400 at Angel Lake.

If Nevada's mountains and desert have gotten to you by the time you reach Wendover, a delicious oasis is the buffet at the **Peppermill Inn & Casino**, Wendover, Nevada, (702) 664-2255, (800) 648-9660. It is one of the finest and very reasonable; even cheaper nice meals are available from its menu.

East of Wendover the **Bonneville Speedway** is a disappointment most of the year because it is under water. Nevertheless, to the person who would like to say that he or she has been there, it is worth the twelve-mile round trip. National Register of Historic Places, started in 1911.

The **Bonneville Salt Flats Rest Area** just east of Wendover is the safest place to park and check out the salt. Yes, it really is salt, but not fit for consumption on hard boiled eggs at your picnic.

Twenty-six miles east of the state line is a salt flat sculpture with two titles, **"Desert Tree Art Sculpture"** and/or **"Tree of Utah,"** the creation of Karl Momen, a Swedish sculptor and architect. It was erected in 1984, eight-three feet tall, concrete, and weighing two hundred tons.* Disliked by some, liked by others, and laughed at by many, it is usually a welcome relief from the bright sun and mirages that make it appear as if you'll drive straight into the lake at any moment. Most people ask, "What is that sculpture doing way out here?" Others just say, "Far out!"

   -- * May, Fred E., and Bill Wilkerson. *Interstate 80: The Historic Route, Salt Lake City, Utah, to Reno, Nevada.* Layton, Utah: Travel Geografix, 1991, page 12.

Sometime on a homeward bound trip the adventurous Californian or Nevadan may wish to take in the **Pony Express route** south of I-80. The scenic route is to take I-15 to Lehi, SR-73 with a brief stop at **Cedar Fort** and the **Stagecoach Inn** to read the historical markers and see the sites, National Register of Historic Places, built 1858. Then on to SR-36 and SR-199 over Johnson Pass to Dugway. At the Dugway Proving Grounds entrance you turn left and explore some of the finest Pony Express station ruins in the West. There is an oasis at **Fish Springs National Wildlife Reserve.** Take all the food and water you may need for nearly an all day trip, as well as a tank full of gas. Don't miss Callao. You may also wish to detour to Gold Hill and Ibapah. By the way, the road is good graded gravel, fine for a sedan in fair weather and well worth the trip. Once, that is. If you love the desert it's an interesting trip; if you don't love the desert, don't go. And, by the way, it's over a hundred miles. Rejoin I-80 at Wendover or go on to Ely via White Horse Pass on US-Alt 93 to US 93 and US-50 for a more scenic route west, cheaper motel rates, more **Pony Express station ruins** and sites, and some unique bars that serve great grilled cheese sandwiches for tired bicyclists. My pedaling son suggests that I explain this last remark as he, at fourteen, with his older brother and me, took ten days to pedal to Provo, Utah from Turlock, California via California SR-4, SR-88, and US-50. They went to a high school debate workshop at Brigham Young University and I to teach at a genealogy workshop, followed by research at the Family History Library. It was a fun, real adventure. The widely spaced bars were to cyclists as stage stations to earlier travelers, but improved considerably, with cold soft drinks, grills, and shade in which to rest.

If you are not intrigued to drive around the southern edge of the Great Salt Lake, at least have someone in the auto read aloud the following book as you travel homeward on I-80:

Stewart, George Rippey. *The California Trail: An Epic with Many Heroes*. Lincoln: University of Nebraska Press, 1983. Paper $9.95. University of Nebraska Press, 901 North 17th Street, Room 327, Lincoln, NE 68588-0520, (800) 755-1105.
  Originally published: New York: McGraw-Hill, 1962.

US-50 FROM ELY AND CARSON CITY, NEVADA

Lehman Caves, which is part of the **Great Basin National Park**, near the Utah border, is well worth the nine-mile partial loop drive. The cave is open all year and has a great number of marvelous formations; an easy walk but lots of stairs.

Wheeler Peak is another (summer only) twenty-mile round trip above Lehman Caves, where a moderate five-mile round trip hike takes you to one of the few **bristle cone pine** forests in the world. If you do not wish to hike, the drive provides a marvelous view of Utah's western desert from the white pine forest near the 10,000 foot level of the 13,063 foot peak.

Night driving on this route is somewhat hazardous, because it passes through open cattle range and the warm roadways attract livestock at night.

INTERSTATES 84, 15, AND US-89 FROM IDAHO

The **Great Salt Lake** is visible from several points south of Ogden along these routes. A sunset view of the Great Salt Lake from the mountain slopes east of any of the communities from Roy to Bountiful is one of the most marvelous sunset sights in the world.

Hill Aerospace Museum, Hill Air Force Base, 777-6868 or 777-6818, closed on Monday, is easily accessible from I-15 at exit 341, Roy.

ROADSIDE GUIDES

Guides to the sights along a highway and the local history of the area traveled are interesting to many travelers. The following are some that can turn travel into an informative experience:

Roylance, Ward Jay. *Utah: A Guide to the State, Part 2, Tour Section.* Revised and enlarged. Salt Lake City: *Utah: A Guide to the State* Foundation, 1982 ($9.95 paper, 506 pages; available from the Western Epics Publishing Co., 254 South Main Street, Salt Lake City, UT 84101, (801) 328-2586.

May, Fred E., and Bill Wilkerson. *Interstate 80: Reno, Nevada, to Salt Lake City, Utah. Eastbound Version, 523 Miles of Fascinating Information, History - Geography - Legends - Animal Life - Geology.* Layton, Utah: Travel Geografix, 1992 ($10.00 paper, 78 pages; available from the Travel Geografix, 439 North Spring Valley Parkway East, Elko NV 89801, (702) 753-8335.

Chapter 16

May, Fred E., and Bill Wilkerson. *Interstate 80: The Historic Route, Salt Lake City, Utah, to Reno, Nevada. Westbound Version for Enroute Travelers.* Layton, Utah: Travel Geografix, 1991 ($10.00 paper, 74 pages).

May, Fred E., and Bill Wilkerson. *Milepost Guidebook to Interstate 15: Las Vegas, Nevada, to Salt Lake City, Utah. Northbound Version.* Layton, Utah: Travel Geografix, in progress.

May, Fred E., and Bill Wilkerson. *Milepost Guidebook to Interstate 15: Salt Lake City, Utah to Las Vegas, Nevada. Southbound Version.* Layton, Utah: Travel Geografix, in progress.

Trimble, Marshall. *Roadside History of Arizona.* Missoula, Mont.: Mountain Press Publishing Co., 1986 ($12.95, 480 pages, P.O. Box 2399, 59806, (406) 728-1900, (800) 234-5308.

McTighe, James *Roadside History of Colorado.* Rev. ed. Boulder, Colo.: Johnson Books, 1989 ($11.95 paper, 628 pages, 1880 South 57th Court, 80301, (303) 443-1576, (800) 662-2665.

Wilson, D. Ray. *Kansas Historical Tour Guide.* 2d ed. Carpentersville, Ill.: Crossroads Communications, 1990 ($9.95 paper, 346 pages, P.O. Box 7, 60110-0007, (708) 426-0008.

West, Carroll Van. *A Traveler's Companion to Montana History.* Helena, Mont.: Montana Historical Society Press, 1986 ($9.95 paper, 239 pages, 225 North Roberts Street, Helena, MT 59620, (406) 444-2890).

Boye, Alan. *The Complete Roadside Guide to Nebraska.* St. Johnsbury, Vt.: Saltillo Press, 1989 ($11.95 paper, 370 pages, 57 Lafayette, 05819).

Fugate, Francis L., and Roberta B. Fugate. *Roadside History of New Mexico.* Missoula, Mont.: Mountain Press Publishing Co., 1989 ($24.95, $15.95 paper, 483 pages).

218

Wilson, D. Ray. *Wyoming Historical Tour Guide.* 2d ed. Carpentersville, Ill.: Crossroads Communications, 1990 ($9.95, 264 pages).

THE GEOLOGICAL SCENE

Because the geological formations of the West are so exposed to view, amateur geologists and geographers can have an exciting field trip driving to Salt Lake City if they utilize one of the many available field guides that are included in the following list:

Chronic, Halka. *Roadside Geology of Utah.* Missoula Mont.: Mountain Press Publishing Co., 1990 ($12.95 paper, 326 pages, P.O. Box 2399, 59806, (406) 728-1900, (800) 234-5308.

Chronic, Halka. *Roadside Geology of Arizona.* Missoula Mont.: Mountain Press Publishing Co., 1983 ($12.95 paper, 321 pages).

Hamblin, W. Kenneth. *Roadside Geology of U.S. Interstate 80 Between Salt Lake City and San Francisco: The Meaning Behind the Landscape.* Sponsored by the American Geological Institute. Van Nuys, Calif.: Varna Enterprises, 1974 ($5.00 paper, 51 pages, American Geological Institute, 4220 King Street, Alexandria VA 22302-1507, (703) 379-2480, (800) 336-4764.

Alt, David D., and Donald W. Hyndman. *Roadside Geology of Northern California.* Missoula, Mont.: Mountain Press Publishing Co., 1975 ($11.95 paper, 244 pages).

Sharp, Robert Phillip. *Field Guide, Southern California.* 2d Rev. ed. K/H Geology Field Guide Series. Dubuque, Iowa: Kendall/Hunt, 1990 ($15.95 paper, 208 pages, 2460 Kerper Blvd, 52001, (319) 588-1451, (800) 338-578.

Chronic, Halka. *Roadside Geology of Colorado.* Missoula Mont.: Mountain Press Publishing Co., 1980 ($11.95 paper, 334 pages).

Chapter 16

Alt, David D., and Donald W. Hyndman. *Roadside Geology of Idaho.* Roadside Geology Series. Missoula, Mont.: Mountain Press Publishing Co., 1989 ($14.95, 393 pages).

Alt, David D., and Donald W. Hyndman. *Roadside Geology of Montana.* Missoula, Mont.: Mountain Press Publishing Co., 1986 ($12.95 paper, 427 pages).

Chronic, Halka. *Roadside Geology of New Mexico.* Missoula Mont.: Mountain Press Publishing Co., 1986 ($9.95 paper, 255 pages).

Alt, David D., and Donald W. Hyndman. *Roadside Geology of Oregon.* Roadside Geology Series. Missoula, Mont.: Mountain Press Publishing Co., 1978 ($11.95 paper, 279 pages).

Alt, David D., and Donald W. Hyndman. *Roadside Geology of Washington.* Missoula, Mont. Mountain Press Publishing Co., 1984 ($12.95 paper, 282 pages).

Lageson, David R., and Darwin Spearing. *Roadside Geology of Wyoming.* Missoula, Mont. Mountain Press Publishing Co., 1988 ($9.95 paper, 274 pages).

This section of *Going* is dedicated to Walter ("Uncle Walt") R. Buss, who forty-two years ago introduced the author to field and roadside guides while he was a geology and geography student of "Uncle Walt's" at Weber College (now Weber State University). Now retired, "Uncle Walt" is still an avid geologist and geographer, but now is also an avid genealogist.

ADDITIONAL READING:

American Automobile Association. *Colorado/Utah.* Heathrow, Fla.: American Automobile Association, 1994.

Weir, Bill. *Utah Handbook*. 4th ed. Chico, Calif.: Moon
Publications, 1995 (P.O. Box 3040, 95927). (800) 345-5473. $16.95
paper. 458 pages.
   Weir's book has lots of historical background coverage.

SUMMARY:

Take some time to relax and drink in the beauties of the still somewhat-
wild West as you drive to and from Salt Lake City and the Family
History Library.

THE FAMILY HISTORY LIBRARY 7:15 A.M.

PART III

BACK HOME AGAIN

Chapter 17

REVIEW, FOLLOW-UP, AND GOING ON

After a visit to the Family History Library make sure that you review your research and add to your pedigrees and family group sheets the information obtained in Salt Lake City. There's a saying that for every hour you spend in the Library you need to devote two hours to studying your findings. Take time to analyze the fruits of your labors, prepare for additional research, and plan for future trips to Salt Lake City and other cities where you may need to continue your research.

Write to people you found who may also be researching your lines. Write county courthouses for records not available in the Family History Library. It may be necessary to hire someone in a county seat if the county court house staff is not helpful.

It may also be necessary to write for certificates of birth, marriage, or death for ancestors who were born, married, or who died in the twentieth century. The addresses and fees of the various United States vital records offices are listed in the U.S. National Center for Health Statistics, *Where to Write for Vital Records: Births, Deaths, Marriages, and Divorces* (Hyattsville, Md.: 1993). Many Family History Centers and public libraries also have Thomas Jay Kemp's *International Vital Records Handbook* (3d ed., Baltimore: Genealogical Publishing Co., 1994) that provides the forms often needed for obtaining certificates of vital records. His book also includes addresses, fees, and telephone numbers for vital records offices in the United States, Canada, the United Kingdom, and Ireland. For addresses of other foreign offices, various how-to-do-it genealogical research books and other resources at your local Family History Center can be of assistance. Before submitting requests to a vital records office in the United States, it is wise to telephone the office. Many of them have recorded messages providing current prices and the latest restrictions concerning the availability of records.

Share your research through gifts of family histories, pedigrees and family group sheets to relatives and others who may ask for your assistance. Submit your family group sheets and pedigrees to the *Ancestral File* and send in corrections if you find errors in it (refer again to chapter 4 of this book for details).

If your first visit to the Family History Library was not as productive as you might have wished, you may need better preparation. Perhaps more use of a Family History Center could fill those needs. Reading additional how-to-do-it books may help. Seminars, workshops, or programs offered by local genealogical societies have helped numerous researchers. Return to the Family History Library with a group that has experienced researchers who are willing to share their expertise with you.

If you are over fifty-five years of age you are eligible, along with your companion of at least age fifty, to enroll in any of the Elderhostel beginning genealogy programs in Provo, Utah, offered by the Brigham Young University, and their advanced courses in Salt Lake City at the Family History Library. In Provo you will have the opportunity for both instruction and daily research in the large campus Family History Center, and, in some courses, assistance in a field trip to the Family History Library. Recent courses in Provo included:

> Advanced Family History
> Beginning Family History Library Research
> Beginning Family History Workshop
> British Isles Research Workshop
> Family History On Personal Computers: Personal Ancestral
>   File Software
> Family History Research At BYU And Salt Lake City Family
>   History Library
> Intermediate Family History Workshop

In Salt Lake City, Brigham Young University offers:
> Advanced Family History: Focus On England, Ireland,
>   Scotland and Wales

Review, Follow-up, and Going On

Write Elderhostel, 75 Federal Street, Boston, MA 02110, (617) 426-8056, for their catalog. Programs currently offered may not continue because of low enrollment, instructors' interest changes, and site administration turnover.

Elderhostel courses in genealogy are also offered at numerous other colleges, universities, and educational centers in Canada and the United States. Those listed in recent Elderhostel catalogs were:

> University of South Alabama, Baldwin County, Beachside, Alabama
> Eastern Arizona College, Thatcher, Arizona
> Grand Canyon University, Phoenix Valley, Arizona
> Mohave Community College, Kingman Campus, Arizona
> Rio Salado College, Central Phoenix, Arizona
> Center for Studies of the Future, Palm Desert, Calif.
> University of Judaism, Los Angeles, California
> Academy of Jewish Studies, Fort Lauderdale, Florida
> Deerhaven Camp and Conference Center, Deerhaven, Fla.
> South Palm Beach County Jewish Federation, Florida
> Columbus College, Pine Mountain, Georgia
> Columbus College, Roosevelt-Warm Springs Institute, Georgia
> Idaho State University, Pocatello, Idaho
> Augustana College, Rock Island, Illinois
> Saint Francis College, Fort Wayne, Indiana
> Kentucky Historical Society, Frankfort, Kentucky
> University of Maine, Fort Kent, Maine
> Columbia Union College, Takoma Park, Maryland
> Towson State University, Towson, Maryland
> Berkshire Community College (Pittsfield), Lee, Massachusetts
> North Adams State College, North Adams, Massachusetts
> Abundant Life Center, Independence, Missouri
> Seashore United Methodist Assembly, Biloxi, Mississippi
> YMCA of the Ozarks, Trout Lodge, Potosi, Missouri
> Franklin Pierce College, Troy, New Hampshire
> New Hampshire Society of Genealogists, Durham, N.H.
> Georgian Court College (Lakewood), Avalon/Stone Harbor, N.J.
> Mid-Atlantic Center for the Arts, Cape May, New Jersey
> Holiday Hills Conference Center, YMCA, Pawling, N.Y.

Stella Niagara Education Park, Center of Renewal, Niagara
    Falls, New York
Tara Circle, Garrison, New York
John C. Campbell Folk School, Murphy, North Carolina
Ohio University, Athens, Ohio
Laurelville Mennonite Church Center, Laurelville, Pa.
Valley Forge Historical Society, Valley Forge National
    Historical Park, Pennsylvania
Coastal Retreat Center, Isle of Palms, South Carolina
University of South Carolina, Columbia, South Carolina
Young Judaea Retreat and Conference Center, Wimberley,
    Texas
Brigham Young University, Provo, Utah
Brigham Young University, Salt Lake City, Utah
Averett College, Danville, Virginia
Chanco Episcopal Conference Center, Surry County, Virginia
Radford University, Radford, Virginia
Southern Virginia College for Women (Buena Vista), Natural
    Bridge, Va.
Concord College (Athens), Pipestem State Park, West Virginia
B'nai B'rith Beber Camp and Conference Center, Mukwonago,
    Wisconsin
George Williams College, Lake Geneva, Wisconsin

University of New Brunswick, Fredericton, N.B., Canada
Memorial University, St. John's, Newfoundland, Canada
Dalhousie University, Nova Scotia, Canada
Gaelic College of Celtic Arts and Crafts, Badderk, Nova
    Scotia, Canada
Ottawa YMCA-YWCA, Ottawa-Carleton, Ontario, Canada
YWCA Woodlawn Residence, Toronto, Ontario, Canada
Canadian Hostelling Association, Saskatchewan Region Inc.,
    Waskesiu, Saskatchewan, Canada

London School of Economics, Rosebery Hall, England
University of Limerick, Limerick, Ireland
University of Edinburgh, Pollock Halls, Edinburgh, Scotland
University of Strathclyde, Glasgow, Scotland
Hantverkets Folkhögskola, Akerö, Leksand, Sweden

CALENDAR DATING

Each genealogist may someday cross the "time line" when the modern calendar system begins for a particular country of research. Understanding the calendar change at that "time line" is vital to correctly interpreting dates.

Why is this time line important? Please examine the following example: Your research uncovers an ancestor's will that was written October 15, 1731, and death took place January 24, 1731. Not a gross error, just the Julian calendar, which was in use from 52 A.D. to October 5, 1582 and until later dates in some countries. Your ancestor died three months after writing his will. For 1731 and all Julian years, the last day of the year was March 24.

In order to convert the overlapping dates of the Julian year, January 1 through March 24, to our present Gregorian calendar, there was need for a way of writing those dates so that they would be understandable. Something that you will need to know when such a date crops up. In presenting your family history you might want to write that your ancestor died 24 January 1731/32.

For American researchers the "time line" is the year 1752. On January 1, 1753 Great Britain and her colonies, including all of her American colonies began the first regular calendar year under the Gregorian calendar. A regular series of leap years adds one extra day every four years, but skips the century years not divisible by 400. This keeps our calculation of time equal to the true length of the year, which is actually 365 and a quarter days, by celestial reckoning.

For 1752 and earlier years, the dates from January 1 through March 24 have been written by some genealogists, historians, and also by people of the time, with the abbreviation 1751 O.S. (Old Style), or sometimes double-dated, 1751/52. When the change to the Gregorian new calendar was made in September, 1752, eleven days were dropped from the calendar (September 3-13) so that the calendar would coincide with the lunar calendar. September 2 was followed the next day by September 14. This one-time adjustment corrected the time difference accrued over the years since the beginning of the Julian calendar in 45 B.C.

Chapter 17

The textbook example of how the old and new calendars work is shown in the various ways the birth date of President George Washington can be written:

b. 11 da 12 mo 1731 — 11 da 12 mo 1731 is the 11th day of the 12th month, February. March is the 1st month of the old Julian calendar.

b. 11 Feb 1731 O.S. — The method for writing Washington's birth date in the Old Style or Julian calendar.

or b. 22 Feb 1732 N.S. — The method for writing Washington's birth date in the New Style or Gregorian calendar.

or b. 11 Feb 1731/32 — Double-dating or dual-dating = 1731 for the old Julian calendar and 1732 for the new Gregorian calendar.

or b. 11/22 Feb 1731/32 — Double-dating of the day and the year for George Washington's birth date.

As the Gregorian calendar was instituted in each country, there was an adjustment of from ten to thirteen days, depending on the century the change was made, to match time with the lunar calendar. Different countries and religious sects accepted the new calendar beginning in 1582 and continuing into the twentieth century.

The list below shows the date on which the following countries changed from the old Julian calendar to the new Gregorian calendar:

	Date changed	Following day's date
Austria	October 6, 1583	October 16
Belgium	December 22, 1582	January 1, 1583
Canada	September 3, 1752	September 14
Catholic	October 5, 1582	October 15
Denmark	February 19, 1700	March 1
England	September 3, 1752	September 14
Finland	February 2, 1918	February 15
France	December 10, 1582	December 20
Germany		
Catholic	November 4, 1583	November 14 (some)
Protestant	November 4, 1699	November 15 (some)
Great Britain	September 3, 1752	September 14
Holland	December 22, 1582	January 1, 1583

Hungary	October 22, 1582	November 1
Ireland	September 3, 1752	September 14
Italy	October 5, 1582	October 15 (some)
Luxembourg	October 5, 1582	October 15
Portugal	October 5, 1582	October 15
Norway	February 19, 1700	March 1
Poland (German)	October 5, 1582	October 15
Austrian	October 5, 1582	October 15
Russian	January 1, 1918	January 14
Portugal	October 5, 1582	October 15
Rumania Greek		
Orthodox	March 5, 1920	March 18
Catholic	March 5, 1919	March 18
Scotland	September 3, 1752	September 14
Spain	October 5, 1582	October 15
Sweden	February 18, 1753	March 1
Switzerland		
Catholic	January 12, 1584	January 22 (some)
Protestant	January 1, 1701	January 12 (some)
United States	September 3, 1752	September 14
Catholic	October 5, 1582	October 15
Quakers	September 3, 1752	September 14
Yugoslavia	March 5, 1919	March 18
Wales	September 3, 1752	September 14

The day after October 4, 1582, ten days were dropped from the calendar, calling the day after October 4, October 15. From 1582 up to February 28, 1700 those adopting the new calendar dropped ten days; between February 28, 1700 and February 28, 1800, eleven days; from February 28, 1800 to February 28, 1900, twelve days; and thirteen days from February 28, 1900 to February 28, 2100.

Another confusing problem of this calendar change is that earlier genealogists, historians, researchers, or recorders may not have indicated which of the above dating systems they used in recording dates for our ancestors. If you cannot figure that out, you may never really know the exact date of your ancestor's birth, marriage, death, or any other date in his/her life's history.

Chapter 17

Solution: When you copy Julian calendar dates just copy the dates provided you as given in the records you are using. If you discover a problem such as the will example provided above, then make a note or footnote of explanation, including one of the four dating methods used for George Washington's example above. It is this author's recommendation that you do not change the dates you copied from the resource from which you obtained them; explain goofy-looking dates with a footnote or note.

For additional reading concerning this subject, including the calendars of other countries, cultures, and religions of the world consult:

Parise, Frank, ed. *The Book of Calendars*. New York: Facts on File, Inc., 1982.

Part of the above country table is based on information in the Parise book and in the *World Almanac*.

PERPETUAL CALENDAR

For various reasons, you may wish to determine on which day of the week a historical event took place in an ancestor's life. Consult a *World Almanac* (700 - 2080) or *Information Please Almanac* (1800 - 2063) for a perpetual calendar.

Those of you who have the computer program, *Personal Ancestral File* (PAF), or have access to it at a Family History Center or at the Family History Library, may use its "Gregorian Date Calculator" for determining the days of the week for earlier (or future) dates. PAF does not have a Julian date calculator.

The directions for finding and using the "Gregorian Date Calculator" are as follows:

From the "ACCESS MENU" of PAF (2.31, 30 Sep 1994) select "1. Family Records."

When the "FAMILY RECORDS PROGRAM" screen appears, press "Enter."

From the "MAIN MENU" of the "Family Records Program" select "9. Facts and Fun."

From the "FACTS AND FUN MENU" select "6. Date Calculator."
At the "GREGORIAN DATE CALCULATOR" screen, type in the
"First Date,"
(example) 15 Oct 1931, press "F1 CALCULATE." The
calendar box on the left will fill in the dates and days for
October 1931; the 15th was on Thursday.
To continue to make determinations of other dates, press "F3
CLEAR."
To exit, press "F2 QUIT" then press "0," "0," "Enter," and "0"
through several menus to return to the computer's system.

You may determine the age, including months and days, at the time of
the death of an ancestor by typing in the birth date in the "First Date"
space and the death date in the "Last Date" space on the "Gregorian
Date Calculator" screen, then press "F1 CALCULATE."

There is another use for the "Gregorian Date Calculator" that may help
you with a research problem that is presented with some cemetery
headstone inscriptions and even some other sources that give the age of
the deceased, 83 years, 5 months, and 22 days, without a birth date.
The birth date may easily be determined by typing nothing in the "First
Date" space, press "Enter"; typing the death date in the "Last Date"
space, press "Enter"; then typing the years of age at death in the
"Years" space, press "Enter"; the number of months in the "Months"
space, press "Enter"; the number of days in the "Days" space; press
"F1 CALCULATE." The answer appears in the "First Date" space and
the birth date is highlighted in the left hand calendar. Classy program!

I. FAMILY HISTORY CENTER USERS:

Order microforms that you did not have time to read while in Salt Lake
City.

II. LOCAL PUBLIC LIBRARY USERS:

Request your reference librarian to interlibrary loan some of the printed
materials or census schedules you were not able to read while in Salt

Chapter 17

Lake City. One example would be to request photocopies of biographical sketches through the interlibrary loan services of your public library. Provide the librarian with the author, title, place of publication, publisher, date of publication, beginning page, and name of biographee. If any library's interlibrary loan service prohibits obtaining a photocopy of a desired biographical sketch, ask for a copy of the *American Library Directory* (New York: Bowker) FHL US/CAN REF AREA 973 J54a. Locate the name and address of the state, county, city or regional library serving the geographical locale of interest. Write to the library directly asking if they will photocopy the biographical sketch for you.

Many libraries are able to obtain microfilm copies of the U.S. federal census schedules through interlibrary loan from their state libraries or through the rental services of the National Archives Microfilm Rental Program, P.O. Box 30, Annapolis Junction, MD 20701-0030, (301) 604-3699 or the American Genealogical Lending Library, P.O. Box 329, Bountiful, Utah 84011-0329, (801) 298-5446, FAX (801) 298-5468.

The U.S. National Center for Health Statistics, *Where to Write for Vital Records: Births, Deaths, Marriages, and Divorces* (Hyattsville, Md.: 1990) mentioned above is usually available in your local public library and in some public libraries may be available under the government publications classification number, HE20.6210/2:990. If your public library does not have it, the U.S. Depository Library in your nearest university library or larger public library probably has it.

III. HOME LIBRARY USERS:

It may be necessary to join some of the book or microfilm home loan programs that are advertised in various genealogical journals. The largest and most reasonable rental collection is owned by the American Genealogical Lending Library, P.O. Box 329, Bountiful UT 84011-0329, (801) 298-5446, FAX (801) 298-5468. They have over 100,000 microforms in their rental collection, including all of the U.S. federal census schedules; state census schedules; nearly all of the U.S. ship passenger lists; and many military records, family histories, and county histories.

The U.S. National Center for Health Statistics, *Where to Write for Vital Records: Births, Deaths, Marriages, and Divorces* (Hyattsville, Md.: 1990) mentioned above may be obtained for your home use for $1.75 from the Superintendent of Documents, U.S. Government Printing Office, Washington, D.C. 20402 (stock number 017-022-01109-3).

ADDITIONAL READING:

All of the following are available at the Family History Library and its Centers.

FamilySearch: Contributing Information to Ancestral File." Salt Lake City: Corporation of the President of The Church of Jesus Christ of Latter-day Saints, 1990. 4 pages.

FamilySearch: Correcting Information in Ancestral File." Series AF, No. 4. Salt Lake City: Corporation of the President of The Church of Jesus Christ of Latter-day Saints, 1991. 4 pages.

SUMMARY:

After a visit to the Family History Library, it is necessary to review, update, analyze, plan for additional research trips, write to others researching your lines, and request additional materials through the interlibrary loan services of a Family History Center, a public library, or through home loan programs. Also share your completed research with others by contributing to the *FamilySearch: Ancestral File.*

> "Look at all of these marvelous records that my cousin sent me!"
> -- Turlock, California researcher, 1992

MICROFORM READERS
TURLOCK CALIFORNIA FAMILY HISTORY CENTER

APPENDIX

FAMILY HISTORY CENTERS
IN THE UNITED STATES AND CANADA

Below is a list of cities, arranged by state or province, in which a Family History Center is located. Some Centers' locations are listed in your telephone book under the Church of Jesus Christ of Latter-day Saints (either white, yellow, or business pages); if not listed, call Tuesday through Saturday evenings or Sundays any of the numbers listed under the Church of Jesus Christ of Latter-day Saints. If you are not able to contact anyone at the Church, call your local public library, local genealogical society, or write or call the Family History Library, 35 North West Temple Street, Salt Lake City UT 84150 (801) 240-3702 to locate the Center serving your area. Cities listed with a number following have more than one Center. There are currently 853 Family History Centers in Canada and the United States.

ALABAMA
Anniston
Birmingham
Cullman
Decatur
Dothan
Eufaula
Florence
Huntsville
Mobile
Montgomery
Tuscaloosa

ALASKA
Anchorage
Fairbanks
Juneau
Ketchikan
Sitka
Soldotna
Wasilla

ARIZONA
Benson

Buckeye
Casa Grande
Cottonwood
Duncan
Eagar
Flagstaff
Globe
Holbrook
Kingman
Mesa
Nogales
Page
Payson
Peoria
Phoenix 7
Prescott
Safford
Scottsdale
Show Low
Sierra Vista
Snowflake
St. Johns
Tucson 2
Willcox

Winslow
Yuma

ARKANSAS
Fort Smith
Hot Springs
Jacksonville
Little Rock
Rogers
Russellville

CALIFORNIA
Anaheim
Anderson
Antioch
Auburn
Bakersfield 3
Barstow
Blythe
Buena Park
Burbank
Camarillo
Carlsbad
Carson

237

Cerritos
Chatsworth
Chico
Chino
Cloverdale
Clovis 2
Concord
Corona
Covina
El Cajon
El Centro
Escondido
Eureka
Fairfield
Fontana
Fremont 2
Fresno 2
Glendale
Grass Valley
Gridley
Hacienda Heights
Hanford
Hemet
Huntington Beach
Huntington Park
La Crescenta
Lake Elsinore
Lancaster 2
Lemon Grove
Lompoc
Long Beach
Los Alamitos
Los Altos
Los Angeles
Manteca
Menlo Park
Merced
Miranda
Mission Viejo
Modesto 2
Monterey Park
Moreno Valley
Mt. Shasta
Napa
Needles

Newbury Park
North Edwards
Northridge
Norwalk
Oakland
Orange
Pacifica
Palm Desert
Palmdale
Pasadena
Placerville
Quincy
Rancho Palos
    Verdes
Redding
Redlands
Ridgecrest
Riverside 3
Sacramento 2
San Bernardino
San Bruno
San Diego 3
San Jose 2
San Luis Obispo
Santa Barbara
Santa Clara
Santa Cruz
Santa Maria
Santa Rosa
Seaside
Sonora
Simi Valley
Stockton
Susanville
Sutter Creek
Thousand Oaks
Torrance
Turlock
Ukiah
Upland
Vacaville
Valencia
Van Nuys
Ventura
Victorville

Visalia
Vista
Weaverville
Westminster
Whittier
Woodland
Yuba City

COLORADO
Alamosa
Arvada
Aurora
Colorado Springs
Cortez
Craig
Denver
Durango
Fort Collins
Frisco
Grand Junction
Greeley
La Jara
Littleton 2
Longmont
Louisville
Montrose
Northglenn
Paonia
Pueblo
Sterling

CONNECTICUT
Bloomfield
Madison
New Canaan
Quaker Hill
Woodbridge

DELAWARE
Dover
Wilmington

FLORIDA
Arcadia
Belle Glade

Boca Raton
Brandenton
Ft. Myers
Gainesville
Homestead
Jacksonville
Key West
Lake City
Lake Mary
Largo
Lecanto
Miami
New Port Richey
Orange Park
Orlando
Palm Beach Gardens
Palm City
Panama City
Pensacola
Plantation
Port Charlotte
Rockledge
Tallahassee
Tampa
Winter Haven

GEORGIA
Albany
Brunswick
Columbus
Douglas
Evans
Gainesville
Jonesboro
Macon
Marietta
Powder Springs
Rome
Roswell
Savannah
Tucker

HAWAII
Hilo
Honolulu 2
Kahului

Kailua-Kona
Kaneohe
Kona
Laie
Lihue
Mililani
Waipahu

IDAHO
Arimo
Basalt
Blackfoot 2
Boise 3
Burley
Caldwell
Coeur D'Alene
Driggs
Emmett
Grangeville
Hailey
Idaho Falls 3
Lewiston
Malad
McCammon
Montpelier
Moore
Mountain Home
Nampa
Pocatello
Preston
Rexburg
Rigby 2
Salmon
Sandpoint
Shelley
Soda Springs
Terreton
Twin Falls
Weiser

ILLINOIS
Buffalo Grove
Champaign
Chicago Heights
Fairview Heights
Naperville

Nauvoo
O'Fallon
Peoria
Rockford
Schaumburg
Wilmette

INDIANA
Bloomington
Columbus
Evansville
Ft. Wayne
Indianapolis
Kokomo
Muncie
New Albany
Noblesville
South Bend
Terre Haute
West Lafayette

IOWA
Ames
Cedar Falls
Cedar Rapids
Davenport
Mason City
Sioux City
West Des Moines

KANSAS
Dodge City
Emporia
Hutchinson
Olathe
Salina
Topeka
Wichita

KENTUCKY
Corbin
Hopkinsville
Lexington

Louisville
Martin
Morgantown
Owingsville
Paducah

LOUISIANA
Alexandria
Baton Rouge
Denham Springs
Monroe
Metairie
Shreveport
Slidell

MAINE
Bangor
Cape Elizabeth
Caribou
Farmingdale

MARYLAND
Annapolis
Ellicott City
Frederick
Gaithersburg
Kensington
Lutherville
Suitland

MASSACHUSETTS
Foxboro
Tyngsboro
Weston
Worcester

MICHIGAN
Ann Arbor
Bloomfield Hills
East Lansing
Escanaba
Grand Blanc
Grand Rapids
Harvey
Hastings

Kalamazoo
Ludington
Midland
Muskegon
Traverse City
Westland

MINNESOTA
Bemidji
Brooklyn Park
Duluth
Minneapolis
Rochester
St. Paul

MISSISSIPPI
Booneville
Clinton
Columbus
Gulfport
Hattiesburg

MISSOURI
Cape Girardeau
Columbia
Farmington
Frontenac
Hazelwood
Independence
Joplin
Kansas City
Liberty
Springfield
St. Joseph

MONTANA
Billings 2
Bozeman
Butte
Glasgow
Glendive
Great Falls
Havre
Helena
Kalispell

Lewiston
Missoula
Stevensville

NEBRASKA
Gordon
Grand Island
Lincoln
Omaha
Papillion

NEVADA
Ely
Elko
Fallon
Henderson
Las Vegas
Logandale
Mesquite
Reno
Tonapah
Winnemucca

**NEW
HAMPSHIRE**
Concord
Portsmouth

NEW JERSEY
Cherry Hill
East Brunswick
Morristown
North Caldwell
Shoal Hills

NEW MEXICO
Alamogordo
Albuquerque 3
Carlsbad
Clovis
Farmington
Gallup
Grants
Las Cruces
Los Alamos

Roswell
Santa Fe
Silver City

NEW YORK
Brooklyn
Elmhurst
Ithaca
Jamestown
Lake Placid
Liverpool
Loudonville
New York City
Pittsford
Plainview
Rochester
Scarsdale
Vestal
Williamsville
Yorktown

NORTH CAROLINA
Charlotte 2
Durham
Fayetteville
Goldsboro
Greensboro
Hickory
Kingston
Raleigh
Skyland
Wilmington
Winston-Salem

NORTH DAKOTA
Bismarck
Fargo
Grand Forks
Minot

OHIO

Cincinnati 2
Dayton
Dublin

Fairborn
Kirtland
Perrysburg
Reynoldsburg
Tallmadge
Westlake
Wintersville

OKLAHOMA
Ardmore
Enid
Lawton
Muskogee
Norman
Oklahoma City 2
Stillwater
Tulsa 2
Woodward

OREGON
Baker City
Beaverton
Bend
Brookings
Corvallis
Eugene
Gold Hill
Grants Pass
Gresham
Hermiston
Hillsboro
John Day
Keizer
Klamath Falls
La Grande
Lake Oswego
McMinnville
Medford
Newport
Northbend
Nyssa
Ontario
Oregon City
Portland 2
Prineville

Roseburg
Salem 2
Sandy
Scio
St. Helens
The Dalles
Tualatin

PENNSYLVANIA
Broomall
Clarks Summit
Erie
Johnston
Kane
Lancaster
Philadelphia
Pittsburgh
Reading
State College
York

RHODE ISLAND
Warwick

SOUTH CAROLINA
Charleston
Columbia
Florence
Greenville

SOUTH DAKOTA
Gettysburg
Pierre
Rapid City
Rosebud
Sioux Falls

TENNESSEE
Bartlett
Chattanooga
Cordova
Franklin
Kingsport
Knoxville
Madison

241

McMinnville

TEXAS
Abilene
Amarillo
Austin 2
Bay City
Bryan
Conroe
Corpus Christi
Dallas
Denton
Duncanville
El Paso 2
Fort Worth 2
Friendswood
Gilmer
Harlingen
Houston 2
Katy
Killeen
Kingwood
Longview
Lubbock
McAllen
Midland
Odessa
Orange
Pasadena
Plano
Port Arthur
San Antonio 2
Spring
Sugarland
The Colony
Tyler
Victoria
Wichita Falls

UTAH
Altamont
American Fork 2
Beaver
Blanding
Bountiful

Brigham City
Castle Dale
Cedar City
Delta
Draper
Duchesne
Enterprise
Eureka
Farmington 3
Ferron
Fillmore
Goshen
Helper
Huntington
Hurricane
Hyrum
Kanab
Kaysville 2
Kerns 3
Laketown
Layton
Lehi
Loa
Logan 2
Magna 2
Manti
Mapleton
Marion
Midvale
Midway
Moab
Monticello
Morgan
Moroni
Mt. Pleasant
Murray 4
Nephi
Ogden
Orem 4
Panguitch
Park City
Parowan
Pleasant Grove
Price
Provo 7

Provo (BYU)
Richfield
Riverton
Roosevelt
Salt Lake City 12
Sandy 9
Santaquin
South Jordan
Springville
St. George
Syracuse
Taylorsville
Tooele
Tremonton
Tropic
Vernal
Wellington
Wendover
West Jordan 3
West Valley City 6

VERMONT
Berlin

VIRGINIA

Alexandria
Annandale
Bassett
Centreville
Charlottesville
Chesapeake
Dale City
Falls Church
Fredericksburg
Hamilton
Newport News
Oakton
Pembroke
Richmond
Salem
Virginia Beach
Waynesboro
Winchester

WASHINGTON
Auburn
Bellevue
Bellingham
Bremerton 2
Centralia
Cheney
Colville
Ellensburg
Elma
Ephrata
Everett
Federal Way
Lake Stevens
Longview
Moses Lake
Mount Vernon
Mountlake Terrace
North Bend
Olympia
Omak
Othello
Port Angeles

Pullman
Puyallup
Quincy
Richland
Seattle 2
Spokane 3
Sumner
Tacoma
Vancouver 3
Walla Walla
Wenatchee
Yakima

WEST VIRGINIA
Charleston
Fairmont
Huntington

WISCONSIN
Appleton
Eau Claire
Hales Corners

Kenosha
Madison
Shawano
Wausau

WYOMING
Afton
Casper
Cheyenne
Cody
Diamondville
Evanston
Gillette
Green River
Jackson Hole
Laramie
Lovell
Lyman
Rawlins
Riverton
Rock Springs
Sheridan
Worland

CANADA

ALBERTA
Calgary
Cardston
Edmonton
Fort Macleod
Grande Prairie
Lethbridge
Magrath
Raymond
Red Deer
Spruce Grove
Taber

**BRITISH
COLUMBIA**
Burnaby
Courtenay
Cranbrook

Fort St. John
Kamloops
Kelowna
Prince George
Terrace
Victoria

MANITOBA
Brandon
Winnipeg

NEW BRUNSWICK
St. John

NEWFOUNDLAND
St. John's

NOVA SCOTIA
Dartmouth

ONTARIO
Brampton
Chatham
Etobicoke
Fort Frances
Glenburnie
Hamilton
Kitchener
London
Oshawa
Ottawa
Sarnia
Sault Ste. Marie
St. Thomas
Thunder Bay

ONTARIO

Timmins
Windsor

QUEBEC
Montreal 2

SASKATCHEWAN
Regina
Saskatoon

A PEEK AT PART OF THE OHIO COLLECTION
FAMILY HISTORY LIBRARY

SUBJECT INDEX

Individual Cards

THE SALT LAKE TEMPLE

The Church of Jesus Christ of Latter-day Saints

SALT LAKE CITY DOWNTOWN ACCOMMODATIONS

In Alphabetical Order

(Area code 801)

Anniversary Inn at Kahn Mansion	363-4900		9
Anton Boxrud Bed & Breakfast	363-8035	(800) 524-5511	11
Armstrong Manor Bed & Breakfast	531-1333		12
Best Western Olympus Hotel	521-7373	(800) 426-0722	28
Carlton Hotel	355-3418		8
Crystal Inn	328-4466	(800) 366-4466	18
Deseret Inn	532-2900		20
Doubletree Hotel	531-7500	(800) 222-8733	6
Embassy Suites Hotel	359-7800	(800) 362-2779	26
Hilton Hotel	532-3344	(800) 445-8667	19
Howard Johnson	521-0130	(800) 366-3684	5
The Inn at Temple Square	531-1000	(800) 843-4668	7
The Kimball	363-4000		3
Little America Hotel and Towers	363-6781	(800) 453-9450	23
Marriott Courtyard	531-6000	(800) 321-2211	16
Marriott Hotel	531-0800	(800) 228-9290	10
Peery Hotel	521-4300	(800) 331-0073	15
Quality Inn - City Center	521-2930	(800) 521-9997	25
Ramada Inn	364-5200	(800) 272-6232	24
Red Lion Hotel	328-2000	(800) 547-8010	14
Residence Inn by Marriott	532-5511	(800) 228-9290	17
Royal Executive Inn	521-3450	(800) 541-7639	1
Salt Lake City Center TraveLodge	531-7100	(800) 578-7878	22
Salt Lake TraveLodge at Temple Square	533-8200 (800) 578-7878		2
Shilo Inn	521-9500	(800) 222-2244	13
Super 8 Motel	534-0808	(800) 843-1991	27

(Key to downtown accommodations map on page 259)

SALT LAKE CITY DOWNTOWN ACCOMMODATIONS

(Key to downtown accommodations map on page 259)

(Area code 801)

1	Royal Executive Inn	521-3450 (800) 541-7639
2	Salt Lake TraveLodge/Temple Square	533-8200 (800) 578-7878
3	The Kimball	363-4000
5	Howard Johnson	521-0130 (800) 366-3684
6	Doubletree Hotel	531-7500 (800) 222-8733
7	The Inn at Temple Square	531-1000 (800) 843-4668
8	Carlton Hotel	355-3418
9	Anniversary Inn at Kahn Mansion	363-4900
10	Marriott Hotel	531-0800 (800) 228-9290
11	Anton Boxrud Bed & Breakfast	363-8035 (800) 524-5511
12	Armstrong Manor Bed & Breakfast	531-1333
13	Shilo Inn	521-9500 (800) 222-2244
14	Red Lion Hotel	328-2000 (800) 547-8010
15	Peery Hotel	521-4300 (800) 331-0073
16	Marriott Courtyard	531-6000 (800) 321-2211
17	Residence Inn by Marriott	532-5511 (800) 228-9290
18	Crystal Inn	328-4466 (800) 366-4466
19	Hilton Hotel	532-3344 (800) 445-8667
20	Deseret Inn	532-2900
22	Salt Lake City Center TraveLodge	531-7100 (800) 578-7878
23	Little America Hotel and Towers	363-6781 (800) 453-9450
24	Ramada Inn	364-5200 (800) 272-6232
25	Quality Inn - City Center	521-2930 (800) 521-9997
26	Embassy Suites Hotel	359-7800 (800) 362-2779
27	Super 8 Motel	534-0808 (800) 843-1991
28	Best Western Olympus Hotel	521-7373 (800) 426-0722

Map key courtesy the Salt Lake Convention & Visitors Bureau

MAP OF SALT LAKE CITY DOWNTOWN ACCOMMODATIONS

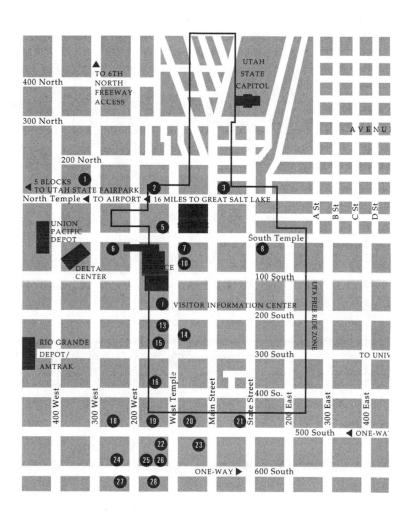

Map courtesy the Salt Lake Convention & Visitors Bureau

JOSEPH SMITH MEMORIAL BUILDING

SALT LAKE CITY DOWNTOWN ATTRACTIONS

In Alphabetical Order

		(Area code 801)
AMTRAK/Rio Grande Depot	34	531-0189
Beehive House	10	240-2671
Capitol Theatre	17	355-2787
Cathedral Church of St. Mark	26	322-3400
Catholic Cathedral of the Madeleine	27	328-8941
City and County Building	36	535-6333
Crossroads Plaza	15	531-1799
Delta Center	33	325-2000
Devereaux House/Triad Center	31	575-5423
FAMILY HISTORY LIBRARY	**3**	**240-3702**
First Presbyterian Church	28	363-3889
Hansen Planetarium	12	538-2098
JOSEPH SMITH MEMORIAL BUILDING	**8**	**240-4400**
LDS Church Office Building	6	240-2842
Lion House	9	363-5466
Maurice Abravanel Concert Hall	2	533-5626
Museum of Church History and Art	4	240-3310
Promised Valley Playhouse	16	364-5696
Salt Lake Art Center	2	328-4201
Temple Square	5	240-2534
Triad Center/Devereaux House	31	575-5423
Utah State Historical Society	34	533-3500
Utah State Capitol	22	538-3000
Visitor Information	1	521-2868
ZCMI Center	14	321-8745

(Key to downtown attractions map on the inside of back cover)

SALT LAKE CITY DOWNTOWN ATTRACTIONS

(Key to downtown attractions map on the inside of back cover)

(Area code 801)

1	Visitor Information	521-2868
2	Salt Palace Convention Center	534-6370
2	Salt Lake Art Center	328-4201
2	Maurice Abravanel Concert Hall	533-5626
3	**FAMILY HISTORY LIBRARY**	**240-3702**
4	Museum of Church History and Art	240-3310
5	Temple Square	240-2534
6	LDS Church Office Building	240-2842
7	Brigham Young Monument/Meridian Marker	
8	**JOSEPH SMITH MEMORIAL BUILDING**	**240-4400**
9	Lion House	363-5466
10	Beehive House	240-2671
11	Eagle Gate	
12	Hansen Planetarium	538-2098
13	Old Social Hall	321-8700
14	ZCMI Center	321-8745
15	Crossroads Plaza	531-1799
16	Promised Valley Playhouse	364-5696
17	Capitol Theatre	355-2787
18	Arrow Press Square Restaurant Complex	531-9700
19	John W. Gallivan Utah Center	532-0459
20	Marmalade District Historic Homes	533-0858
21	Pioneer Memorial Museum	538-1050
22	Utah State Capitol	538-3000
23	Council Hall	538-1030
24	Memory Grove Park/City Creek Canyon	
25	Brigham Young Grave	
26	Cathedral Church of St. Mark	322-3400
27	Catholic Cathedral of the Madeleine	328-8941
28	First Presbyterian Church	363-3889
29	Enos A. Wall Mansion (LDS Business College)	524-8100
31	Triad Center/Devereaux House	575-5423
32	Union Pacific Railroad Depot	595-3600
33	Delta Center	325-2000
34	Rio Grande Depot/AMTRAK	531-0189
34	Utah State Historical Society	533-3500
35	Exchange Place Historic District	
36	City and County Building	535-6333